Managing and Leveraging Events

This book explores and advances the latest concepts and developments in event management theory and practice.

Drawing on the ever-growing event management literature – and supported by theories and concepts from parent disciplines – the book examines challenges and opportunities related to maximising business and social benefits for those working in different event management positions in a variety of contexts. Written by an international team of five management scholars, the book investigates event management and leverage from various angles, including international business, event business studies, sport management, community development, and business strategy. It does so by offering a combination of theoretical approaches as well as contemporary cases from around the world.

This book will be of interest to undergraduate and postgraduate students of event management, as well as scholars researching in social and business-related areas of event management and leverage.

Nico Schulenkorf is Associate Professor of Sport Management at the University of Technology Sydney, Australia. His research focuses on the social, cultural, and health-related outcomes of sport and event projects. Nico's recent books and edited volumes include *Global Sport Leadership* (Routledge, 2019); *Critical Issues in Global Sport Management* (Routledge, 2017), and *Managing Sport Development: An International Perspective* (Routledge, 2016).

Katie Schlenker is Associate Professor of Event Management at the University of Technology Sydney, Australia. Katie's research interests and publications are in the areas of event evaluation, the social impacts of events, event legacies, events and social capital, and business events.

Hussain Rammal is Associate Professor of International Business and Strategy at the University of Technology Sydney, Australia. His research focuses on cross-border knowledge management, trade in services, and international business negotiations. Hussain is Co-Editor-in-Chief of the *Review of International Business and Strategy* journal and Founding Editor of the *Emerging Issues in International Business and Global Strategy* book series.

Jon Welty Peachey is Associate Professor of Sport Management in the Department of Recreation, Sport and Tourism at the University of Illinois Urbana-Champaign, USA. His research examines how sport for development programmes and events should be best designed, managed, and led to achieve individual- and community-based outcomes. Jon is a frequent invited speaker and consultant internationally on leadership, event management, and sport for development. He has published more than 100 scholarly articles and book chapters and given over 150 presentations at academic conferences around the word.

Ashlee Morgan is Lecturer in Sport Management at Edith Cowan University, Perth, Australia. Her research examines both the business of sport, such as sponsorship and strategic alliance management, and diversity and inclusion in sport and events.

Routledge Advances in Event Research Series

Edited by Warwick Frost and Jennifer Laing
Department of Marketing, Tourism and Hospitality, La Trobe University, Australia

Exhibitions, Trade Fairs and Industrial Events
Edited by Warwick Frost and Jennifer Laing

Power, Construction and Meaning in Festivals
Edited by Allan Jepson and Alan Clarke

Royal Events
Rituals, Innovations, Meanings
Jennifer Laing and Warwick Frost

Accessibility, Inclusion, and Diversity in Critical Event Studies
Edited by Rebecca Finkel, Briony Sharp, and Majella Sweeney

Tourism Events in Asia
Marketing and Development
Edited by Azizul Hassan and Anukrati Sharma

Marginalisation and Events
Edited by Trudie Walters and Allan Stewart Jepson

Festival and Event Tourism Impacts
Edited by Dogan Gursoy, Robin Nunkoo and Medet Yolal

Death and Events
International Perspectives on Events Marking the End of Life
Edited by Ian R Lamond and Ruth Dowson

Managing and Leveraging Events
Business and Social Dimensions
Nico Schulenkorf, Katie Schlenker, Hussain Rammal, Jon Welty Peachey and Ashlee Morgan

For more information about this series, please visit: www.routledge.com/ Routledge-Advances-in-Event-Research-Series/book-series/RAERS

Managing and Leveraging Events

Business and Social Dimensions

Nico Schulenkorf, Katie Schlenker, Hussain Rammal, Jon Welty Peachey and Ashlee Morgan

LONDON AND NEW YORK

First published 2022
by Routledge
2 Park Square, Milton Park, Abingdon, Oxon OX14 4RN

and by Routledge
605 Third Avenue, New York, NY 10158

Routledge is an imprint of the Taylor & Francis Group, an informa business

© 2022 Nico Schulenkorf, Katie Schlenker, Hussain Rammal, Jon Welty Peachey, and Ashlee Morgan

The right of Nico Schulenkorf, Katie Schlenker, Hussain Rammal, Jon Welty Peachey, and Ashlee Morgan to be identified as authors of this work has been asserted by them in accordance with sections 77 and 78 of the Copyright, Designs and Patents Act 1988.

All rights reserved. No part of this book may be reprinted or reproduced or utilised in any form or by any electronic, mechanical, or other means, now known or hereafter invented, including photocopying and recording, or in any information storage or retrieval system, without permission in writing from the publishers.

Trademark notice: Product or corporate names may be trademarks or registered trademarks, and are used only for identification and explanation without intent to infringe.

British Library Cataloguing-in-Publication Data
A catalogue record for this book is available from the British Library

Library of Congress Cataloging-in-Publication Data
A catalog record for this book has been requested

ISBN: 978-0-367-42827-3 (hbk)
ISBN: 978-1-032-12311-0 (pbk)
ISBN: 978-1-003-00277-2 (ebk)

DOI: 10.4324/9781003002772

Typeset in Times New Roman
by Apex CoVantage, LLC

Contents

List of illustrations	vii
Foreword by Laurence Chalip	viii
Acknowledgements	xi

PART 1
Event management and leverage: definitions and conceptualisations — 1

1 Managing and leveraging events: background, focus, and context	3
2 The strategic event management framework	11
3 Event leverage	25
4 Event impact evaluation	40

PART 2
Event management and leverage in practice: cases, contexts, and challenges — 57

5 Events and commercial engagement: business and social factors	59
6 Events and international business opportunities	76
7 Events, strategic alliance, and network management	89
8 Business events, knowledge management, and strategic responses	104
9 Social dimensions of community events	116
10 A new social field: events-for-development	131

vi *Contents*

PART 3
Event management and leverage: reflections and outlook 149

11 Critical issues and future research in event management
and leverage 151

Index 159

Illustrations

Figures

2.1	Strategic Event Management (SEM) Framework	15
8.1	Institutional Barriers to Knowledge Transfer in Business Events and Strategic Response	111

Tables

6.1	2020 Global Cities Index	80
6.2	Projected Outcomes of the Expo 2020 Dubai	84

Foreword

For several decades, it was common to hear about event impacts – that is, what effects an event was said to have. Typically, those were considered with reference to economic impact, although it was not uncommon for event impacts to be described in terms of social, political, and/or environmental impacts. Discussions of impact became bogged down in methodological squabbles. So, for economic estimates, were the input–output (I/O) analyses, which were most commonly used to gauge economic impact, really accurate? Were computable general equilibrium (CGE) models more accurate? Or would cost–benefit models provide the best policy information? Similar debates occurred over models applied to evaluate social, political, or environmental effects from events.

There were additional debates over how best to formulate models of impact. Not all I/O estimates from similar events yielded similar conclusions. Changes in assumptions or measurements could change the estimates. Ex ante estimates always seemed more optimistic than did ex post estimates. Similar problems were noted with other assessment methods and foci. Assumptions and timing seemed to alter findings. But surely, it was presumed, there are impacts, and we need to know them. How could we obtain reliable and valid estimates?

Then it was noticed that no matter what technique was used, events rarely lived up to their promises. Effects on the economy were unevenly distributed, making events as much an income transfer as an economic boon. Behaviours were rarely altered, and if there were behavioural effects, they were short-lived. Environmental protections were rarely adequate.

Yet, events can be fun. They may earn a fond place in public memory. They can elevate the status of business and political organisers who enable them. So, there is substantial incentive for the rich-and-powerful to make events happen.

If so, then what could be done to enable better justification than the unreliable and often fanciful impact of forecasts and evaluations? Several clever solutions were advanced. The economic and social value might be estimated jointly, so we could ask people about intangible benefits and perhaps even ask what they might be willing to pay for them. So, even if the measurable economic value was not much, we could assert that psycho-social value be compensated. Never mind that the measurable social benefits didn't fully support any such claim.

Foreword ix

Well, if that wasn't really a solution, maybe we could pretend that what we got in the short term was compensated by long-term benefits. It became fashionable to talk about event legacies. A great deal of effort was expended creating categories of potential legacy. Event organisers even began to promise legacies. Of course, after the event was over, there was no need to manage or deliver legacies. The caravan could move on. After all, legacies eventuate only once you're dead.

Despite the many disappointments, events multiplied. Some even grew and became increasingly elaborate. After all, events can be fun; they can be politically attractive; we are attracted by their glamour and their promise. So, what can we do to enable the benefits we want to claim from events? If we are going to do events, can we enhance what we obtain from them?

Those are radical questions because they demand that the black box be opened. No longer could we simply assert that events have an impact. Now we would need to know what we do with and through events to render outcomes we might seek. What we might get from an event could depend on what we do with it – how we manage it, market it, and integrate it into the social, economic, and political fabric of host communities, regions, and nations. Impact is not merely the result from having hosted an event; it is a set of outcomes that we create through choices we make regarding event design, implementation, and integration into public policy processes. It's no longer sufficient merely to host the event; we need to think about what we can and will do with it.

The result was a paradigm shift. Suddenly, impacts became epiphenomenal. Yes, they might still be interesting to know, but by themselves, they were no longer meaningful. What mattered was what we do to render those impacts. This was not merely evaluative; it was a way of learning how to do events better. Strategy pursuant to outcome became paramount.

Something else happened in consequence. We realised that the event itself was insufficient to enable the outcomes being sought. Effects depend on what is done with and for event visitors, event ambiance, and event media. Each event is a non-incremental addition to the product-and-service mix of the host community, its region, and its nation. Outcomes depend on how the event is combined with that mix and then utilised. It's not about the event *per se*; it's about ways the event is integrated into its policy context.

Which leads to another insight: That's a lot of work with a lot of stakeholders to be formulated, managed, and executed. Event organisers are too busy planning and implementing the event to be solely responsible for event leverage. Other businesses and agencies need to become partners. They need to be encouraged and enabled to take advantage of opportunities the event offers. Policy goals need to be identified, and the necessary partnerships and alliances need to be forged to pursue those goals. Events are opportunities, but they do not deliver benefits by themselves.

That can seem daunting or downright risky. How do we manage the many stakeholders? How do we keep expectations realistic? How do we hold alliances together, especially when business rivals must cooperate? What is the difference between a partnership for purposes of event leverage and old-fashioned ambush

x *Foreword*

marketing? Can we use event leverage to help sponsors activate their sponsorships? We continue to seek fully developed answers to questions like these.

The challenge is that event leverage is not merely a paradigm shift; it is a new one. If we are going to leverage events, we have to organise, run, and utilise them in ways that are still new to us while not forsaking lessons from the past. We are learning. Insights need to be collated and integrated.

This book is the first to undertake that challenge. It is a vital step forward.

Laurence Chalip
George Mason University

Acknowledgements

This book was conceived with the assistance of several key people. We would like to thank our colleagues at the University of Technology Sydney, the University of Illinois Urbana-Champaign, and Edith Cowan University for their support and critical feedback that helped to shape the book. We also wish to acknowledge the encouragement and professionalism of the Taylor & Francis editorial team: Emma Travis (Senior Editor Tourism, Events and Hospitality) and Lydia Kessell (Editorial Assistant). And perhaps most importantly, we would like to express our gratitude to our families who cheered from the COVID-safe sidelines as this book evolved.

As an interdisciplinary team of authors, we were conscious of the need to make this book research driven yet accessible and relevant for a wide audience of students, academics, and practitioners of event management. Hence, we aimed to combine and explain theory and practice across the book and included applied and contemporary examples wherever possible. We also subjected all chapters to strenuous editorial feedback – a process that has been important to secure continuity and connections in the development of the concepts and issues presented. We are confident that our applied approach has resulted in an attractive book that brings event management studies to life and that assists in making reading and learning truly relevant, meaningful, and enjoyable.

Part 1

Event management and leverage

Definitions and conceptualisations

1 Managing and leveraging events

Background, focus, and context

Introduction

Whether you are in charge of organising music festivals, planning business-to-business webinars, running sport tournaments, or hosting beer brewing workshops, as an event creator you have a desire to entertain and inspire your attendees. At the same time, you aim to achieve your business goals which may simply mean staying within your allocated budget or, in a for-profit context, maximising revenues from staging events. Taken together, the social and business-related dimensions are central aspects of successful event management operations, and those responsible for events require strong socio-managerial knowledge and skills to succeed in their chosen profession.

From a business perspective, the events industry has grown into a professionally organised and financially lucrative sector. In 2018, the size of the global events industry was valued at $1,100 billion, and it was expected to grow at a compound annual growth rate of 10.3% to reach $2,330 billion by 2026 (Roy & Deshmukh, 2019). There is no doubt – events mean big business. Sport events alone are outpacing the GDP growth in nearly every country in the world (Collignon & Sultan, 2014). If we look at business events – which include conferences and conventions, exhibitions, and incentives – they are now a global phenomenon and play a pivotal role for cities, regions, and countries in regard to their economic prosperity. As such, they are important destination marketing tools; they boost the visitor economy through local, national, and international visitation (such as transport, hotels, retail, and restaurants), facilitate small business growth by connecting buyers and sellers, allow for knowledge sharing that leads to innovation and business collaboration (both locally and globally), and they provide a platform or catalyst for entrepreneurship, international trade, and investment (see, e.g. Davidson, 2018; Dwyer & Jago, 2012; Hayduk, 2019; Mair, 2012; Manzenreiter & Horne, 2017; Smith, 2012).

From a social perspective, the general public's interest in topics such as community development, social justice, and sustainability has led to a significant increase in policy makers and event planners focusing on the social domains of event management. The analysis of social event impacts – which in contrast to their economic counterparts are largely intangible and difficult to quantify – has received

DOI: 10.4324/9781003002772-2

4 *Event management and leverage*

significant research attention over the past two decades, with studies investigating topics such as sport-for-development, (inter-)community well-being, and social cohesion (see, e.g. Levermore, 2011; Meir & Fletcher, 2019; Schulenkorf & Edwards, 2012; Schulenkorf, Giannoulakis, & Blom, 2019; Welty Peachey, Borland, Lobpries, & Cohen, 2015). It has been shown that if properly managed, events can enhance individual and collective capacities, improve people's level of self-efficacy, create social capital, and, where poverty is implicated, promote social and economic justice and well-being (Misener & Mason, 2006; Richardson & Fletcher, 2020; Schulenkorf, 2010, 2013, 2016; Schulenkorf, Thomson, & Schlenker, 2011; Sherry, Karg, & O'May, 2011; Zhou & Kaplanidou, 2018). Importantly, the social experiences at events are often the key motivator for people to get involved in the first place; for instance, people want to socialise, be entertained, develop contacts, friendships and networks, and celebrate or enhance cultural traditions. On a wider level, these social aspects can then lead to what event proponents label as improved community spirit or pride at the local, national, and/or international levels (Heere et al., 2013; Pawlowski, Downward, & Rasciute, 2014; Storm & Jakobsen, 2020).

In addition to business and social dimensions, there are a number of related event impact categorisations that are important to organisers and attendees. Event researchers have classified event impacts into political, psychological, physical, and environmental domains (see Allen, O'Toole, Harris, & McDonnell, 2011; Preuss & Solberg, 2006). Recent studies on sport events have further added health impacts as well as sport participation impacts to the mix (see, e.g. Richards, Foster, Townsend, & Bauman, 2014; Veal, Toohey, & Frawley, 2012, 2019), while educational and reputational impacts have also been identified (see, e.g. Parent, MacDonald, & Getz, 2017; Potwarka & Snelgrove, 2017; Schulenkorf & Schlenker, 2017). We suggest that these additional categories provide an ample opportunity to investigate managerial processes and strategies for development and leverage; however, they are not taking centre stage in this book. We are well aware though that different dimensions interrelate and overlap with each other. For example, an improvement in transport and communications (physical) can influence interaction and cooperation among people (social), whereas urban transformation and renewal (physical) may result in job creation (economic) and/or problems with social dislocation (social). As such, event impacts and their managerial domains cannot and should not be viewed in isolation, and we are committed to respecting this in our book.

What the aforementioned examples also show is that we cannot see event impacts as either solely positive or negative, because potential knock-on effects may be perceived differently in various contexts (Small, 2007; Small, Edwards, & Sheridan, 2005). For instance, social spaces can enable increased interactivity and celebration at music events, which may result in a party-like atmosphere. For some, this describes a socialisation or engagement benefit (Welty Peachey et al., 2015), while others in the host community may perceive increased noise levels as a disturbance. This means that when discussing event management across different dimensions, a critical appraisal and a reflective approach are required. For

Managing and leveraging events 5

too long, event proponents across government and community have conveniently ignored the warnings of event critics who have shown that events may leave host communities and organisers with a significant economic or environmental burden, and – from a social perspective – they may well *reduce* the quality of life of people who are directly or indirectly affected by their existence. There are numerous events that have, for instance, led to an increase in antisocial behaviour, criminal activity, violence, and arrests during the festivities (Getz, 2019; Yolal, Gursoy, Uysal, Kim, & Karacaoğlu, 2016).

Moreover, in 2020 and 2021, the event industry had to battle the most severe external disruption it has ever faced. The COVID-19 pandemic has brought many live events to a halt and event organisers were required to quickly adapt to "the new Covid normal". The consequences were drastic. With social distancing requirements enforced by legislators, educational events such as conferences and congresses had to shift to online modes of delivery. Sport events were conducted with restricted capacity or no fans in the stadium. Meanwhile, live acts such as theatre performances or music festivals were largely cancelled with dramatic negative impacts on event businesses, staff, and performers. Figures from the Business Events Council of Australia showed that in 2020, the Australian economy alone was set to lose over \$35 billion in direct expenditure, as nearly all business events scheduled for 2020 (96%) had to be cancelled or postponed. Overall, it is fair to say that COVID-19 has challenged the events industry like nothing before, and it will likely be a bumpy road towards a full recovery. Again, this is particularly true for the social and business-related domains of event management where aspects of social engagement and financial revenue – two of the core benefits of special events – have been majorly interrupted.

With this book, we are committed to a critical yet balanced investigation into recent events, including the different dimensions and strategic decision-making. While a focus on social and business dimensions has provided the impetus and starting point for our writing, we will refer to other related domains whenever suitable. We do so because we believe that to be a successful event planner and organiser, a holistic, proactive, and strategic approach to management is required.

Purpose of the book

The purpose of this book, *Managing and Leveraging Events: Business and Social Dimensions*, is to explore and advance the latest concepts and developments in event management theory and practice. Drawing on the ever-growing event management literature – and supported by theories and concepts from parent disciplines such as international business and community development – the book will examine challenges and opportunities related to maximising business and social benefits for those working in different event management positions in a variety of contexts. The book has been written by an international, interdisciplinary team of management scholars, each of whom has practical and theoretical expertise in different fields of event management. As such, the book set out to investigate and advance critical developments in event management from various angles,

6 *Event management and leverage*

including international business, event business studies, sport management, community development, and business strategy. It does so by offering a combination of different theoretical approaches as well as contemporary examples and case studies from around the world.

Structure of the book

Whilst the event industry is constantly growing – and despite an increased academic focus on event management in recent decades – it is surprising how little work has been completed around the managerial aspects and processes associated with event leverage and impact studies. However, momentum is gathering with dedicated event impact and legacy subjects offered at event management university courses around the world, and special issues published in high-quality academic journals including one on strategies for leveraging sport mega-events, published in the *Journal of Sport Policy and Politics* (Grix, Brannagan, Wood, & Wynne, 2017), and another on impacts and strategic outcomes from non-mega sport events for local communities, published in *European Sport Management Quarterly* (Taks, Chalip, & Green, 2015). In short, *Managing and Leveraging Events: Business and Social Dimensions* set out to capitalise on this momentum to bring together a book that explores how the latest event impact and leverage research can inform the growing field of event management.

In this introductory chapter we have briefly provided the background, purpose, and context for *Managing and Leveraging Events: Business and Social Dimensions*. In the remaining ten chapters of this book, we invite readers to explore, learn, discuss, and reflect on the latest concepts, issues, and trends in managing and leveraging events. With a clear focus on the social and business-related aspects of event management, readers will enjoy interrelated chapters that cover (a) theoretical definitions and conceptualisations; (b) practical cases, contexts, and challenges; as well as (c) critical event management issues and future research opportunities.

The first section (Chapters 1–4) will set the scene by focusing on key definitions and conceptualisations in the context of managing and leveraging events for business and social benefit. In addition to this introduction, Chapter 2 presents a conceptual framework for event-related social and business management and a discussion of key stakeholders, management processes, impacts, and outcomes. Next, Chapter 3 provides a critical discussion of the managerial aspects of event leverage, including recent theoretical advances and practical examples. The final chapter of the first section highlights the importance of event evaluation; it presents current assessment approaches and provides applied examples of impact evaluation.

With the groundwork firmly laid, the second section (Chapters 5–10) explores in depth the managerial challenges and opportunities related to maximising the business and social opportunities of events. The six chapters in this section are supported by a variety of cases and contexts, ranging from international large-scale events to small-scale festivals in local communities. Moreover, the section will feature examples from high-income countries as well as low- and middle-income settings – an area that has so far been largely overlooked in event leverage research (Schulenkorf & Schlenker, 2017). In particular, Chapter 5 brings together business and social factors around commercial event engagement. Here, the focus is placed on sponsorship management and using the digital landscape as an important dimension of event leverage. Next, Chapter 6 investigates special events and international business opportunities. With a focus on business relationships and event partnerships, this chapter also provides a critical appraisal of the roles of governments and cities in staging events. In Chapter 7, research from the area of strategy – including strategic alliances and network management – is applied to an event context where aspects such as alliance portfolios, stakeholder networks, and business relationships are critically discussed. This is followed by Chapter 8, which focuses on business events and knowledge management. This chapter is underpinned by academic literature on strategic responses and organisational learning which is applied to an event management context. Meanwhile, Chapter 9 shifts the focus to the social dimensions of events and does so from a smaller community perspective. Drawing on contemporary case studies, this chapter highlights critical event strategies and managerial implications for enhancing the social value of events. Finally, Chapter 10 introduces the reader to a relatively new socio-managerial field, namely events-for-development. It first defines and explains this new concept and then engages with examples that highlight the potential and challenges of using events as strategic vehicles for development in disadvantaged social settings.

The third and final section of the book is presented in Chapter 11. This section reflects on the status quo in event management and highlights the "lessons learnt". Furthermore, it explores future challenges and research opportunities for events in a post-COVID-19 era that will advance our knowledge on special event management and leverage for business and social impact.

Conclusion and outlook

Special events hold significant business and social value to countries and communities around the world. With this book, we are exploring the latest concepts and developments in event management theory and practice, and we do so from a variety of angles and academic disciplines. With a specific focus on managing and leveraging business and social dimensions of events, we offer a combination of theoretical approaches as well as contemporary examples and case studies from a variety of socio-economic contexts. We hope that the interdisciplinary nature of this book will provide a stimulating environment to explore, learn about, and discuss the latest concepts and trends in event management. With this in mind, we turn to Chapter 2, where we introduce a conceptual framework for event-focused social and business management, combined with a discussion of critical management processes and their resulting impacts and outcomes.

8 *Event management and leverage*

References

Allen, J., O'Toole, W., Harris, R., & McDonnell, I. (2011). *Festival and special event management* (5th ed.). Milton: Wiley.

Collignon, H., & Sultan, N. (2014). *Winning in the business of sports*. Retrieved from www.kearney.com/communications-media-technology/article?/a/winning-in-the-business-of-sports

Davidson, R. (2018). *Business events*. Abingdon: Routledge.

Dwyer, L., & Jago, L. (2012). The economic contribution of special events. In S. J. Page & J. Connell (Eds.), *The Routledge handbook of events* (pp. 129–147). Abingdon: Routledge.

Getz, D. (2019). Event evaluation and impact assessment: Five challenges. In J. Armbrecht, E. Lundberg, & T. D. Andersson (Eds.), *A research agenda for event management* (pp. 48–56). Cheltenham: Edward Elgar Publishing.

Grix, J., Brannagan, P. M., Wood, H., & Wynne, C. (2017). State strategies for leveraging sports mega-events: Unpacking the concept of "legacy". *International Journal of Sport Policy and Politics, 9*(2), 203–218. doi:10.1080/19406940.2017.1316761

Hayduk, T. (2019). Leveraging sport mega-events for international entrepreneurship. *International Entrepreneurship and Management Journal*. doi:10.1007/s11365-019-00573-w

Heere, B., Walker, M., Gibson, H., Thapa, B., Geldenhuys, S., & Coetzee, W. (2013). The power of sport to unite a nation: The social value of the 2010 FIFA World Cup in South Africa. *European Sport Management Quarterly, 13*(4), 450–471. doi:10.1080/16184742.2013.809136

Levermore, R. (2011). Sport-for-development and the 2010 Football World Cup. *Geography Compass, 5*(12), 886–897.

Mair, J. (2012). A review of business events literature. *Event Management, 16*(2), 133–141. doi:10.3727/152599512X13343565268339

Manzenreiter, W., & Horne, J. (2017). Socio-economic impacts of sports mega-events. In N. Schulenkorf & S. Frawley (Eds.), *Critical issues in Global Sport Management* (pp. 128–140). Abingdon: Routledge.

Meir, D., & Fletcher, T. (2019). The transformative potential of using participatory community sport initiatives to promote social cohesion in divided community contexts. *International Review for the Sociology of Sport, 54*(2), 218–238.

Misener, L., & Mason, D. S. (2006). Creating community networks: Can sporting events offer meaningful sources of social capital? *Managing Leisure, 11*(1), 39–56. doi:10.1080/13606710500445676

Parent, M. M., MacDonald, D., & Getz, D. (2017). The sport event owners' perspective. In *Routledge handbook of sports event management* (pp. 109–126). Abingdon: Routledge.

Pawlowski, T., Downward, P., & Rasciute, S. (2014). Does national pride from international sporting success contribute to well-being? An international investigation. *Sport Management Review, 17*(2), 121–132. doi:10.1016/j.smr.2013.06.007

Potwarka, L. R., & Snelgrove, R. (2017). Managing sport events for beneficial outcomes: Theoretical and practical insights. *Event Management, 21*(2), 135–137. doi:10.3727/152599517X14878772869522

Preuss, H., & Solberg, H. A. (2006). Attracting major sporting events: The role of local residents. *European Sport Management Quarterly, 6*(4), 391–411. doi:10.1080/16184740601154524

Richards, J., Foster, C., Townsend, N., & Bauman, A. (2014). Physical fitness and mental health impact of a sport-for-development intervention in a post-conflict setting: Randomised

Managing and leveraging events   9

controlled trial nested within an observational study of adolescents in Gulu, Uganda. *BMC Public Health, 14*(1), 619. doi:10.1186/1471-2458-14-619

Richardson, K., & Fletcher, T. (2020). Community sport development events, social capital and social mobility: A case study of Premier League Kicks and young black and minoritized ethnic males in England. *Soccer & Society, 21*(1), 79–95.

Roy, A., & Deshmukh, R. (2019). *Events industry market: Opportunities and forecasts 2019–2026 report.* Retrieved from www.alliedmarketresearch.com/events-industry-market

Schulenkorf, N. (2010). Sport events and ethnic reconciliation: Attempting to create social change between Sinhalese, Tamil and Muslim sportspeople in war-torn Sri Lanka. *International Review for the Sociology of Sport, 45*(3), 273–294. doi:10.1177/1012690210366789

Schulenkorf, N. (2013). Sport-for-development events and social capital building: A critical analysis of experiences from Sri Lanka. *Journal of Sport for Development, 1*(1), 25–36.

Schulenkorf, N. (2016). The contributions of special events to sport-for-development programs. *Journal of Sport Management, 30*(6), 629–642. doi:10.1123/JSM.2016–0066

Schulenkorf, N., & Edwards, D. (2012). Maximizing positive social impacts: Strategies for sustaining and leveraging the benefits of intercommunity sport events in divided societies. *Journal of Sport Management, 26*(5), 379–390. doi:10.1123/jsm.26.5.379

Schulenkorf, N., Giannoulakis, C., & Blom, L. (2019). Sustaining commercial viability and community benefits: Management and leverage of a sport-for-development event. *European Sport Management Quarterly, 19*(4), 502–519. doi:10.1080/16184742.2018. 1546755

Schulenkorf, N., & Schlenker, K. (2017). Leveraging sport events to maximize community benefits in low- and middle-income countries. *Event Management, 21*(2), 217–231. doi: 10.3727/152599517X14878772869766

Schulenkorf, N., Thomson, A., & Schlenker, K. (2011). Intercommunity sport events: Vehicles and catalysts for social capital in divided societies. *Event Management, 15*(2), 105–119. doi:10.3727/152599511X13082349958316

Sherry, E., Karg, A., & O'May, F. (2011). Social capital and sport events: Spectator attitudinal change and the Homeless World Cup. *Sport in Society, 14*(1), 111–125. doi:10.10 80/17430437.2011.530015

Small, K. (2007). Social dimensions of community festivals: An application of factor analysis in the development of the Social Impact Perception (SIP) scale. *Event Management, 11*(1), 45–55.

Small, K., Edwards, D., & Sheridan, L. (2005). A flexible framework for socio-cultural impact evaluation of a festival. *International Journal of Event Management Research, 1*(1), 66–77.

Smith, A. (2012). *Events and urban regeneration: The strategic use of events to revitalise cities.* New York: Routledge.

Storm, R. K., & Jakobsen, T. G. (2020). National pride, sporting success and event hosting: An analysis of intangible effects related to major athletic tournaments. *International Journal of Sport Policy and Politics, 12*(1), 163–178.

Taks, M., Chalip, L., & Green, B. C. (2015). Impacts and strategic outcomes from non-mega sport events for local communities. *European Sport Management Quarterly, 15*(1), 1–6. doi:10.1080/16184742.2014.995116

Veal, A. J., Toohey, K., & Frawley, S. (2012). The sport participation legacy of the Sydney 2000 Olympic Games and other international sporting events hosted in Australia.

10 *Event management and leverage*

Journal of Policy Research in Tourism, Leisure and Events, 4(2), 155–184. doi:10.1080/19407963.2012.662619

Veal, A. J., Toohey, K., & Frawley, S. (2019). Sport participation, international sports events and the "trickle-down effect". *Journal of Policy Research in Tourism, Leisure and Events, 11*(sup1), s3–s7.

Welty Peachey, J., Borland, J., Lobpries, J., & Cohen, A. (2015). Managing impact: Leveraging sacred spaces and community celebration to maximize social capital at a sport-for-development event. *Sport Management Review, 18*(1), 86–98. doi:10.1016/j.smr.2014.05.00

Yolal, M., Gursoy, D., Uysal, M., Kim, H. L., & Karacaoğlu, S. (2016). Impacts of festivals and events on residents' well-being. *Annals of Tourism Research, 61*, 1–18.

Zhou, R., & Kaplanidou, K. (2018). Building social capital from sport event participation: An exploration of the social impacts of participatory sport events on the community. *Sport Management Review, 21*(5), 491–503. https://doi.org/10.1016/j.smr.2017.11.001

2 The strategic event management framework

Introduction

Special events come in all shapes and sizes. From small community festivals to mega-events such as the Olympic Games, they present a reason for celebration and engagement for people and communities. To achieve desired event outcomes and to leverage business and social opportunities, event organisers are tasked with strategically planning, implementing, and evaluating events. As such, event managers rarely work in isolation; they collaborate with key partners and engage with a variety of external stakeholders to maximise an event's overall potential.

In this chapter, we explore the roles and responsibilities of event organisers, host communities, and key stakeholders who all contribute to event management processes aimed at achieving not only positive immediate impacts but also sustainable long-term outcomes. We discuss their contributions and involvement in the context of the newly designed Strategic Event Management (SEM) Framework. Importantly, the SEM Framework provides a managerial foundation for the rest of this book as it assists in illustrating the processes of event organisers and stakeholders in their attempts to achieve critical business and social benefits. Before we introduce the SEM Framework in more detail, it seems important to provide an overview of existing event models and frameworks and their inherent strengths and limitations. As we will discuss, most of the original frameworks were designed to assess events ex post by measuring event impacts or comparing event inputs and outputs. More recently, the perspectives have started to change and we are seeing a number of qualitative process-oriented frameworks that help to better understand – and plan for – event benefits ex ante. The discussion in the following sections will allow us to illustrate the recent shifts in managerial foci and conceptual thinking that have underpinned the design and development of the SEM Framework.

Review of event management frameworks

Conceptual frameworks are used in research to outline the links between different literature areas and concepts and to show their distinct relationships with each other (Veal, 2006). A number of previous studies have made a contribution in this

DOI: 10.4324/9781003002772-3

12 *Event management and leverage*

space, including a variety of event impact frameworks and evaluation models. In particular, within the area of event and tourism management, categorisation and assessment frameworks have been proposed in an attempt to classify and measure the various impacts generated by special events. Back in 1984, Ritchie published a seminal article that portrayed a framework for the evaluation of hallmark events. He included six types of impacts into his framework, namely economic, tourism/commercial, physical, sociocultural, psychological, and political. Since then, others have advanced the understanding and development of event and tourism impact frameworks, but the focus largely remained on quantitative measures, appraisals, and evaluations. For example, Lindberg and Johnson (1997) applied the Contingent Valuation method to the measurement of social impacts of tourism, which was originally developed to measure consumers' willingness to pay for goods. In simple words, the study asked local residents to assign a monetary value to different tourism impacts. While *some* tourism impacts can perhaps be analysed more effectively by lending them an economic value, it is important to note that not all social impacts can be assessed or understood this way. The same argument applies to the measurement of quantitative social indicators within different types of Social Impact Assessments (see Esteves, Franks, & Vanclay, 2012; Getz, 2019), which can be designed to support the identification of social consequences of events, such as a prediction of the increased level of crime through an analysis of police records.

To cater for both quantitative and qualitative impacts, Dwyer, Mellor, Mistilis, and Mules (2000) were the first to develop a framework for evaluating and forecasting both tangible impacts (such as visitor expenditure) and intangible impacts (such as free publicity) of special events. Their research focused predominantly on economic and social aspects of event management – the two areas that the authors consider of critical importance for the host destination or community. In the following years, Dwyer et al.'s (2000) work provided the backdrop for researchers interested in a holistic triple bottom line (TBL) evaluation of event impacts where scholars started to add environmental considerations to the mix (see, e.g. Collins & Cooper, 2017; Fredline, Raybould, Jago, & Deery, 2004; Mair & Laing, 2013; Sherwood, Jago, & Deery, 2004).

With a heightened focus on community feelings and perceptions, research has also been done to assess people's opinions, values, and attitudes regarding the hosting of special events. Such research can and has been conducted in the lead up to mega-events such as the Olympic Games, or ex post to depict the overall success or failure of an event (Delamere, Wankel, & Hinch, 2001; Fredline, Jago, & Deery, 2003; Small & Edwards, 2003).

Looking more closely at understanding and managing the actual experiences of event customers, Liu, Sparks, and Coghlan (2017) take a holistic approach to analysing a food and wine event. Drawing on an ecosystem concept from service design and the concept of co-creation of value, their conceptual framework aims to capture the complexity of customer experience in situ. Liu et al.'s (2017) study shows that both positive and negative customer experiences are affected by an event's ecosystem, which, in turn suggests that when designing event programmes,

The strategic event management framework 13

event managers should be aware of the importance of balance within the ecosystem. This finding is important given that developing positive experiences as well as long-term benefits is often a key promise made by event organisers, especially those in charge of large-scale and mega-events (see Frawley, 2017; Schulenkorf, Schlenker, & Thomson, 2017).

Process-based qualitative frameworks

As the previous section indicates, the analysis of social and business impacts of events has largely been conducted from an ex post rather than ex ante perspective. In other words, most available frameworks are designed to quantitatively assess events by measuring event impacts or comparing event inputs and outputs. In recent years, the perspectives have started to change and there are now a number of qualitative process-oriented frameworks available that aim to better understand the various impact dimensions of events. As part of this shift, we have also seen first iterations of specific event frameworks that describe and visualise the social *processes* of event management and therefore focus on collaborations and strategies through which outcomes are obtained or enhanced. While there is still an ample opportunity for future developments in this critical space, we now briefly look back at these studies to provide an important backdrop for the development of our newly proposed Strategic Event Management (SEM) Framework.

First, in 2009, Schulenkorf introduced the Social Inter-Community Event (SICE) Framework that focused specifically on the processes towards generating social impacts in inter-community event settings. The SICE Framework was initially developed to guide event planning and management in the context of creating sociocultural benefits in divided societies, but it has since been used and adapted to inform empirical event studies as well as newly designed conceptualisations (see, e.g. Schulenkorf, 2012). Second, Soteriades and Dimou (2011) proposed a systematic conceptual framework to enhance efficient event management, with a particular focus on optimising their contribution to wider long-term development objectives. With a particular focus on tourism, the process-oriented framework takes account of the political, social, and economic contexts and covers critical aspects of strategic planning, management, and evaluation with a focus on event experiences. Related to this, Ziakas's (2016) integrative framework for fostering the social utility of events was designed to shed light on the multi-layered processes that specifically underpin *social* event management. The author combined the theoretical tenets of social leverage, event dramaturgy, and social capital to understand and explain the key dynamics associated with event planning and implementation of leveraging strategies – and to guide future interdisciplinary research towards strategically incorporating events in community development. Against this background – and with a focus on the business and social dimensions of events – we will now turn towards introducing the SEM Framework that aims to guide scholars and practitioners in their desire to better understand critical event management processes.

14 *Event management and leverage*

Introducing the SEM Framework

When working on event projects, several authors highlight the importance of establishing a clear strategy and setting lucid goals to achieve sustainable development outcomes (Lawson, 2005; Naparstek, Dooley, & Smith, 1997; Wickham, Donnelly, & French, in press). As such, strategic planning and cooperative participation are required from all stakeholders to not only implement the event and generate direct event impacts but then leverage these impacts to achieve long-lasting positive outcomes (Chalip, 2004, 2006; Kellett, Hede, & Chalip, 2008; O'Brien, 2007; O'Brien & Chalip, 2007; Schulenkorf, 2009). Importantly, from the beginning of the event management process the host community and event organisers should engage with key stakeholders in a forward-looking planning process; in other words, strategic event management goes beyond the operational aspects and includes a clear commitment to achieving specific long-term event outcomes or legacies. This strategic ex ante approach to event management is presented in the SEM Framework (see Figure 2.1).

The process-based SEM Framework provides the underpinning foundation for the discussions in our book. In a nutshell, the SEM Framework portrays a strategic event management process which begins with the planning phase where host communities and event organisers engage with key stakeholders to map out their responsibilities, the event's programme, as well as short-term objectives (i.e., desired impacts) and long-term goals (i.e., desired outcomes and legacies). In the implementation phase, the event is staged and direct impacts are created – and they are likely to include both positive and negative examples. The maximisation phase then looks at sustaining positive impacts for the longer term, as well as growing and leveraging (particularly social and business) opportunities beyond event borders. Finally, the evaluation phase looks back at the event and assesses its diverse impacts and outcomes. We are now moving towards explaining – in a more detailed and applied way – the conceptual thinking behind the SEM Framework.

Planning

As both the sources and intended beneficiaries of special events, host communities and event organisers are central to all event planning efforts. Planning per se is *the* fundamental management function; it precedes all other management activities and is concerned with defining goals for an event's programme and future direction and determining the resources to achieve those targets (Dowson & Bassett, 2018). As a systematic activity, it involves deciding beforehand, what is to be done, when it is to be done, how it is to be done and who is going to do it. Here, event organisers, the host community and key stakeholders come together and engage in an intellectual process which identifies joint goals and objectives and the course of action (Jordan, Gibson, Stinnett, & Howard, 2019; Mallen & Adams, 2017). Critically, the planning phase is also of strategic importance for any organisation as it addresses not only short-term objectives

The strategic event management framework 15

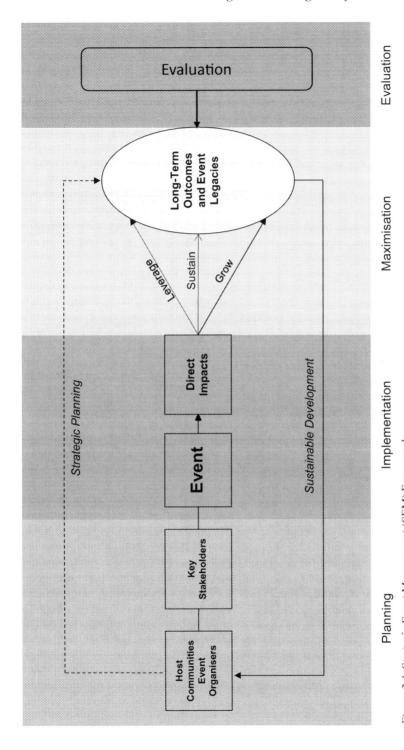

Figure 2.1 Strategic Event Management (SEM) Framework
Source: (adapted from Schulenkorf, 2009, 2010, 2012)

16 *Event management and leverage*

but also long-term goals and requires detailed thinking before any action or event takes place.

For events in particular, the planning phase involves preparing an attractive programme and specific course of action. Here, the event organiser, host community, and key stakeholders try to balance the wants and needs of the audience, performers, business partners, etc. – and all available skills and resources. During the planning phase, event managers take the role of facilitators to administer and/or supervise all business practices with the final goal of creating the highest level of efficiency possible (Mallen & Adams, 2017). In addition to those operational aspects of planning, event organisers and stakeholders also discuss strategic planning aspects, including event sustainability, growth and leverage strategies (Jordan et al., 2019). Here, the organisers, host community, and key stakeholders take a strategic ex ante approach towards realising desired long-term event outcomes. In other words, they look forward and prepare plans to generate and maximise longer-term event outcomes (see Maximisation phase for details).

Implementation

In the implementation phase, managers execute their plans and turn them into actions. This means that in an event context, organisers and stakeholders are enacting their programme; in other words, they are staging the event in an attempt to achieve all predetermined goals and objectives. In most cases, this means delivering a successful event that leads to a range of positive direct impacts, including those categorised under the traditional fields of economic, social/cultural, physical/environmental impacts (see Allen et al., 2011) but also in related areas including reputation, health, or sport development (Bell & Daniels, 2018; Misener, 2015; Misener, McGillivray, Gayle, & Legg, 2015; Potwarka & Snelgrove, 2017; Schulenkorf & Edwards, 2012; Schulenkorf, Giannoulakis, & Blom, 2019; Schulenkorf & Schlenker, 2017; Schulenkorf & Siefken, 2019; Taks, Misener, Chalip, & Green, 2013).

Given that our book is centred on the business and social dimensions of events, we focus our review of event impact studies and discussions of critical issues on these two areas. From a business perspective, the staging of events has long played a significant part in strategic tourism development initiatives, as special events can attract large numbers of visitors to a town, city, or region (Dwyer, Jago, & Forsyth, 2016; Prayag, Hosany, Nunkoo, & Alders, 2013; Yolal, Gursoy, Uysal, Kim, & Karacaoğlu, 2016). Moreover, special events – and particularly the large-scale and mega-events – have the capacity to stimulate business activity, create income and jobs, and allow for new expenditure to be injected into a host region for urban development or regeneration (Dwyer et al., 2016). It should also be noted that negative or unintended economic impacts can occur from the staging of events, including community and local business resistance to tourism, inflated prices, opportunity costs, and – if events fail to deliver promised returns – financial loss and damage to reputation (see Allen, O'Toole, Harris, & McDonnell, 2011; Preuss & Solberg, 2006).

The strategic event management framework 17

From a social and cultural perspective, there is evidence that events can impact on individual and collective social agendas. For instance, events allow individual participants and attendees to develop contacts, friendships, and networks (O'Brien, 2007; Schulenkorf, 2010, 2013). Moreover, events have the ability to contribute to the building of community networks and social capital, the celebration and enhancement of cultural traditions, the opportunity to develop community spirit and pride, education and awareness, and – where poverty is implicated – promote social and economic justice and well-being (Chalip & McGuirty, 2004; Gibson & Connell, 2015; Jepson & Stadler, 2017; Kellett et al., 2008; Misener & Mason, 2006; Nicholson & Hoye, 2008; O'Brien, 2007; O'Brien & Chalip, 2008; Skinner, Zakus, & Cowell, 2008). Meanwhile, negative and generally unintended social impacts that may result from events include congestion and overcrowding in towns, community alienation or backlash, as well as antisocial behaviour including an increase in crime, violence, and substance abuse (see Allen et al., 2011; Preuss & Solberg, 2006). In the specific context of mega-events, Manzenreiter and Horne (2017) further highlight a number of additional unintended social consequences, including a) changes in conceptions of freedom and democracy because of increased surveillance; b) the unequal distribution of gains from events among the host community; and c) the potential for exclusionary or even xenophobic impact of an event. All of these are critical for event managers to consider and address, especially as they are at odds with the often-portrayed political sentiment that special events provide an exclusively positive experience for members of the community.

Maximisation

The maximisation aspect of event management revolves around opportunities to sustain, grow, and leverage positive event impacts. In line with the initially determined strategic goals of the event (see Planning phase), event organisers move beyond the planning of direct event impacts towards focusing on strategic paths which aim to secure ongoing or long-term benefits for the host community, event organisers, and relevant stakeholders. For reoccurring events, the sustainability and growth aspects are particularly critical. They link to evaluation and learning efforts that are undertaken to improve the event in future iterations. As such, planning for the next event takes into account the newly identified weaknesses and opportunities to advance the event to the next level.

Even when sustainability per se is not a central criterion – for instance, at a one-off event that is not part of a wider event portfolio – one strategic maximisation aspect remains critical for organisers, stakeholders, and communities: the aspect of event leverage. This concept is defined as the strategic maximisation of event benefits beyond event borders (Chalip, 2004, 2006; Kellett et al., 2008); in other words, leverage represents a strategic managerial attempt to "making bigger things happen", rather than leaving them to chance. Much of the early research on event leverage referred to opportunities stemming from large-scale or mega-events, particularly in the context of maximising tourism and business opportunities (Chalip, 2004, 2006; Chalip & Leyns, 2002; Chalip & McGuirty,

18   *Event management and leverage*

2004; Kellett et al., 2008; O'Brien, 2006; O'Brien & Gardiner, 2006; Sparvero & Chalip, 2007). While discussions on leveraging large-scale and mega-events have continued (see, e.g. Smith, 2014; VanWynsberghe, Derom, & Maurer, 2012), in recent years researchers have also started to provide empirical evidence supporting the claim that community events and/or charity events can use and benefit from social and business-related event leveraging (e.g. Filo, Lock, Sherry, & Quang Huynh, 2018; Goodwin, Snelgrove, Wood, & Taks, 2017; O'Brien, 2007; Snelgrove & Wood, 2010; Woolf, Heere, & Walker, 2013). An increasing number of empirical studies have also investigated events as part of the burgeoning sport-for-development (SFD) movement; here, research has become available on leveraging opportunities that facilitate sustainable social development in disadvantaged social settings and/or in a developing world context (Bell & Daniels, 2018; Schulenkorf & Edwards, 2012; Schulenkorf et al., 2019; Schulenkorf & Schlenker, 2017; Welty Peachey, Borland, Lobpries, & Cohen, 2015). Chapter 10 will focus on the new events-for-development space in more detail.

Overall, it has become evident that regardless of the size of the event, the most significant opportunities for leverage exist in economic and social areas. For example, in the area of economic leverage, organisers can employ strategies during the event that encourage repeat visitation by event participants and attendees as future tourists to the host region (Chalip & Leyns, 2002; Chalip & McGuirty, 2004; Costa & Chalip, 2005; O'Brien, 2006). Special events can be used to foster long-term business relationships between the community and sponsors by encouraging future trade, investment, and employment. From a social perspective, Chalip (2004, 2006) argues that liminality and *communitas* can be seen as "raw material" for social leverage, as they result from a sense of celebration and social camaraderie that can exist around events. The key, then, is to leverage liminoid experiences and the sense of togetherness to achieve lasting social benefits for the community beyond events. Sport events, in particular, provide a promising arena for social leverage because participants and attendees often experience authentic human interactions not bounded by socio-economic and sociopolitical positions, status, and roles. Specifically designed sport events may be used as a platform to highlight pressing community issues or to change people's perception regarding certain social problems or values. The staging of the annual Homeless World Cup is an example of this. Here, organisers align the sport event with a particular social issue and they cooperate with the media to showcase and publicise both the current challenges and future potential of homeless people in the community (see Magee & Jeanes, 2013; Sherry, 2010; Sherry, Karg, & O'May, 2011).

Importantly, when attempting to leverage special events with the intention to reach the wider community, event organisers need to expand their connections with key decision-makers to generate additional political, educational, promotional, and financial benefits. For example, support from different levels of government may secure political backing, financial contributions, and permission for the staging and leveraging of events. Similarly, active engagement with local businesses is needed to achieve economic leverage. Event organisers and the host community can, for example, cooperate with local businesses and sponsors to

The strategic event management framework 19

create "an event-related look-and-feel" (Chalip, 2004, p. 230) in the host community. This may be achieved by creating relevant ancillary events and executing specifically designed event-related products, promotions, and theming tactics. From a sociopolitical perspective, Kellett et al. (2008) have previously shown that cities and their people can obtain valuable benefits from leveraging relationships with visiting sport teams. In a study around visiting teams training for the Melbourne 2006 Commonwealth Games, the authors found that the town of Port Phillip formulated and implemented a detailed strategic leverage plan, which contributed to the formation of new social and business relationships, cultural insights, and improved organisational networks with its visiting team from Papua New Guinea (PNG). For this, the town strategically planned a "PNG Week" and an array of festivals, workshops, and activities which included cultural displays, story readings, a barbecue and bowls game, visits to schools by PNG nationals, traditional face painting, music, song and dance, and a culminating "PNG Association Ball". Overall, with everyone on board, it was possible to achieve valuable social leverage outcomes that went well beyond the immediate purpose of the PNG team's visit, that is, participation in the Commonwealth Games.

Overall, the maximisation of positive event impacts largely depends on clever and holistic strategic management. In other words, long-term vision and strategic planning are required to successfully leverage events for expanded experiences and wider community assets. As such, event organisers, the host community, and key stakeholders need to work closely together to activate and boost an event's potential. This strategic focus is also visualised in the SEM Framework, where the long-term social outcomes are to be anticipated in the planning stage and embedded in a cyclical process towards sustainable development and community empowerment following the event's evaluation.

Evaluation

Evaluation is the final stage of the management process in which the event is systematically examined and assessed against its goals and objectives to accurately assess its overall quality, value, and achievements (Allen et al., 2011; Meyrick et al., 2015). Here, a critical appraisal of different impacts and long-term outcomes is necessary to provide evidence of the profundity of the event, as well as the longevity of potential benefits. Indeed, if the goal of an event initiative is to advance social development and business opportunities within a community, then the sustainability of relationships, business partnerships, and social networks beyond the event provide key areas for ongoing assessment (see Schulenkorf, 2012).

Evaluation efforts should be undertaken from different perspectives, including that of the organiser, community, and key stakeholders. In the end, all stakeholders want to know – and have a right to know – what exactly the event has achieved; in other words, they deserve to find out if event investments have created the promised results in terms of economic or social benefits (Schulenkorf & Edwards, 2013). Hence, reporting back to stakeholders and engaging in joint discussions are an important part of any event's ongoing success, as critical dialogue

20 *Event management and leverage*

around assessments and "lessons learnt" can lead to positive changes in future event planning and development (Presbury & Edwards, 2010).

An open and transparent event evaluation process is critical, as the provision of key information – including data collection and analysis methods – will assist in achieving accountability, credibility, and legitimacy (Carlsen, 2004; Getz, 2019; Meyrick et al., 2015). To achieve this goal, a range of quantitative and qualitative methods are available to evaluate events and it comes down to the purpose, focus, and size of the event to determine the nature of the most adequate evaluation approach. In short, quantitative methods allow for the precise assessment and measurement of an event's performance, while qualitative methods provide an in-depth way to understand the "why" and "how" of event (management) decisions and experiences. We are not going into detail about the different methods and approaches and instead refer the reader to Chapter 4 of this book. Also worthwhile is the recent event impact collection by Armbrecht and Andersson (2017) as well as Dwyer et al.'s (2016) critical appraisal of current event evaluation techniques, including the two major approaches of cost–benefit analysis and economic impact assessment.

At this stage, we want to conclude by suggesting that any newly gained knowledge from the event evaluation process can and should contribute to the future planning, management, and development of event activities. This is visualised in the SEM Framework where the evaluation phase connects back to the planning stage through a cyclical process that facilitates sustainable development and continuous improvement (see Figure 2.1).

Conclusion and outlook

People often have the naïve belief that anyone can organise an event. As we have seen, this belief does not hold true and instead detailed strategic planning, purposeful design, and in-depth research are needed to inform the elements of a quality event experience. Moreover, only a solid understanding of different event stakeholders, and their varying motivations and involvements, will allow organisers to create and maximise positive impacts and to achieve truly memorable and engaging event experiences. In this chapter, we have introduced the newly designed SEM Framework and have used it to discuss the roles and responsibilities of event organisers, host communities, and key stakeholders who all contribute to critical event management processes. For the remainder of the book, the SEM Framework will provide a managerial foundation for understanding the processes of event organisers and stakeholders to achieve critical social and business benefits. As such, the reader can refer back to the SEM Framework's interrelated stages of event planning, implementation, maximisation, and evaluation in the context of the latest social and business-related event management discussions.

References

Allen, J., O'Toole, W., Harris, R., & McDonnell, I. (2011). *Festival and special event management* (5th ed.). Milton: Wiley.

The strategic event management framework 21

Armbrecht, J., & Andersson, T. D. (2017). *Event impact* (2nd ed.). Abingdon: Routledge.

Bell, B., & Daniels, J. (2018). Sport development in challenging times: Leverage of sport events for legacy in disadvantaged communities. *Managing Sport and Leisure*, *23*(4–6), 369–390. doi:10.1080/23750472.2018.1563497

Carlsen, J. (2004). The economics and evaluation of festivals and events. *Festivals and Events Management*, 246–259.

Chalip, L. (2004). Beyond impact: A general model for host community event leverage. In B. Ritchie & D. Adair (Eds.), *Sport tourism: Interrelationships, impacts and issues* (pp. 226–252). Clevedon, UK: Channel View.

Chalip, L. (2006). Towards social leverage of sport events. *Journal of Sport and Tourism*, *11*(2), 109–127. doi:10.1080/14775080601155126

Chalip, L., & Leyns, A. (2002). Local business leveraging of a sport event: Managing an event for economic benefit. *Journal of Sport Management*, *16*(2), 132–158. Retrieved from http://journals.humankinetics.com/doi/abs/10.1123/jsm.16.2.132

Chalip, L., & McGuirty, J. (2004). Bundling sport events with the host destination. *Journal of Sport Tourism*, *9*(3), 267–282. doi:10.1080/1477508042000320241

Collins, A., & Cooper, C. (2017). Measuring and managing the environmental impact of festivals: The contribution of the ecological footprint. *Journal of Sustainable Tourism*, *25*(1), 148–162. doi:10.1080/09669582.2016.1189922

Costa, C. A., & Chalip, L. (2005). Adventure sport tourism in rural revitalisation: An ethnographic evaluation. *European Sport Management Quarterly*, *5*(3), 257–279.

Delamere, T. A., Wankel, L. M., & Hinch, T. D. (2001). Development of a scale to measure resident attitudes toward the social impacts of community festivals, part I: Item generation and purification of the measure. *Event Management*, *7*(1), 11–24.

Dowson, R., & Bassett, D. (2018). *Event planning and management: Principles, planning and practice* (2nd ed.). London: Kogan Page Publishers.

Dwyer, L., Jago, L., & Forsyth, P. (2016). Economic evaluation of special events: Reconciling economic impact and cost: Benefit analysis. *Scandinavian Journal of Hospitality and Tourism*, *16*(2), 115–129. doi:10.1080/15022250.2015.1116404

Dwyer, L., Mellor, R., Mistilis, N., & Mules, T. (2000). A framework for assessing "tangible" and "intangible" impacts of events and conventions. *Event Management*, *6*(3), 175–189.

Esteves, A. M., Franks, D., & Vanclay, F. (2012). Social impact assessment: The state of the art. *Impact Assessment and Project Appraisal*, *30*(1), 34–42. doi:10.1080/1461551 7.2012.660356

Filo, K., Lock, D., Sherry, E., & Quang Huynh, H. (2018). "You belonged to something": Exploring how fundraising teams add to the social leverage of events. *European Sport Management Quarterly*, *18*(2), 216–236. doi:10.1080/16184742.2017.1368684

Frawley, S. (Ed.). (2017). *Managing sport mega-events*. New York: Routledge.

Fredline, E., Jago, L., & Deery, M. (2003). The development of a generic scale to measure the social impacts of events. *Event Management*, *8*(1), 23–27.

Fredline, E., Raybould, M., Jago, L., & Deery, M. (2004). Triple bottom line evaluation: Progress toward a technique to assist in planning and managing an event in a sustainable manner. Paper presented at *the Tourism: State of the Art II International Scientific Conference*, Glasgow, CD (no page numbers).

Getz, D. (2019). Event evaluation and impact assessment: Five challenges. In J. Armbrecht, E. Lundberg, & T. D. Andersson (Eds.), *A research agenda for event management* (pp. 48–56). Cheltenham, UK: Edward Elgar Publishing.

Gibson, C., & Connell, J. (2015). The role of festivals in drought-affected Australian communities. *Event Management*, *19*(4), 445–459. doi:10.3727/152599515X14465748512560

22 Event management and leverage

Goodwin, A., Snelgrove, R., Wood, L., & Taks, M. (2017). Leveraging charity sport events to develop a connection to a cause. *Event Management*, *21*(2), 175–184. doi:10.3727/1 52599517X14878772869603

Jepson, A., & Stadler, R. (2017). Conceptualizing the impact of festival and event attendance upon family quality of life (QOL). *Event Management*, *21*(1), 47–60.

Jordan, T., Gibson, F., Stinnett, B., & Howard, D. (2019). Stakeholder engagement in event planning: A case study of one rural community's process. *Event Management*, *23*(1), 61–74. doi:10.3727/152599518X15378845225339

Kellett, P., Hede, A.-M., & Chalip, L. (2008). Social policy for sport events: Leveraging (relationships with) teams from other nations for community benefit. *European Sport Management Quarterly*, *8*(2), 101–121. doi:10.1080/16184740802024344

Lawson, H. A. (2005). Empowering people, facilitating community development, and contributing to sustainable development: The social work of sport, exercise, and physical education programs. *Sport, Education and Society*, *10*(1), 135–160.

Lindberg, K., & Johnson, R. (1997). The economic values of tourism's social impacts. *Annals of Tourism Research*, *24*(1), 90–116.

Liu, W., Sparks, B., & Coghlan, A. (2017). Event experiences through the lens of attendees. *Event Management*, *21*(4), 463–479. doi:10.3727/152599517X15015178156222

Magee, J., & Jeanes, R. (2013). Football's coming home: A critical evaluation of the Homeless World Cup as an intervention to combat social exclusion. *International Review for the Sociology of Sport*, *48*(1), 3–19.

Mair, J., & Laing, J. H. (2013). Encouraging pro-environmental behaviour: The role of sustainability-focused events. *Journal of Sustainable Tourism*, *21*(8), 1113–1128. doi:1 0.1080/09669582.2012.756494

Mallen, C., & Adams, L. J. (2017). *Event management in sport, recreation and tourism: Theoretical and practical dimensions*. Abingdon: Routledge.

Manzenreiter, W., & Horne, J. (2017). Socio-economic impacts of sports mega-events. In N. Schulenkorf & S. Frawley (Eds.), *Critical issues in Global Sport Management* (pp. 128–140). Abingdon: Routledge.

Meyrick, J., Barnett, T., Brown, S., Getz, D., Pettersson, R., & Wallstam, M. (2015). Event evaluation: Definitions, concepts and a state of the art review. *International Journal of Event and Festival Management*, *6*(2), 135–157.

Misener, L. (2015). Leveraging parasport events for community participation: Development of a theoretical framework. *European Sport Management Quarterly*, *15*(1), 132–153. doi:10.1080/16184742.2014.997773

Misener, L., & Mason, D. S. (2006). Creating community networks: Can sporting events offer meaningful sources of social capital? *Managing Leisure*, *11*(1), 39–56. doi:10.1080/13606710500445676

Misener, L., McGillivray, D., Gayle, M., & Legg, D. (2015). Leveraging parasport events for sustainable community participation: The Glasgow 2014 Commonwealth Games. *Annals of Leisure Research*, *18*, 450–469. doi:10.1080/11745398.2015.1045913

Naparstek, A. J., Dooley, D., & Smith, R. (1997). *Community building in public housing*. Washington, DC: U.S. Department of Housing and Urban Development.

Nicholson, M., & Hoye, R. (2008). *Sport and social capital*. Oxford: Butterworth-Heinemann.

O'Brien, D. (2006). Event business leveraging: The Sydney 2000 Olympic Games. *Annals of Tourism Research*, *33*(1), 240–261. doi:10.1016/j.annals.2005.10.011

O'Brien, D. (2007). Points of leverage: Maximizing host community benefit from a regional surfing festival. *European Sport Management Quarterly*, *7*(2), 141–165. doi: 10.1080/16184740701353315

O'Brien, D., & Chalip, L. (2007). Executive training exercise in sport event leverage. *International Journal of Culture, Tourism and Hospitality Research*, *1*(4), 296–304.

The strategic event management framework 23

O'Brien, D., & Chalip, L. (2008). Sport events and strategic leveraging: Pushing towards the triple bottom line. In A. Woodside & D. Martin (Eds.), *Tourism management: Analysis, behaviour and strategy* (pp. 318–338). Wallingford, UK and Cambridge, MA: CABI.

O'Brien, D., & Gardiner, S. (2006). Creating sustainable mega-event impacts: Networking and relationship development through pre-event training. *Sport Management Review, 9*(1), 25–48.

Potwarka, L. R., & Snelgrove, R. (2017). Managing sport events for beneficial outcomes: Theoretical and practical insights. *Event Management, 21*(2), 135–137. doi:10.3727/15 2599517X14878772869522

Prayag, G., Hosany, S., Nunkoo, R., & Alders, T. (2013). London residents' support for the 2012 Olympic Games: The mediating effect of overall attitude. *Tourism Management, 36*, 629–640.

Presbury, R., & Edwards, D. (2010). Managing sustainable festivals, meetings and events. In J. Liburd & D. Edwards (Eds.), *Understanding the sustainable development of tourism*. London: Goodfellow Publishers.

Preuss, H., & Solberg, H. A. (2006). Attracting major sporting events: The role of local residents. *European Sport Management Quarterly, 6*(4), 391–411. doi:10.1080/ 16184740601154524

Schulenkorf, N. (2009). An ex ante framework for the strategic study of social utility of sport events. *Tourism and Hospitality Research, 9*(2), 120–131.

Schulenkorf, N. (2010). Sport events and ethnic reconciliation: Attempting to create social change between Sinhalese, Tamil and Muslim sportspeople in war-torn Sri Lanka. *International Review for the Sociology of Sport, 45*(3), 273–294. doi:10.1177/1012 690210366789

Schulenkorf, N. (2012). Sustainable community development through sport and events: A conceptual framework for sport-for-development projects. *Sport Management Review, 15*(1), 1–12. doi:10.1016/j.smr.2011.06.001

Schulenkorf, N. (2013). Sport-for-development events and social capital building: A critical analysis of experiences from Sri Lanka. *Journal of Sport for Development, 1*(1), 25–36.

Schulenkorf, N., & Edwards, D. (2012). Maximizing positive social impacts: Strategies for sustaining and leveraging the benefits of intercommunity sport events in divided societies. *Journal of Sport Management, 26*(5), 379–390. doi:10.1123/jsm.26.5.379

Schulenkorf, N., & Edwards, D. (2013). Planning and evaluating sport events for sustainable development in disadvantaged communities. In T. Pernecky & M. Lück (Eds.), *Events, society and sustainability: Critical and contemporary approaches* (pp. 79–94). Abingdon, Oxon: Routledge.

Schulenkorf, N., Giannoulakis, C., & Blom, L. (2019). Sustaining commercial viability and community benefits: Management and leverage of a sport-for-development event. *European Sport Management Quarterly, 19*(4), 502–519. doi:10.1080/16184742.2018. 1546755

Schulenkorf, N., & Schlenker, K. (2017). Leveraging sport events to maximize community benefits in low- and middle-income countries. *Event Management, 21*(2), 217–231. doi :10.3727/152599517X14878772869766

Schulenkorf, N., Schlenker, K., & Thomson, A. (2017). Strategic leveraging of large-scale and mega-events. In S. Frawley (Ed.), *Managing sport mega-events* (pp. 139–149). Abingdon: Routledge.

Schulenkorf, N., & Siefken, K. (2019). Managing sport-for-development and healthy lifestyles: The sport-for-health model. *Sport Management Review, 22*(1), 96–107. https:// doi.org/10.1016/j.smr.2018.09.003

24   Event management and leverage

Sherry, E. (2010). (Re)engaging marginalized groups through sport: The Homeless World Cup. *International Review for the Sociology of Sport, 45*(1), 59–71. doi:10.1177/1012690209356988

Sherry, E., Karg, A., & O'May, F. (2011). Social capital and sport events: Spectator attitudinal change and the Homeless World Cup. *Sport in Society, 14*(1), 111–125. doi:10.1080/17430437.2011.530015

Sherwood, P., Jago, L., & Deery, M. (2004). Sustainability reporting: An application for the evaluation of special events. Paper presented at *the Annual Council of Australian Tourism and Hospitality Educators' Conference*, Brisbane.

Skinner, J., Zakus, D. H., & Cowell, J. (2008). Development through sport: Building social capital in disadvantaged communities. *Sport Management Review, 11*(3), 253–275. doi:10.1016/S1441-3523(08)70112-8

Small, K., & Edwards, D. (2003). Evaluating the socio-cultural impacts of a festival on a host community: A case study of the Australian festival of the book. Paper presented at *the 9th Annual Conference of the Asia Pacific Tourism Association*, Sydney.

Smith, A. (2014). Leveraging sport mega-events: New model or convenient justification? *Journal of Policy Research in Tourism, Leisure and Events, 6*(1), 15–30. doi:10.1080/19407963.2013.823976

Snelgrove, R., & Wood, L. (2010). Attracting and leveraging visitors at a charity cycling event. *Journal of Sport & Tourism, 15*(4), 269–285.

Soteriades, M. D., & Dimou, I. (2011). Special events: A framework for efficient management. *Journal of Hospitality Marketing & Management, 20*(3–4), 329–346. doi:10.1080/19368623.2011.562418

Sparvero, E., & Chalip, L. (2007). Professional teams as leverageable assets: Strategic creation of community value. *Sport Management Review, 10*(1), 1–30. doi:10.1016/S1441-3523(07)70001-3

Taks, M., Misener, L., Chalip, L., & Green, B. C. (2013). Leveraging sport events for participation. *Canadian Journal of Social Research, 3*(1), 12–23.

VanWynsberghe, R., Derom, I., & Maurer, E. (2012). Social leveraging of the 2010 Olympic Games: "Sustainability" in a city of Vancouver initiative. *Journal of Policy Research in Tourism, Leisure and Events, 4*(2), 185–205. doi:10.1080/19407963.2012.662618

Veal, A. J. (2006). *Research methods for leisure and tourism: A practical guide* (3rd ed.). New York: Financial Times, Prentice Hall.

Welty Peachey, J., Borland, J., Lobpries, J., & Cohen, A. (2015). Managing impact: Leveraging sacred spaces and community celebration to maximize social capital at a sport-for-development event. *Sport Management Review, 18*(1), 86–98. doi:10.1016/j.smr.2014.05.00

Wickham, M., Donnelly, T., & French, L. (in press). Strategic sustainability management in the event sector. *Event Management.* https://doi.org/10.3727/152599519X15506259856318

Woolf, J., Heere, B., & Walker, M. (2013). Do charity sport events function as "brandfests" in the development of brand community? *Journal of Sport Management, 27*(2), 95–107.

Yolal, M., Gursoy, D., Uysal, M., Kim, H., & Karacaoğlu, S. (2016). Impacts of festivals and events on residents' well-being. *Annals of Tourism Research, 61*, 1–18. https://doi.org/10.1016/j.annals.2016.07.008

Ziakas, V. (2016). Fostering the social utility of events: An integrative framework for the strategic use of events in community development. *Current Issues in Tourism, 19*(11), 1136–1157. doi:10.1080/13683500.2013.849664

3 Event leverage

Introduction

Throughout history, events of various types and forms have been a staple in every culture and society. From the ancient Greeks who utilised sport events as a form of worship to the gods in ancient Olympia to the Roman Empire which promulgated gladiator contests and other combative events to entertain a growing discontented populace, and to the promotion of major and mega festivals and events in contemporary society transmitted throughout the world through online and traditional forms of media, every culture and country has invested significant time and energy into hosting events of all shapes and sizes. These events can be small, community-based offerings such as a football tournament for young children and music concerts and festivals in villages and towns or large, major, and mega-events such as the Federation International Football Association (FIFA) World Cup and the Summer and Winter Olympic Games.

Why do communities, cities, and nations wish to play host to events? What can they potentially bring to and do for communities? Communities and cities may desire to host events for myriad reasons, such as to promote economic development, job opportunities, and tourism (Chalip, 2004; Chalip & Leyns, 2002); to enhance the image and sense of pride in a community (Chalip, 2006); to raise awareness of and combat a social or cultural issue (Schulenkorf, Giannoulakis, & Blom, 2019; Welty Peachey, Borland, Lobpries, & Cohen, 2015); to address environmental concerns (Chalip, 2006); and to increase participation in other activities, such as sports, which a community, city, or nation offers on a routine basis (Chalip, Green, Taks, & Misener, 2017; Derom & VanWynsberghe, 2015), among others. However, we must be cautious in claiming that these outcomes will automatically come about simply because the community hosts the event – this is furthest from the truth. Just hosting a regional football tournament in a mid-sized city, for example, may not significantly bring increased dollars into the community unless strategies and tactics are put in place to capitalise on the presence of the tournament in the city. On a grander scale, consider the Tokyo 2020 Summer Olympic Games that had to be postponed to 2021 due to the COVID-19 pandemic. Auspiciously, Japan and the city of Tokyo were hoping to see enhanced economic activity and development over the long term as a result of hosting the

DOI: 10.4324/9781003002772-4

26 *Event management and leverage*

Games, such as job creation, increased tourism, increased business development, and infrastructure improvements. Organisers may also wish to enhance the image of the city, strengthen pride in the city, or even utilise the Games to stimulate ongoing sport participation and healthy lifestyle choices in residents. These laudable outcomes, however, will not be realised unless Games organisers and community officials and partners strategically plan for these outcomes, launching tactics to capitalise on the Games to realise these objectives. This is the concept of event leverage, which is the focus of this chapter.

Event leverage can be defined as "activities that need to be undertaken around the event itself, which seeks to maximise long-term benefits from events" (Chalip, 2004, p. 228). As such, the event acts as a resource or catalyst from which other benefits can be levered (Smith, 2014). The concept of event leverage has come about only fairly recently, signalling a paradigm shift from event thinking focused primarily on the impacts of events and post hoc event evaluations, or what is commonly referred to as event legacy (Preuss, 2007; Smith, 2014). This new paradigm encourages event planners and researchers to plan for and identify targeted strategies and tactics that are effective in catalysing specified outcomes (Chalip, 2006; Misener, 2015). The leveraging approach is about envisioning desired outcomes for a community *before* the event takes place, and then deriving strategies to maximise benefits towards these outcomes, whether they be economic, environmental, or social (Chalip, 2006; O'Brien & Chalip, 2007). However, the leveraging paradigm is not infallible. While research has shown that some communities have effectively engaged in event leverage towards a variety of economic, environmental, cultural, political, social, and sport-related outcomes (Chalip et al., 2017; Karadakis, Kaplanidou, & Karlis, 2010), other scholarship has identified events which have not been leveraged effectively (Hodgetts & Duncan, 2015; Taks, Green, Misener, & Chalip, 2014; Ziakas, 2015).

Given the new focus in practice and scholarship on event leverage, the purpose of this chapter is to provide an in-depth discussion of the event leverage concept and then to illuminate recent advances in leverage thinking, and where warranted, engage with criticisms about this approach. Managerial implications for event leverage and thoughts on future outlook for practice and scholarship will also be advanced. Throughout, examples of events that are engaging in the leveraging approach, from smaller, community-based offerings to mega-events, will be highlighted, including the strategies and tactics associated with leverage for economic and social outcomes.

Distinction between legacy and leverage

Historically, much of the conversation about events has focused on legacy or the lasting impacts that an event may have on a community, culture, and nation (Preuss, 2007). As suggested by Preuss (2007), "Irrespective of the time of production and space, legacy is all planned and unplanned, positive and negative, tangible and intangible structures created for and by a sport event that remain longer than the event itself" (p. 211). While the focus on legacy has primarily been associated

Event leverage   27

with mega-sport events such as the Olympic Games, the concept is also applicable to smaller, community-based events and to non-sport events as well. Legacies of events can occur in economic, social, and environmental areas (Karadakis et al., 2010). However, the key here is that more often than not legacies or impacts are assumed to occur as a result of hosting the event and do not focus on strategically planning and designing the event in order to bring about these outcomes of interest (Taks, Misener, Chalip, & Green, 2013). Studies have shown that host communities do not always benefit from positive legacies of events due to the trickle-down effect or demonstration effect (Misener, Taks, Chalip, & Green, 2015; Smith & Fox, 2007). As such, and gradually within the last two decades, conversation has moved more towards the concept of event leverage or the strategic planning of events to achieve targeted outcomes (Chalip, 2006; O'Brien & Chalip, 2007). The leveraging approach has been advanced as more sustainable and as a long-term strategic process that is a marked improvement over the legacy concept of retrospective, ex post, impact research and thinking (O'Brien & Chalip, 2007). Thus, more and more scholarship and conversation have embraced the paradigm shift from legacy to leverage thinking. Next, we turn to the historical development of leverage theory and outline its key tenets.

Leverage theory development and principles

Chalip and Leyns (2002) and Chalip (2004) were the first to crystallise the shifting paradigm from legacy thinking to event leverage and strategic planning for outcomes. Early scholarship in event leverage centred upon strategically designing events to maximise economic benefits and developing the specific tactics to do so (Chalip, 2004; Chalip & Costa, 2005; Chalip & Leyns, 2002). Subsequently, the conversation advanced to also include the leverage of events for social outcomes (Chalip, 2006), as well as to raise awareness in the public about environmental issues, or environmental leverage (O'Brien & Chalip, 2007). As such, the triple bottom line approach to leverage (economic, social, and environmental) began to gain traction (Girginov, Peshin, & Belousov, 2017; O'Brien & Chalip, 2007). As articulated by Beesley and Chalip (2011), "a strategic approach to event planning and management, referred to as leveraging, not only can stimulate economic development, but also can be used to encourage change in social . . . and environmental agendas" (p. 324). More recently, Chalip and colleagues (2017) have further advanced the event leverage concept by proposing a model for leveraging sport events for enhanced sport participation in non-host regions. All of these approaches to event leverage will be discussed in more detail in the following sections.

In terms of key principles, leverage thinking necessitates that host regions consider the resources that are available, and the opportunities they wish to capitalise upon, when hosting an event of any size (Misener, Lu, & Carlisi, 2020). Resources are those tied to event-related activities in order to develop strategic, community-based outcomes, such as human capital, financial resources, community networks, and stadia and infrastructure (Grix, 2014). In addition, to fully

28 *Event management and leverage*

activate event leverage strategies, collective community action and alliance building are vital (Chalip et al., 2017; Chen & Misener, 2019). There needs to be an effective coordination of the network surrounding the event (local agencies, businesses, communities, various levels of government) to ensure that the positive benefits from event leverage strategies are realised (Chalip et al., 2017). As another key principle, it is important to consider existing local strategies, resources, sociocultural, and political conditions for effective leverage to be activated (Beesley & Chalip, 2011; Chen & Misener, 2019). Events must be planned for and considered within the existing destination product and service mix of a location – events cannot just be planned and administered in isolation from these other endeavours (Chalip, 2006).

It is also helpful to differentiate between event-led leveraging and event-themed leveraging (VanWynsberghe, 2014). Event-led leveraging occurs when leverage strategies/projects are closely tied to the events and attempt to optimise desired positive impacts, such as leveraging a mega-sport event for positive economic return in a host destination. With event-themed leverage, there are looser ties to the actual event, as the projects are often general initiatives in the community that attempt to capitalise on the opportunities presented by an event to address other key priorities, such as a marathon event being utilised to draw awareness to a community's existing priorities on developing physically active local residents (Smith, 2012).

In a broad sense, much of the conceptual thinking and scholarship on event leverage, as illumined earlier, to date has focused on large-scale and mega-events such as the Olympic Games, with less attention given to the leverage of smaller, community-based events (Schulenkorf et al., 2019). However, there has been some recent scholarship that is beginning to examine how smaller-scale, community-based events can also be leveraged, particularly with regard to social outcomes (Schulenkorf & Schlenker, 2017). This new advancement will be discussed in further detail later. Finally, it is readily apparent that almost all leverage scholarship has taken place in the context of sport events, which is not surprising given that the event leverage concept emerged with Chalip (2004) and Chalip and Leyns's (2002) economic leverage models pertaining to sport events. Thus, this accentuates the need for future research on event leverage models and strategies with other types of events (e.g. music and food festivals, outdoor recreation events, and many more).

The next section presents a discussion of the various types of leverage, namely economic leverage, social leverage, and the more recent advance of leveraging events for sport participation and physical activity, particularly in non-host regions.

Economic leverage

As mentioned earlier, the paradigm shift from legacy to leverage began with Chalip and Leyns (2002) and Chalip's (2004) work on sport events and economic leverage. Early research with economic leverage found that many businesses in

Event leverage 29

the area of a sport event – the Gold Coast Honda Indy in Australia in this case – were not capitalising on the leverageable opportunities associated with the event (Chalip & Leyns, 2002). The potential for leverage went unrealised, and there was inertia that had to be overcome in order for businesses to engage in leverage thinking, which could explain why the economic benefits of sport events are generally not optimised. To maximise the potential for economic benefits, Chalip and Leyns (2002) advocated that event organisers must engage in active coordination efforts with local businesses to capitalise on the opportunity.

This early work led Chalip (2004) to advance a general model for event leverage that has guided subsequent thinking and investigations into events, economic leverage, and brand enhancement. Chalip highlighted that the strategic goals of event leveraging are focused on short- and long-term outcomes. The leverageable resource is the portfolio of events in a community, which then creates opportunities to maximise event visitors and trade, along with event media coverage to enhance a host community's image. To maximise total trade and revenue from an event, four tactics can be employed in the short term: (1) entice visitor spending; (2) lengthen visitor stays in the region; (3) retain event expenditures within the local community in order to keep revenues from the event in the community; and (4) utilise the event to enhance existing and new business relationships (Chalip, 2004; O'Brien, 2007). To engage in longer-term event leveraging, Chalip (2004) then posited that tactics need to be developed to enhance a host community's image through event and destination marketers aligning their marketing messages. Principally, this can be accomplished through effective event media management by engaging in two primary tactics: (1) showcase the region through event advertising and reporting; and (2) use the event in regional advertising and reporting. On the whole, Chalip suggested that there needs to be a strong link between the event and the destination marketing mix in the community, with event marketers making use of destination images in their advertising and promotion efforts, while destination marketers incorporate event images in their destination marketing and promotions. To accomplish these objectives for optimising economic return to a community from an event and enhancing the brand, coordination between event organisers and community leaders, government officials, and local businesses is critical (Chalip & Leyns, 2002; O'Brien, 2007).

With the majority of work in event leverage thus far focused on economic and tourism impacts of mega-events (Taks, Chalip, & Green, 2015), O'Brien (2007) made an important advance to Chalip's (2004) leverage model by illuminating how a local or regional, smaller-scale sport event can also apply these tactics to maximise economic leverage and enhance destination image. O'Brien's work made two conceptual extensions to Chalip's model. First, his work demonstrated that sustainable business relationships and reputation enhancement are vital for both immediate and long-term leverage, not just for one or the other. Second, and specific to sport events, O'Brien posited that the integration of a sport subculture into event programming can enhance immediate and longer-term leverage, and thus, Chalip's model was revised to include the centrality of a sport subculture to event leverage. In other words, it is important for event organisers and destination

30 *Event management and leverage*

marketers to create programming and marketing messages that tap into the particular subculture of a sport in order to entice visitor spending and lengthen visitor stays. Event visitors wish to identify with an event and the values of a particular sport, and this capitalisation on sport subculture values can make this linkage for consumers and thus increase affinity for the event and attendance (O'Brien, 2007).

More recent work on economic leverage and sport events has also focused on smaller, regional events. A study in three Australian cities with regional sport events (a triathlon, marathon, and sailing regatta) revealed that there are six key determinants to business engagement in event leveraging with these smaller events: (1) event cooperation; (2), tourism dependency; (3) business size; (4) promotion; (5) strategic direction; and (6) skills (Mackellar, 2015). Local businesses must effectively engage with the regional sport event in order to maximise its economic contribution to the area, ongoing success of the event, and visitor satisfaction. In addition, recent advances have also demonstrated that tourism in a region can be enhanced and invigorated through the strategic leveraging of a portfolio of events, together with cross-leveraging (different organisations working synergistically together to strategically plan events for mutually agreed-upon outcomes), strong coordination between agencies, and planning of ancillary events around the focal events (Pereira, Mascarenhas, Flores, & Pires, 2015).

Social leverage

As highlighted earlier, the initial work in event leverage embraced economic leverage concepts. Building on this model of leverage focusing on economic and brand image enhancement (Chalip, 2004), Chalip (2006) proposed a model of social leverage of events, a critical conceptual advance. In this model, events must first focus on cultivating liminality and then leveraging it. Through the process, communitas is generated and also leveraged for various social outcomes (Chalip, 2006; O'Brien & Chalip, 2007). Liminality, as described by Turner (1979), is conceptualised as "being-on-a-threshold" and in a state that is "betwixt-and-between the normal, day-to-day cultural and social states" (p. 465). It is a "time of enchantment, when anything might, and even should, happen" (Turner, 1979, p. 465). Sport events and other types of festivals and events can create a liminoid space, where fans and event attendees experience the unexpected, excitement, enthusiasm, and community cohesion that result through spontaneous celebration and building of relationships, or communitas (Welty Peachey et al., 2015). Communitas, then, occurs when individuals step outside of their normal bounds and form unexpected relationships, where the event elicits feelings of equality, belonging, and group devotion to a goal that transcend individual lives and interests (Arnould & Price, 1993).

Taking into account the aforementioned, Chalip (2006) advanced a number of strategies for an event to cultivate liminality, which can then generate communitas and serve as the precondition for social impact: (1) enabling sociability among event visitors; (2) creating event-related social events; (3) facilitating informal

Event leverage 31

social opportunities; (4) producing ancillary events surrounding the main event; and (5) theming, or using decorations, symbols, colours, rituals, and narratives at the event. O'Brien and Chalip (2008) then made an important advance to Chalip's (2006) model, articulating four tactics that event planners can strategically utilise to leverage liminoid experiences and communitas for social outcomes and social change, through adjusting people's perceptions about social issues and problems. These tactics are: (1) align sport events with targeted social issues; (2) create a "fit" between targeted social issues and sport subcultures; (3) lengthen visitor stays for social purposes; and (4) entice engagement with the targeted social issues. In addition, O'Brien and Chalip (2008) advanced that event media is also a leverageable opportunity that can be optimised for a social cause.

Using Chalip (2006) and O'Brien and Chalip (2008) as the foundation, there have been a number of recent studies which have examined the capacity of sport events to be leveraged socially. Many of these events fall within the remit of sport-for-development (SFD) and can be positioned as a new avenue of events-related scholarship, that of events-for-development (see Chapter 10 for a full exploration of this recent trend). It has been posited that smaller-scale or community events have even more potential for leveraging social issues than do large-scale or mega-events (Misener, 2015). Small events do not have the capital expenditures and financial risks as larger events, and thus do not have to be justified through financial investments (Smith, 2012). In addition, with smaller-scale events, there is "the potential for tighter social networks and connectedness of the local population with the event, be it as politicians, spectators, volunteers, marketing destination managers, or event organisers" (Misener et al., 2015, p. 4).

For example, Schulenkorf and Edwards (2012) investigated the opportunities and strategic tactics for leveraging social event benefits resulting from small-scale, intercommunity sport events in ethnically divided Sri Lanka. Their work was an important conceptual advance, as previous scholarship had not examined how to leverage events for social change in a region in conflict and political turmoil. Their findings suggested that to leverage these small-scale, community events for social change and local capacity building, host communities needed to utilise children as catalysts for change; design ethnically mixed sport activities; plan event-related sociocultural opportunities; integrate events with ongoing SFD programming; and engage in social, cultural, political, and educational event leverage. More recent work by Schulenkorf and Schlenker (2017) has examined how to maximise the social potential and leverageable opportunities in low- and middle-income countries, a previously unexplored area. They advanced leverage thinking by identifying the mechanisms through which these events engaged in sociocultural, participatory, educational, health, and reputational leverage. Similarly, Schulenkorf and colleagues (2019) examined how a smaller, community-led event in Greece was leveraged for social, cultural, economic, and sporting benefits. Here, it was found that the management team of a mini-marathon event engaged in a participatory management approach and strategic leverage thinking to leverage the local culture and historic sites, align the event with relevant social issues and work with local community residents to become engaged with and

32 *Event management and leverage*

involved in the event. Within these forms of smaller SFD and community events, external change agents play a vital role in helping to leverage the events for sustainable development (Schulenkorf, 2010).

Focusing on a different social issue, Welty Peachey and colleagues (2015) examined the Street Soccer USA annual tournament for teams of individuals suffering from homelessness to see how the event was being leveraged socially to develop social capital for these individuals. They found that event organisers were successful in cultivating a buzz in Washington, D.C., about homeless issues through the event by employing many of the tactics suggested by Chalip (2006) and O'Brien and Chalip (2008) for cultivating liminality and communitas. They were then able to leverage these intangible resources for social capital development and integrate homeless individuals back into their communities. As an important conceptual advance, they found that inclusive play, or where coaches played with the homeless players, was a key ingredient for social capital development through the event.

Other recent work has examined the social leverage of parasport events, where able-bodied athletes and athletes with a disability compete alongside each other, making important advancements to the social leverage literature (Misener, 2015; Misener et al., 2015; Misener et al., 2020). Work by Misener and colleagues (2015) examined how an integrated parasport event was being leveraged to create opportunities for community participation and influence attitudes towards disability. Using the 2014 Commonwealth Games in Glasgow as a case, it was found that while there were attempts at an integrated policy approach to leveraging the event for accessibility outcomes, the leveraging attempt was not as successful as it could have been, mainly because there were not additional programmes or projects envisioned that could lead to impact beyond the temporal nature of a large-scale sport event. With this unrealised potential, a later study by Misener and colleagues (2020) examined how parasport events can create and catalyse alliances and partnerships around leveraging resources of the event for social impact. Focusing on the cross-sectoral partnership of the Ontario Parasport Legacy Group, the study showed that resource conditions, window of collaborative opportunity, and cultural influence were important drivers of leadership and strategic initiatives. However, to maintain effective partnership delivery, it is critical to enhance engagement of all parties, maintain shared motivation, and improve joint capacity.

Thus, on the whole, there has been a growing body of work which has engaged with the concept of social leverage of events, although there are still many directions left to explore and crystallise.

Leverage for sport participation, physical activity, and physical health

In addition to economic and social leverage of events, other more recent scholarship has examined how events can be leveraged for related outcomes, such as sport participation, physical activity, and physical health benefits (Chalip et al., 2017; Chen & Misener, 2019; Derom & VanWynsberghe, 2015; Lane, Murphy, &

Event leverage 33

Bauman, 2013). Lane and colleagues (2013) began this line of research by examining the leverage effect of participation in a small-scale community sport event (the Women's Mini-Marathon in Ireland) that capitalised on existing community-based resources to enhance physical activity among physically inactive women. In this experimental design, participants who received community-based resources (packet with physical activity options in their community, training plans, a pedometer, among others) demonstrated increased physical activity after the event compared to control group members who did not receive these materials. Essentially, this research points towards the importance of strategically utilising resources, targeted communication, and planning for how an event can be leveraged to increase physical activity post-event. In another study, Derom and Van-Wynsberghe (2015) explored the leveraging of a bicycling event for public health benefit and to increase physical activity. Here, the Tour of Flanders (Belgium's most popular annual cycling event) was successfully leveraged by the community and event planners through strategically capitalising on the cycling heritage in the region to increase bicycle tourism and ongoing active participation in cycling. Importantly, this study also argued for the critical need to strategically integrate social and economic leverage opportunities in events, not considering them in isolation from each other. In the main, smaller-scale events such as the ones described earlier may be better equipped in the long run to encourage physical activity in a community than one-off mega-events such as the Olympic Games, as they can serve as constant reminders about the benefits of physical health and activity and are more integrated into the fabric of the community (Schulenkorf & Schlenker, 2017).

One of the most intriguing conceptual advances in this area is Chalip and colleagues' (2017) work, which posits a conceptual model for leveraging sport events, more specifically mega-events such as the Olympic Games, for ongoing sport participation and development. Through a panel of 12 experts, a model was developed consisting of three critical elements. First, the hierarchal nature of the context must be considered, such as culture, opinions, attitudes, and systems and structures. Second, the model elucidates that there are three types of organisations that have a stake in the leveraging process – event, sport, and non-sport entities. Finally, the model suggests that human, physical, and knowledge resources are necessary ingredients to successfully leverage the event for sport participation and development. Critically, Chalip and colleagues advance that sport events have the potential to enhance longer-term sport participation in regions, but this is dependent upon the formation of alliances between sport organisations, event organisers, and non-sport stakeholders in order to integrate the events into the marketing mix of sport organisations. However, there are barriers and challenges to leveraging events for sport participation which must be mitigated, such as a region's lack of capacity to absorb new sport participants, the crowding out of local participation by the event, and disincentives that may result from watching elite performances that are unattainable by the average person.

Taking Chalip and colleagues' (2017) model on board, Chen and Misener (2019) more recently extended this model by examining a non-host region of the London 2012 Olympic and Paralympic Games to explore the strategic planning

34   *Event management and leverage*

and leveraging processes for sport participation in a non-host area. Specifically, they found that effective event leverage for sport participation in a non-host area requires the formation of key, early leadership and strategic alliances and that a specific leveraging team plays a pivotal role. However, over time, various partners found it challenging to continue with event leverage strategies due to conflicts of interest and goal misalignment. Conceptually, Chen and Misener augmented Chalip et al.'s (2017) model by positioning policy, politics, and economic environment at the broad level which influence leveraging capabilities, replacing event organisers with a specific committee targeted at leverage opportunities and highlighting the critical role of strategic partnerships.

Overall, while advances have been made when considering the potential of large- and small-scale sport events to be leveraged for sport participation, physical activity, and physical health, this area of study is still in its infancy and requires further conceptual work and empirical engagements.

Event leverage for other outcomes

Finally, it is worth highlighting that event leverage scholarship has also focused on the potential for events to be leveraged for additional outcomes other than the three main areas discussed earlier. These areas include infrastructure development and capacity building (Girginov et al., 2017; Solberg & Preuss, 2007); development of national soft power (Brannagan & Giulianotti, 2015); political leverage resulting from community-based events (Schulenkorf, 2010); heritage restoration (Smith, 2014); quality of life for local residents (Gursoy & Kendall, 2006); and volunteer development (Fairley, Cardillo, & Filo, 2016). Common to many of these studies is the identified need to form strategic alliances and partnerships in order to fully activate the leverage potential of small- and large-scale events and the critical need to integrate the event into the ongoing fabric of the community – socially and economically – through its destination marketing mix.

Challenges to leverage thinking

While there is much potential for events and communities to capitalise on event leverage towards a myriad of economic, social, environmental, and other outcomes, as alluded to earlier, there are challenges to leverage thinking and the potential success of leveraging events for any targeted outcome. For instance, some have questioned the entire philosophy behind event leverage and whether this is really a new direction or rather a public relations tool utilised by event organisers and individuals in power to deflect criticisms from those responsible for legacy of events (Misener et al., 2015; Smith, 2014). Smith (2014) advocates that event-themed leverage provides a more effective strategy for host regions than event-led approaches, as this form of leverage is less reliant on the requirements of the event which are determined by others who may not have a vested interest in the host community. Others have argued that the leverageable benefits of events are not equally experienced by all and that they are not equally distributed (Ziakas, 2015). Marginalised and disenfranchised populations and communities

Event leverage 35

do not receive the benefits of events as equitably as those networked into the social and economic fabric of a community. As such, Ziakas (2015) argued that future event leverage scholarship needs to embrace a critical lens and "account for the influence of power structures and social-ordering processes on developing and implementing strategic leveraging programs" (p. 689). In addition, it is important to recognise that leveraging of events can be aligned with beneficial or unscrupulous purposes and that "the task is therefore to find the means to protect leverage from corrupting forces" (Ziakas, 2015, p. 694).

Businesses, too, often experience barriers to engaging with events to leverage their benefits (Mackellar, 2015). Active engagement on the part of businesses with events can occur when barriers are low, and "when businesses have skills, information, coordination, capital, and strategic direction to become involved" (Mackellar, 2015, p. 24). However, when the barriers are higher, there is less opportunity for the business to engage with the event and even a disincentive to do so. Taks et al. (2015) also suggested that the lack of ownership over the leveraging approach due to limited community capacity hinders the potentialities of leverage for medium-sized participatory events.

In addition, there are a host of challenges related to effective alliances and partnerships between organisations and stakeholders for activating effective and sustainable event leverage. One of the issues here is the potential problems related to knowledge transfer between partners, which can undermine goal alignment and inhibit effective leverage (Beesley & Chalip, 2011; Gao, Heere, Todd, & Mihalik, 2020). In examining partnerships and alliances for leverage of the London 2012 Olympics, Bell and Gallimore (2015) noted that a good number of partners were limited in the capacity to deliver on the benefits laid out in the strategic plan for the Games, however, a steering group was effective in the short term at helping to maintain the collaborative approach to realising the benefits from the event. Over time, though, it is argued that the political, personnel, and organisational change since the 2012 Games has undermined the legacy of the event and its leverageable potential, with agencies and institutions reverting to their silos post-event. Thus, the leverageable benefits are lost (Bell & Gallimore, 2015). Similarly, it was found that event leverage potential was not fully realised with the 2019 Federation of International Basketball Associations World Cup in China because stakeholders and organisations did not have knowledge about social leverage; the media promoted current values and beliefs of stakeholders; and the Chinese culture has implicit and explicit influence on organisational relationships which can limit leverage thinking (Gao et al., 2020).

Even with the myriad of challenges and barriers articulated earlier, there is still much potential for leveraging of events going forward. In the next section, we focus on reviewing managerial implications for leveraging events and how managers and organisations can optimise leverage thinking.

Managerial implications

Drawing from the earlier review and discussion, there are a number of key implications for event managers and organisers to consider for optimally engaging in

36 *Event management and leverage*

event leverage. Managers should consider forming event leverage teams comprising event planners and various community stakeholders in that the most effective way to achieve leveraging goals will often be in a bottom-up approach with community members providing input, guidance, and leadership (Ziakas, 2015). This team can then be charged with conceptualising and implementing the strategies and tactics for leveraging the event for targeted outcomes and for integrating the event into the ongoing destination marketing mix of the community. These teams will be ineffective if they do not comprise key community, business, and government leaders, and in many ways, leadership of these teams should reside with stakeholders outside of the event to increase the opportunity for sustainable leverage planning that is truly integrated into short- and long-term community development goals. Membership on these leverage teams should also comprise key individuals and institutions who are highly respected in the community to increase buy-in from community stakeholders and partners (Schulenkorf & Schlenker, 2017). Outside of the event leverage team, for smaller-scale community-based events, community members should be involved in the design, management, and implementation of the event to facilitate not only effective and efficient event operations but also sustainable leverage opportunities. Long-term leverage strategies are ultimately carried out by community stakeholders, so their involvement in all facets of the event bolsters sustainable leverage towards community-based outcomes identified in the planning stages. In addition, to effectively leverage events, strategic partnerships are needed between the event and various government and business entities. Leveraging cannot be effective without key partnerships that allow the event to be fully integrated into ongoing community strategic efforts for economic or social development or for enhancing sport participation and healthy lifestyles. The danger, as illustrated earlier, is that events can be missed opportunities for community and social development whose potential effects do not last much past the events themselves. Inter-organisational partnerships will help to ensure that the benefits obtained from events will be sustainable and enrich the quality of life in communities.

Conclusion and outlook

So where does all of this leave us? What are the next steps revolving around event leverage? Of course, the current COVID-19 pandemic that has necessitated the cancellation of most events impedes upon leverage considerations in the immediate future, but still, there may be leverageable opportunities associated with event cancellations. For instance, some marathon events are now offering virtual race opportunities to participants in lieu of the physical event. How might these virtual races be leveraged for social outcomes such as sense of community and social capital? How do event organisers strategically plan for the leveraging of these virtual opportunities? This would be a fruitful and exciting line of research that would enhance event scholarship and practice in the face of a challenging pandemic. In addition, as noted earlier, most of the thinking and scholarship around event leverage has been situated within the sport event context. Thus,

Event leverage 37

there are many opportunities in research and practice to apply leverage thinking to non-sport events such as festivals, concerts, and other smaller community-based events. How might leveraging strategies and tactics be different in these contexts? What different types of outcomes may organisers wish to target? Expanding scholarship and practice in event leverage to broader contexts will be critical to advancing leverage thinking and possibilities in the near future. In the final chapter, we will expand upon future research ideas on event leverage concepts.

As this chapter has shown, the concept of event leverage is vital to the design, planning, and implementation of events of all sizes, from smaller community-based offerings to large, mega-events with prominence on the national and international stage. Leverage thinking in many ways is still in its infancy – the concept is relatively new to many event organisers – and scholarship is only now emerging and pushing forward a critical research agenda related to leveraging concepts. The outlook and potential for event leverage is still largely untapped, providing exciting opportunities for event professionals and scholars to truly marshal novel ideas to realise how events can best contribute to the social fabric, and ultimately, deliver positive outcomes for communities and individuals.

References

Arnould, E. J., & Price, L. L. (1993). River magic: Extraordinary experience and the extended service encounter. *Journal of Consumer Research, 20*(1), 24–45.

Beesley, L. G., & Chalip, L. (2011). Seeking (and not seeking) to leverage mega-sport events in non-host destinations: The case of Shanghai and the Beijing Olympics. *Journal of Sport & Tourism, 16*, 323–344.

Bell, B., & Gallimore, K. (2015). Embracing the games? Leverage and legacy of London 2012 Olympics at the sub-regional level by means of strategic partnerships. *Leisure Studies, 34*, 720–741.

Brannagan, P. M., & Giulianotti, R. (2015). Soft power and soft disempowerment: Qatar, global sport and football's 2022 World Cup finals. *Leisure Studies, 34*, 703–719.

Chalip, L. (2004). Beyond impact: A general model for sport event leverage. In B. W. Ritchie & D. Adair (Eds.), *Sport tourism: Interrelationships, impacts and issues* (pp. 226–252). Toronto: Channel View Publications.

Chalip, L. (2006). Towards social leverage of sport events. *Journal of Sport & Tourism, 11*(2), 109–127.

Chalip, L., & Costa, C. A. (2005). Sport event tourism and the destination brand: Towards a general theory. *Sport in Society, 8*(2), 218–237.

Chalip, L., Green, B. C., Taks, M., & Misener, L. (2017). Creating sport participation from sport events: Making it happen. *International Journal of Sport Policy and Politics, 9*, 257–276.

Chalip, L., & Leyns, A. (2002). Local business leveraging of a sport event: Managing an event for economic benefit. *Journal of Sport Management, 16*(2), 132–158.

Chen, S., & Misener, L. (2019). Event leveraging in a nonhost region: Challenges and opportunities. *Journal of Sport Management, 33*, 275–288.

Derom, I., & VanWynsberghe, R. (2015). Extending the benefits of leveraging cycling events: Evidence from the Tour of Flanders. *European Sport Management Quarterly, 15*(1), 111–131.

38 *Event management and leverage*

Fairley, S., Cardillo, M. L., & Filo, K. (2016). Engaging volunteers from regional communities: Non-host city resident perceptions towards a mega-event and the opportunity to volunteer. *Event Management, 20*, 433–447.

Gao, F., Heere, B., Todd, S., & Mihalik, B. (2020). The initial intentions for social leveraging of a mega sport event among stakeholders of a newly formed interorganisational relationship. *Journal of Sport Management*. Advance online publication. doi:10.1123/jsm.2018-0026

Girginov, V., Peshin, N., & Belousov, L. (2017). Leveraging mega-events for capacity building in voluntary sport organizations. *Voluntas, 28*, 2081–2102.

Grix, J. (Ed.). (2014). *Leveraging legacies from sports mega-events: Concepts and cases.* London: Palgrave Macmillan.

Gursoy, D., & Kendall, K. W. (2006). Hosting mega-events: Modeling locals' support. *Annals of Tourism Research, 33*, 603–623.

Hodgetts, D., & Duncan, M. J. (2015). Quantitative analysis of sport development event legacy: An examination of the Australian Surf Life Saving Championships. *European Sport Management Quarterly, 15*, 364–380. doi:10.1080/16184742.2015.1021824

Karadakis, K., Kaplanidou, K., & Karlis, G. (2010). Understanding the legacies of a host Olympic city: The case of the 2010 Vancouver Olympic Games. *Sport Marketing Quarterly, 19*(2), 110–117.

Lane, A., Murphy, N., & Bauman, A. (2013). An effort to "leverage" the effect of participation in a mass event on physical activity. *Health Promotion International, 30*, 542–551.

Mackellar, J. (2015). Determinants of business engagement with regional sport events. *European Sport Management Quarterly, 15*(1), 7–26.

Misener, L. (2015). Leveraging parasport events for community participation: Development of a theoretical framework. *European Sport Management Quarterly, 15*(1), 132–153.

Misener, L., Lu, L. D., & Carlisi, R. (2020). Leveraging events to develop collaborative partnerships: Examining the formation and collaborative dynamics of the Ontario Parasport Legacy Group. *Journal of Sport Management*. Advance online publication. https://doi.org/10.1123/jsm.2019-0283

Misener, L., Taks, M., Chalip, L., & Green, B. C. (2015). The elusive "trickle-down effect" of sport events: Assumptions and missed opportunities. *Managing Sport and Leisure, 20*(2), 135–156.

O'Brien, D. (2007). Points of leverage: Maximising host community benefit from a regional surfing festival. *European Sport Management Quarterly, 7*(2), 141–165.

O'Brien, D., & Chalip, L. (2007). Executive training exercise in sport event leverage. *International Journal of Culture, Tourism and Hospitality Research, 1*(4), 296–304.

O'Brien, D., & Chalip, L. (2008). Sport events and strategic leveraging: Pushing towards the triple bottom line. In A. Woodside & D. Martin (Eds.), *Tourism management: Analysis, behavior and strategy* (pp. 318–338). Wallingford, UK and Cambridge, MA: CABI.

Pereira, E., Mascarenhas, M., Flores, A., & Pires, G. (2015). Nautical small-scale sports events portfolio: A strategic leveraging approach. *European Sport Management Quarterly, 15*(1), 27–47.

Preuss, H. (2007). The conceptualisation and measurement of mega sport event legacies. *Journal of Sport & Tourism, 12*(3–4), 207–227.

Schulenkorf, N. (2010). The roles and responsibilities of a change agent in sport event development projects. *Sport Management Review, 13*(2), 118–128.

Schulenkorf, N., & Edwards, D. (2012). Maximising positive social impacts: Strategies for sustaining and leveraging the benefits of intercommunity sport events in divided societies. *Journal of Sport Management, 26*, 379–390.

Schulenkorf, N., Giannoulakis, C., & Blom, L. (2019). Sustaining commercial viability and community benefits: Management and leverage of a sport-for-development event. *European Sport Management Quarterly, 19*(4), 502–519.

Schulenkorf, N., & Schlenker, K. (2017). Levering sport events to maximise community benefits in low- and middle-income countries. *Event Management, 21*, 217–231.

Smith, A. (2012). Events and social regeneration: From social impacts to social leverage. In *Events and urban regeneration: The strategic use of events to revitalise cities* (pp. 134–168). New York, NY: Routledge.

Smith, A. (2014). Leveraging sport mega-events: New model or convenient justification? *Journal of Policy Research in Tourism, Leisure and Events, 6*(1), 15–30.

Smith, A., & Fox, T. (2007). From "event-led" to "event-themed" regeneration: The 2002 Commonwealth Games legacy programme. *Urban Studies, 44*(5), 1125–1143.

Solberg, H. A., & Preuss, H. (2007). Major sport events and long-term tourism impacts. *Journal of Sport Management, 21*, 213–234.

Taks, M., Chalip, L., & Green, C. (2015). Impacts and strategic outcomes from non-mega sport events for local communities. *European Sport Management Quarterly, 15*(1), 1–6.

Taks, M., Green, B. C., Misener, L., & Chalip, L. (2014). Evaluating sport development outcomes: The case of a medium-sized international sport event. *European Sport Management Quarterly, 14*, 213–237. doi:10.1080/16184742.2014.882370

Taks, M., Misener, L., Chalip, L., & Green, B. C. (2013). Leveraging sport events for participation. *Canadian Journal for Social Research, 3*(1), 12–23.

Turner, V. (1979). Frame, flow and reflection: Ritual and drama as public liminality. *Japanese Journal of Religious Studies, 6*(4), 465–499.

Vanwynsberghe, R. (2014). Applying event leveraging using OGI data: A case study of Vancouver 2010. *Leisure Studies*, 583–599.

Welty Peachey, J., Borland, J., Lobpries, J., & Cohen, A. (2015). Managing impact: Leveraging sacred spaces and community celebration to maximise social capital at a sport-for-development event. *Sport Management Review, 18*, 86–98.

Ziakas, V. (2015). For the benefit of all? Developing a critical perspective in mega-event leverage. *Leisure Studies, 34*, 689–702. doi:10.1080/02614367.2014.986507

4 Event impact evaluation

Introduction

As events around the world have temporarily come to a halt due to the COVID-19 pandemic, people have been provided the opportunity to reflect on the important role that events play in their lives. As individuals, events are how we choose to spend much of our leisure time and our discretionary income. We interact with family and friends, members of our community, and those who share our passions and pastimes as we are entertained, cheer on our team, and celebrate occasions together. Governments and destinations support a programme of events that bring communities together, bring visitors to a destination, stimulate urban development and regeneration, infrastructure use, and the economy (Allen, Harris, & Jago, 2021; Getz & Page, 2016; Smith, 2012).

COVID-19 has compromised our opportunities to engage in events as part of our everyday lives. While some events have transitioned to take place in a virtual space, others have continued with reduced crowd capacities or no spectators at all. These instances have served only to reinforce the significant impacts events offer. Event impact evaluation is vital to measuring the worth of an event and capturing the benefits they offer to individuals, communities, and destinations, and the importance of this role will only grow as the industry bounces back from COVID-19. With even greater competition for funding, there will be a reliance on credible event impact evaluation studies to provide the evidence base to justify funding decisions and government investment in events that will deliver significant positive impacts for various stakeholders.

In this chapter, we explore the topic of event impact evaluation, with the central focus placed on designing and delivering credible impact evaluations that so often serve as an important basis for decision-making in events. We begin by exploring the broader context for event impact evaluation and then examine available definitions and an overarching framework that guides the impact evaluation process. After discussing some of the key considerations and challenges, we draw on literature to discuss specific methodological approaches to assessing the economic and social impacts of events. Given the focus of this book, we specifically review existing efforts across these two domains; however, we also recognise the need for advancing truly holistic evaluation models that seek to encompass

DOI: 10.4324/9781003002772-5

Event impact evaluation 41

the triple bottom line of social, economic, and environmental impact domains. Together with other key challenges, these models will be discussed in more detail in the final chapter of this book, where we discuss future research opportunities in impact evaluation research.

The context for event impact evaluation

Research into the impacts of events has been driven not only by the growth in the number of events being held around the world but also because of a growing recognition of the impacts, both positive and negative, that these events can have on attendees, economies, cultures, and host communities (Getz & Page, 2020; Woosnam, Jiang, Van Winkle, Kim, & Maruyama, 2016). Governments have long recognised the potential for events to play a significant role in supporting particular cultural, sport, tourism, or economic goals for a destination (Allen et al., 2021). Events act as a catalyst for urban regeneration, investment, the development of arts and culture, as well as destination positioning and tourism (Allen et al., 2021; Mair & Whitford, 2013). Further to this, from a social perspective, we recognise events as an opportunity to bring people together to share experiences, celebrate, and be entertained. They are also capable of fostering social cohesion, trust, community identity, and pride (Bagiran & Kurgun, 2016; Black, 2016; Small, 2007; Yürük, Akyol, & Şimşek, 2017). However, not all impacts are positive, and negative impacts can be felt by the host destination and/or community as a result of staging an event. Inflated prices, damage to reputation, and opportunity costs are potential negative impacts (Allen et al., 2021), as are issues of inconvenience, traffic congestion, and overcrowding (Bagiran & Kurgun, 2016), as well as antisocial behaviour (Deery & Jago, 2010) that can impact host communities in particular.

Event impact evaluation is thus an important activity that helps take stock of these positive and negative impacts of events and provides us with a deeper understanding of the possible contributions events can make. Such understanding is of interest to multiple stakeholders but is of particular use in seeking answers to one of the most basic questions in relation to hosting any event: is it worth it? (Mahadevan & Ren, 2019). Event impact evaluation helps answer this question and can provide the evidence needed to justify an event's initial staging or ongoing existence, to build legitimacy, or determine outcomes and impacts (Nordvall & Brown, 2020). Which particular focus an evaluation might take will be context specific and driven by the event size and scope, its aims and objectives, and the range of stakeholders involved (Jaimangal-Jones, Fry, & Haven-Tang, 2018). Event organisers, for example, may need to justify value to their attendees and host community to ensure success and longevity of the event. They might also be required to demonstrate value to their funding bodies or sponsors as part of a contractual requirement (Brown, Getz, Pettersson, & Wallstam, 2015). Governments often use evaluation data to justify significant public investments required to bid for and host large-scale and mega-events (Thomson, Schlenker, & Schulenkorf, 2013), as well as to justify decisions on which events receive government support.

42   *Event management and leverage*

It should be noted that event impact evaluation is evolving in line with the increasing complexity and professionalism of events. In a more competitive environment, as events compete for audiences, funding support, and sponsorships, and stakeholder expectations increase, event organisers need increasing skills in event impact evaluation (Robertson, Rogers, & Leask, 2009). This increased accountability to multiple stakeholders, and needing to meet their requirements for evaluation, increases the complexity of the task for event organisers. Also, recognising the importance of evaluation studies and how their results are used as a basis to make decisions about an event, event impact evaluation is an increasingly politically charged task (Brown et al., 2015).

It is therefore important that evaluation studies are designed, conducted, and reported in ways that guarantee stakeholders, and those making decisions based on the results, that the evaluation is credible and conducted using best practice methodologies and frameworks (Nordvall & Brown, 2020). With this context in mind, the next section moves onto defining event impact evaluation.

Defining event impact evaluation

Event evaluation has been defined as "the holistic assessment of an event through the utilization of a broad range of measures and approaches to determine its value and impacts in an agreed or prescribed context" (Brown et al., 2015, p. 136). This definition puts the focus on an event's value and impacts, which we know are increasingly used to justify an event's existence and/or build legitimacy with stakeholders (Brown et al., 2015). Nordvall and Brown (2020), in their recent review of event evaluation literature, identified the most commonly included data in an event evaluation to be economic impacts, social and cultural impacts, environmental impacts, visitor profiles, event experience quality, and media coverage. Exactly which of these is to be included in an event evaluation will depend on the context – the particular nature of the event, its size and scope, and the purpose of the evaluation. But what is evident is the broadening of event evaluation requirements to include specifically, an evaluation of the impacts created by the staging of an event, which we refer to as event impact evaluation. This reflects the increasing complexity of events and the fact that events are increasingly accountable to multiple stakeholders and their associated criteria for evaluation.

Armbrecht and Andersson (2016) suggest a useful conceptualisation of event impact evaluation studies based on the idea of "subjects" and "objects" of study. They define the three major objects of event impact studies as the economic, sociocultural, and environmental impacts. The subject of study then refers to the perspective from which the evaluation is conducted, that is, taking into account the particular subject (stakeholder group/s) affected by the impact. Thus, any impact dimension (economic, sociocultural, or environmental) can be studied from different perspectives such as the individual level, community level, industry, or region.

In an attempt to assist event managers in their efforts towards event impact evaluation, Wood (2008) presents an overarching framework that guides the process of event impact evaluation, developed specifically in the context of community festivals. The starting point for impact evaluation is gauging the objectives of the event, the event programme, or hosting authority. Understanding whether the event is designed to achieve objectives around community involvement, social inclusion, or civic pride or whether it is designed to achieve objectives around tourism income, investment, and place image should guide the decision as to what type of impacts will be evaluated. Next, consideration can be given to the levels at which the impacts should be investigated, which in the context of community festivals have been categorised as societal, regional, community, and personal. Appropriate methods and measures for evaluation are then selected in line with this. Finally, this framework highlights the need for evaluation and comparison against previous data, other published reports and benchmarks, and the role these learnings should play in inputting into future design and planning. "This helps to ensure that, in practice, there is learning and development rather than mere measurement" (Wood, 2008, p. 179). Importantly, regardless of its focus on community festivals, the principles driving event impact evaluation outlined in this framework hold for events of other types and scales.

Wood's (2008) framework presents an excellent example of an impact evaluation process that aims to incorporate consideration of multiple stakeholder perspectives and which recognises that the specific context surrounding an evaluation will influence the type of evaluation conducted, how it is conducted, and by whom. Here, the focus is not to offer specific methods or measures for impact evaluation, but importantly, the framework serves to bring attention to several considerations in the event impact evaluation process, such as who should conduct an evaluation and associated issues of transparency, objectivity, and accountability. These and other considerations surrounding event impact evaluation are discussed in the next section.

Considerations in event impact evaluation

While impact evaluations are essential to assess the value of events, they come with significant challenges and considerations. Here, we focus on three key considerations that ought to be taken into account early in the evaluation process. Decisions about the timing and time frame of an evaluation, who should conduct the evaluation, and any overarching political agendas that may influence the process represent important considerations that can challenge the objectivity, credibility, and usefulness of impact evaluation studies.

The first consideration relates to the timing and time frame of evaluations. Specifically, impact studies can be classified as one of two types – ex ante (prior to the event) or ex post (after the event). An ex ante approach involves forecasting the impacts an event is likely to have, and such studies are common in the case of mega-events such as the Olympic Games (Kasimati, 2003) and particularly with respect to economic impacts. Many authors agree that such studies tend to exaggerate the positives and underestimate the costs or negative impacts associated with hosting an event (Baade & Matheson, 2016; Scandizzo & Pierleoni,

44 *Event management and leverage*

2018; Walton, Longo, & Dawson, 2008). This in part relates to the timing but also the purpose of the study, commissioned prior to the event – often by those with a vested interest – who need the results to justify an event bid or generate public support for the use of significant taxpayer funds (Baade & Matheson, 2016; Mahadevan & Ren, 2019).

Ex post impact studies, conducted after an event, tend to be more common and precise (Wallstam, Ioannides, & Pettersson, 2020; Williams & Bowdin, 2007). Such studies seek to take stock of the outcomes of an event in order to depict its overall value, success, or failure. Arguments for ex post impact studies focus on the advantage offered by being able to take into account the *actual* experiences and perceptions of various stakeholders who have lived through and been impacted by the event (Mahadevan & Ren, 2019), rather than generating forecasts of what might be likely.

Another consideration in event impact evaluation is who should conduct the evaluation, that is, whether it is conducted "in-house" or outsourced. Conducting a full event impact evaluation internally can represent a challenge for some events, with limited time and/or expertise to carry out such studies (Jaimangal-Jones et al., 2018). One advantage, however, is greater control over the study, including what specifically is evaluated and the methods to be used (Brown et al., 2015). Outsourcing an event impact evaluation to an external organisation or consultancy is suggested to offer greater objectivity and comprehensiveness (Brown et al., 2015) as well as independence (Wood, 2008). An associated risk, however, is putting decisions about evaluation tools and methodologies in the hands of consultants, who may, for example, overlook best practice methodologies in order to deliver results they think the client wants (Carlsen, Getz, & Soutar, 2000). Thus, the question of who conducts the evaluation is not a simple one, as it brings with it associated concerns about objectivity, transparency, and accountability.

This brings us to a final, related consideration, which is the political nature of event impact evaluation. Brown et al. (2015) recognise that "evaluation occurs within policy, planning, and decision-making processes" (p. 135), and thus political agendas can often be at play. This is particularly evident in the context of large-scale or mega-events where governments engage in competitive – and politically driven – bidding to win the right to host events at their destination (Allen et al., 2021). Such activities usually play out with great media interest and attention and public scrutiny of governments surrounding the use of taxpayer funds, recognition of opportunity costs, or potential financial losses to be incurred (Carlsen et al., 2000). As evaluation plays such a critical role in legitimising these types of government decisions, the potential exists for political agendas to drive decisions on the types of impacts to evaluate, the methods to use, the reporting of data, and use of the findings (Wood, 2008). For example, particular methods might be chosen as they deliver a more positive result, or findings could be interpreted or reported in a way that suits a particular political purpose (Getz & Page, 2020). This consideration speaks of the importance of transparency in event impact evaluation and that at least in the context of government-funded or supported events, it is "definitely in the interest of the public and many other stakeholders to insist upon an open and standardized evaluation process" (Brown et al., 2015, p. 138).

Current approaches to evaluating event impacts

In line with contemporary values and community expectations, we have seen the field of event impact evaluation evolve. Early studies in this area focused primarily on the economic impacts of events and it is well documented that the focus on social and environmental impacts – and associated tools for their measurement – was slower to develop (Armbrecht & Andersson, 2016; Mair & Whitford, 2013; Page & Connell, 2011; Wallstam et al., 2020). Given the focus of this book on economic and social dimensions, we will now turn towards the development of best practice approaches to event impact evaluation across these two critical domains.

Economic impacts

The initial focus of event impact research was on the economic dimension. In fact, economic impacts remain a priority for many stakeholders, particularly government agencies and funding bodies, hence they remain the most commonly evaluated and researched (Brown et al., 2015; Nordvall & Brown, 2020). Additionally, this focus on measuring the success of events in economic terms is in part due to the relative ease with which economic impacts can be assessed. As economic impacts are more tangible, their measurement is considered more straightforward than other types of impacts (Mahadevan & Ren, 2019), and there is the advantage of being able to communicate outcomes in monetary terms, which can often be more easily interpreted and as Getz and Page (2016) argue, "often more politically effective" (p. 614).

The key input to any study of the economic impacts of an event is the injection of new money into a region. This new money (also referred to as inscope expenditure) is defined as "expenditure that would not have occurred in the host region had the event not taken place" (Jago & Dwyer, 2006, p. 8). It includes the event-induced expenditure of a range of stakeholders in the event, such as event attendees, exhibitors, event organisers, promoters, and all others as a result of the staging of the event. However, it is more than this initial event-induced expenditure that represents the economic impacts of an event. Further flow-on effects are created as the initial injection of money because of an event is spent and re-spent in an economy. These flow-on or secondary effects include indirect impacts (the spending due to inter-business transactions flowing from the initial direct expenditure) and induced impacts (the increase in consumer spending due to an increase in income) (Saayman & Saayman, 2012). Thus events, through their initial direct expenditure, have the potential to stimulate further economic activity such as changes in business activity, sales, output, job creation, and household income (Dwyer, Jago, & Forsyth, 2016; Kim et al., 2017).

A substantial body of research has grown from the early studies that focused on evaluating the economic impacts of events (Crompton, Lee, & Shuster, 2001;

46 *Event management and leverage*

Dwyer, Forsyth, & Spurr, 2006; Tyrrell & Johnston, 2006). Over many decades – and with much debate and significant theoretical development of best practice methodologies – it has been shown that economic impacts of an event are most commonly evaluated through an Economic Impact Analysis (EIA) (Dwyer & Forsyth, 2019). An EIA takes the initial expenditure associated with an event and through application of an economic model (based on the concept of a multiplier), determines the secondary (indirect and induced) effects to estimate changes to overall economic activity within a host region. Two of the most prominent methods used in an EIA are Input–Output (I/O) modelling and Computable General Equilibrium (CGE) modelling.

I/O models are used to determine the flow-on effects of the initial injection of money because of an event on other sectors of a local economy (Hodur & Leistritz, 2006). I/O models are based on an assumption of unlimited resources and capacity, meaning that they tend to account for only the positive impacts of an event and ignore the negative impacts that may be occurring in other parts of the economy as a result. I/O models have been criticised for these unrealistic assumptions and for the typically exaggerated (or overly positive) estimates they consequently provide (Allen et al., 2021). This inability to account for negative impacts occurring in other sectors is particularly problematic for larger events whose impacts on other parts of the economic are likely to be greater than would be the case for smaller events.

As an alternative to I/O modelling, CGE models have gained favour, particularly for larger events, as they are thought to recognise more economy-wide impacts. By imposing restrictions on the availability of labour and capital (absent in I/O models), CGE models recognise that "the greater resource requirements associated with event-related expenditure are likely to result in lower resource use, and output, in other areas of economic activity" (Dwyer & Forsyth, 2019, p. 898). By accounting for these potential negative impacts, such an approach is thought to provide more realistic results (Blake, 2005). However, in order to achieve such results, CGE models incorporate a variety of assumptions based on a large number of variables, making them complex and often costly to use (O'Sullivan, Pickernell, & Senyard, 2009).

The literature demonstrates that while both methods have their critics, both also continue to be used in recent studies of the economic impacts of events. For example, I/O modelling has been used in studies of a jazz music festival (Bracalente et al., 2011) and in the analysis of major sports events (Huang, Mao, Kim, & Zhang, 2014; Kim et al., 2017), and it is suggested that where the area of interest is a local economy rather than a wider regional or national economy, that I/O modelling remains appropriate (Dwyer et al., 2006). In contrast, CGE is argued to be more appropriate than I/O modelling in the context of mega-events (Giesecke & Madden, 2011), with several studies adopting CGE modelling in analysing the economic impacts of the Olympic Games (Ap & Crompton, 1993; Blake, 2005; Li, Blake, & Thomas, 2013).

In order to overcome issues of inflated impacts and potentially dubious multipliers associated with I/O and CGE modelling (see Andersson & Lundberg, 2013), several authors have recommended that direct expenditure should be used as the baseline data for reporting on the economic performance of an event (Davies, Coleman, & Ramchandani, 2013; Getz & Page, 2020; Jago & Dwyer, 2006). Variously referred to as the Direct Expenditure Approach (Davies et al., 2013), Direct Economic Contribution (Getz & Page, 2020), or Inscope expenditure calculation (Jago & Dwyer, 2006), this approach is concerned only with the first-round "direct" economic expenditures injected into a host economy because of an event. Importantly, direct expenditure measures the economic contribution of an event and should therefore not be confused with the wider notion of economic impact, which includes the secondary (indirect and induced) effects of the initial direct expenditure.

Several studies have used this direct expenditure approach as an evaluation method within its own right (Davies et al., 2013; Edwards, Foley, Dwyer, Schlenker, & Hergesell, 2014; Laitila & Herpen, 2018). While not always suitable for major or mega-events, which have interactive effects on other sectors of the economy, a significant advantage of the direct expenditure is that it can be used to compare quite simply the economic performance of an event over time, as well as between events, and thus represents a solid basis that can underpin decision-making about events, including on levels of support from government and other funding bodies (Edwards et al., 2014). Importantly, when employing this approach, care must be taken to include only "new money" (inscope expenditure) that comes from outside the host region and which would otherwise have not occurred if not for the event. Accurate estimation of inscope expenditure generated by an event is crucial to the study of economic impacts, and there has been significant theoretical discussion and methodological guidance on the inclusions and exclusions of inscope expenditure, including the treatment of local residents, casual visitors, and time-switchers, as well as dealing with retained expenditure and crowding-out effects (Crompton, 2006; Jago & Dwyer, 2006).

Social impacts

Originating from an appreciation of the potential that events have to significantly interrupt the normal life of a community (Deery & Jago, 2010), event impact studies progressed from being purely focused on the economic dimension, to those that examined social impacts (Delamere, 1997; Fredline & Faulkner, 2000; Kim & Petrick, 2005; Reid, 2004; Waitt, 2003). Social impacts range from the inconvenience associated with crowding and traffic congestion to the opportunities for entertainment and socialisation, development of social capital, community identity, and pride that come from the hosting of an event (Nordvall & Brown, 2020; Wallstam et al., 2020). Noting the complexity of some of these concepts, we often see social impacts referred to as "intangibles" (Kim & Petrick, 2005; Oshimi, Harada, & Fukuhara, 2016; Waitt, 2003). While both Deery and Jago (2010) and Getz and Page (2016) argue that the social impacts literature is now well established, tools for measuring the social impacts of events were slow to develop, in part, related to the difficulty of quantifying many of these "intangible" social impacts.

One way in which researchers have attempted to measure such intangible social impacts is through an objective approach which seeks to assign a surrogate

48 *Event management and leverage*

monetary value to them. In an early attempt, Burns, Hatch, and Mules (1986) assigned surrogate monetary values to represent the cost of certain social impacts to local residents in their research on the Australian Grand Prix held in Adelaide. For example, a monetary value was assigned to represent the time lost by residents because of increased traffic congestion. Other studies since have sought to assign a monetary value to social impacts using a Contingent Valuation (CV) approach, which asks residents to estimate a willingness-to-pay (WTP) and willingness-to-accept (WTA) value in relation to a particular event (Walton et al., 2008). CV accounts for both the use values of individuals who attend the event in question and the non-use values, which are attributed to those individuals who do not attend the event but who are affected by its externalities (Andersson & Lundberg, 2013). These can be positive externalities such as the creation of national pride, contribution to a positive destination image, and positive impact on community and culture (Walton et al., 2008; Wicker, Hallmann, Breuer, & Feiler, 2012), or negative externalities such as the crowding and disruption caused by the hosting of an event (Atkinson, Mourato, Szymanski, & Ozdemiroglu, 2008). CV has, for example, been used to estimate the value of such intangible social impacts in the hosting of major sport events and Olympic Games (Mahadevan & Ren, 2019; Walton et al., 2008; Wicker et al., 2012).

Recently, Andersson and Lundberg (2013) used a CV approach to elicit the WTP and WTA values of local residents of Gothenburg, Sweden in relation to the Way Out West music festival. The study is based around the scenario of whether local residents would support public funding of the Way Out West music festival. Those in favour of public support were asked to estimate their WTP in terms of an increase in their local taxes to support the festival. For those who were against public support of the festival, they were asked to estimate their WTA in terms of a decrease in their local taxes in order for public support to be given to the festival. In short, these estimates provide dollar amounts that speak to the social costs and benefits of the festival and the level of public support within the community.

Whilst it is thought there will be some benefit in valuing social impacts using a monetary value, including them being more easily interpreted and communicated (Getz & Page, 2016), CV methods have attracted some criticism. First, CV is a stated preference technique and thus the WTP and WTA figures are hypothetical. In other words, a hypothetical WTP may not reflect the actual amount a person would pay (Andersson & Lundberg, 2013; Wicker et al., 2012). Second, and more fundamentally, respondents may experience difficulty with this process, based on an unfamiliarity with ascribing economic values to such a scenario, and particularly in relation to valuing typically intangible social impacts (Ohmann, Jones, & Wilkes, 2006).

Noting the difficulties with assigning a monetary value to some intangible impacts, the other main way in which social impacts have been evaluated is via a subjective approach which examines residents' perceptions (Getz & Page, 2016; Nordvall & Brown, 2020; Wallstam et al., 2020). Rather than attempting

Event impact evaluation   49

to quantify social impacts, the residents' perceptions approach allows people to comment on the impacts they perceive an event to have had on them. Importantly, if residents perceive that certain impacts are occurring, it is this belief – rather than any objective reality – that affects their attitudes and behaviours towards an event (Ohmann et al., 2006; Small, 2007). This, in turn, suggests that examining social impacts via the residents' perceptions approach can provide valuable information for decision-makers with respect to an understanding of the ways in which a community is affected by the hosting of an event. Importantly, this can provide the basis for event organisers to improve outcomes for this stakeholder group (Liu, 2016).

Based on a recognition of the need for appropriate tools to measure residents' perceptions of event social impacts, a number of early studies focused on event impact scale development in the context of small-scale community festivals. Delamere, Wankel, and Hinch (2001) developed a Festival Social Impact Attitude Scale (FSIAS) for the measurement of residents' perceptions of the social impacts of community-based festivals and Delamere (2001) then verified and refined this scale by applying it to the Edmonton Folk Music Festival in Canada. Factor analysis identified two factors of social benefits and social costs. Secondary factor analysis found that the first factor (social benefits) had two subfactors of "community benefits" and "individual benefits". The second factor (social costs) did not reveal any subfactors. This early study was important for event evaluation researchers as it sought to create a scale specific to the social impacts of festivals and distinct from the tourism social impact scales that had existed previously.

Later, Small (2007) developed the Social Impact Perception (SIP) scale. Initially tested in the context of two Australian music festivals, the SIP scale is incorporated into a questionnaire that seeks to measure residents' perceptions of social impacts. Respondents are asked, for each of the 41 social impact statements, if they perceive the impact to have occurred (Yes, No, or Don't Know). For those who answered "yes" or "no", they are then asked to indicate the level of impact they believe it had using a five-part directional scale. This scale ranges from -5 to $+5$, with 0 as the midpoint representing "no impact", 1 representing a "very small impact", 2 representing a "small impact", 3 representing a "moderate impact", 4 representing a "large impact", and 5 representing a "very large impact". Values on the negative side of the scale represent varying levels of negative impacts, while values on the positive side represent varying levels of positive impacts. The design of the scale is particularly important and it supports the findings of previous research which found that consensus is not always achieved with respect to the nature of impacts on residents and that people can perceive the same impacts as having different effects (Small, Edwards, & Sheridan, 2005). Consequently – and distinct from Delamere's (2001) FSIAS – the underlying dimensions of social impacts identified in this study have not been labelled as simply positive or negative in nature. Rather, the factors are broadly labelled as: inconvenience, community identity and cohesion, personal

50 *Event management and leverage*

frustration, entertainment and socialisation opportunities, community growth and development, and behavioural consequences, with respondents making the distinction on whether the individual impacts within these factors affect them positively or negatively.

Overall, the investigation of residents' perceptions remains the most common way of examining social impacts (Getz & Page, 2016; Nordvall & Brown, 2020; Schlenker, Foley, & Getz, 2010; Small, 2007; Wallstam et al., 2020). This is evident in the continued growth of studies that use such an approach, including those that focus on the social impacts of large-scale and mega sport events including the Tour de France (Balduck, Maes, & Buelens, 2011), FIFA World Cup (Kim & Petrick, 2005; Ohmann et al., 2006), Cricket World Cup (Lorde, Greenidge, & Devonish, 2011), and the Olympic Games (Waitt, 2003). Scale development work that often accompanies residents' perception studies also continues. Early scales such as the FSIAS for community festivals have been further tested and refined (Bagiran & Kurgun, 2016; Woosnam et al., 2016; Woosnam, Van Winkle, & An, 2013), and scales specific to large-scale sport events have been progressed by several authors (Kim, Gursoy, & Lee, 2006; Kim & Petrick, 2005; Kim, Jun, Walker, & Drane, 2015; Mao & Huang, 2016). This is important given that larger scale events, particularly sport events, are likely to have more substantive impact dimensions to smaller community festivals.

Moving towards holistic event impact evaluation

The previous section has outlined the state of play and current approaches used in evaluating the economic and social impacts of events. The literature shows us that the majority of event impact evaluation studies tend to be based on only one of these impact dimensions. However, in a move towards delivering more comprehensive forms of event impact evaluation, there have been some attempts to combine these two impact dimensions – and indeed to incorporate the evaluation of environmental impacts as well – as part of a triple bottom line approach (see Fredline, Raybould, Jago, & Deery, 2005; Sherwood, 2007). Whilst environmental impacts are not a focus of this book, it is important to acknowledge the inclusion of this dimension in attempts to develop more holistic evaluation models, which we will discuss briefly here and revisit in our final chapter.

Several authors have attempted to develop "toolkits", designed to offer a standardised approach to event impact evaluation. For example, Pasanen, Taskinen, and Mikkonen (2009), drawing on best practice evaluation methodologies, developed the Finnish Event Evaluation Tool (FEET) to evaluate both economic and sociocultural impacts of events. Schlenker et al. (2010) proposed a toolkit based on an expansion of the existing ENCORE Festival and Event Evaluation Kit. Originally developed as a toolkit to guide the measurement of direct economic impacts via inscope expenditure calculation, the toolkit was revised to also include the measurement of social and environmental impacts. Such toolkits respond to calls for a more standardised approach to event impact evaluation (Brown et al., 2015; Nordvall & Brown, 2020). Use of the same methods provides consistency and therefore comparability, allowing for benchmarking across different events (Schlenker et al., 2010). The challenge however, recognised by both Pasanen et al. (2009) and Schlenker et al. (2010), is that even when a standard tool can be developed, there must be sufficient flexibility to ensure that there can be customisation to meet the evaluation needs of a particular event.

Whilst addressing the needs for a more standardised evaluation approach, what such toolkits fail to address is the issue of commensurability (Andersson & Lundberg, 2013). That is, the ability to generate one comprehensive measure of an event's total impact, which combines its various impacts into a common metric. Andersson and Lundberg (2013) have advanced work in this regard, developing a measurement model that puts a monetary value on a festival's total impact, comprising economic, social, and environmental dimensions. This approach, like triple bottom line (TBL) (see Fredline et al., 2005; Sherwood, 2007) and cost–benefit analysis (CBA) approaches (see Dwyer & Forsyth, 2019; Dwyer et al., 2016), seeks to integrate multiple impact dimensions into one common – usually monetary – metric.

One advantage of using a monetary figure to express social (and environmental) impacts is that the economic impacts are already expressed in monetary units and therefore, the social and environmental impacts become more comparable (Andersson & Lundberg, 2013). This method is thus useful in showing the relative importance of the various impact dimensions against each other and in relation to the total festival impact. However, consideration must be given to the ease of communicating the total value of an event in one uniform metric and the value this provides to various stakeholders versus the potential to undermine the importance of particularly social impacts that many argue are best defined descriptively (Singh, Shalender, & Su, 2019).

Conclusion and outlook

This chapter has served to overview event impact evaluation as an area of study. The specific methodological approaches to assessing economic and social impacts of events have been discussed, as have existing efforts towards advancing more holistic evaluation models. Throughout this chapter, the central focus has remained firmly on the context for event impact evaluation and its use as a basis for decision-making. With much at stake, being able to credibly speak to the outcomes and impacts of an event on multiple stakeholders is crucial for event managers to build legitimacy, justify funding support, maintain community support, and argue for an event's continued existence. And as we seek to re-establish the events industry post-COVID-19, those that can best demonstrate the value they create – and their ability to deliver significant positive impacts for various stakeholders – will be those most likely to thrive.

This chapter has also highlighted that numerous challenges remain in the event evaluation space. These include, inter alia, standardised approaches to event

52 *Event management and leverage*

impact evaluation that allow for comparability but which do not come at the expense of contextualisation; and the communication of event impacts which includes finding a balance between commensurability and being able to understand impacts in a nuanced way. With this in mind, we will return to discussing a number of evaluation challenges in the final chapter of this book.

References

Allen, J., Harris, R., & Jago, L. (2021). *Festival and special event management essentials.* Milton, Queensland: John Wiley and Sons.

Andersson, T. D., & Lundberg, E. (2013). Commensurability and sustainability: Triple impact assessments of a tourism event. *Tourism Management, 37*, 99–109. doi:10.1016/j.tourman.2012.12.015

Ap, J., & Crompton, J. L. (1993). Residents' strategies for responding to tourism impacts. *Journal of Travel Research, 32*(1), 47–50.

Armbrecht, J., & Andersson, T. D. (2016). Subjects and objects of event impact analysis. *Scandinavian Journal of Hospitality and Tourism: Event Impact, 16*(2), 111–114. doi:10.1080/15022250.2016.1162417

Atkinson, G., Mourato, S., Szymanski, S., & Ozdemiroglu, E. (2008). Are we willing to pay enough to "back the bid"?: Valuing the intangible impacts of London's bid to host the 2012 Summer Olympic Games. *Urban Studies, 45*(2), 419–444. doi:10.1177/0042098007085971

Baade, R. A., & Matheson, V. A. (2016). Going for the gold: The economics of the Olympics. *The Journal of Economic Perspectives, 30*(2), 201–218. doi:10.1257/jep.30.2.201

Bagiran, D., & Kurgun, H. (2016). A research on social impacts of the Foça Rock Festival: The validity of the Festival Social Impact Attitude Scale. *Current Issues in Tourism, 19*(9), 930–948. doi:10.1080/13683500.2013.800028

Balduck, A., Maes, M., & Buelens, M. (2011). The social impact of the Tour de France: Comparisons of residents' pre- and post-event perceptions. *European Sport Management Quarterly, 11*(2), 91–113. doi:10.1080/16184742.2011.559134

Black, N. (2016). Festival connections: How consistent and innovative connections enable small-scale rural festivals to contribute to socially sustainable communities. *International Journal of Event and Festival Management, 7*(3), 172–187. doi:10.1108/IJEFM-04-2016-0026

Blake, A. (2005). *The economic impact of the London 2012 Olympics, research report 2005/5.* Nottingham, UK: Christel DeHaan Tourism and Travel Research Institute, Nottingham University.

Bracalente, B., Chirieleison, C., Cossignani, M., Ferrucci, L., Gigliotti, M., & Ranalli, M. G. (2011). The economic impact of cultural events: The Umbria Jazz music festival. *Tourism Economics, 17*(6), 1235–1255. doi:10.5367/te.2011.0096

Brown, S., Getz, D., Pettersson, R., & Wallstam, M. (2015). Event evaluation: Definitions, concepts and a state of the art review. *International Journal of Event and Festival Management, 6*(2), 135–157. doi:10.1108/IJEFM-03-2015-0014

Burns, P., Hatch, J., & Mules, T. (1986). *The Adelaide Grand Prix: The impact of a special event.* Adelaide: The Centre for South Australian Economic Studies.

Carlsen, J., Getz, D., & Soutar, G. (2000). Event evaluation research. *Event Management, 6*(4), 247–257. doi:10.3727/152599500108751408

Crompton, J. L. (2006). Economic impact studies: Instruments for political shenanigans? *Journal of Travel Research, 45*(1), 67–82. doi:10.1177/0047287506288870

Crompton, J. L., Lee, S., & Shuster, T. J. (2001). A guide for undertaking economic impact studies: The Springfest example. *Journal of Travel Research, 40*(1), 79–87.

Davies, L., Coleman, R., & Ramchandani, G. (2013). Evaluating event economic impact: Rigour versus reality? *International Journal of Event and Festival Management, 4*(1), 31–42.

Deery, M., & Jago, L. (2010). Social impacts of events and the role of anti-social behaviour. *International Journal of Event and Festival Management, 1*(1), 8–28. doi:10.1108/17852951011029289

Delamere, T. A. (1997). Development of scale items to measure the social impact of community festivals. *Journal of Applied Recreation Research, 22*(4), 293–315.

Delamere, T. A. (2001). Development of a scale to measure resident attitudes toward the social impacts of community festivals, part II: Verification of the scale. *Event Management, 7*, 25–38.

Delamere, T. A., Wankel, L. M., & Hinch, T. D. (2001). Development of a scale to measure resident attitudes toward the social impacts of community festivals, part I: Item generation and purification of the measure. *Event Management, 7*, 11–24.

Dwyer, L., & Forsyth, P. (2019). Evaluating special events: Merging two essential approaches. *Event Management, 23*(6), 897–911. doi:10.3727/152599519X15506259856417

Dwyer, L., Forsyth, P., & Spurr, R. (2006). Assessing the economic impacts of events: A computable general equilibrium approach. *Journal of Travel Research, 45*(1), 59–66. doi:10.1177/0047287506288907

Dwyer, L., Jago, L., & Forsyth, P. (2016). Economic evaluation of special events: Reconciling economic impact and cost: Benefit analysis. *Scandinavian Journal of Hospitality and Tourism, 16*(2), 115–129. doi:10.1080/15022250.2015.1116404

Edwards, D., Foley, C., Dwyer, L., Schlenker, K., & Hergesell, A. (2014). Evaluating the economic contribution of a large indoor entertainment venue: An inscope expenditure study. *Event Management, 18*(4), 407–420. doi:10.3727/152599514X14143427352076

Fredline, E., & Faulkner, B. (2000). Host community reactions: A cluster analysis. *Annals of Tourism Research, 27*(3), 763–784.

Fredline, E., Raybould, M., Jago, L., & Deery, M. (2005). Triple bottom line event evaluation: A proposed framework for holistic event evaluation. Paper presented at *the Third International Event Management Research Conference: The Impacts of Events*, Sydney.

Getz, D., & Page, S. J. (2016). Progress and prospects for event tourism research. *Tourism Management (1982), 52*(C), 593–631. doi:10.1016/j.tourman.2015.03.007

Getz, D., & Page, S. J. (2020). *Event studies: Theory, research and policy for planned events* (4th ed.). Abingdon, Oxon: Routledge.

Giesecke, J., & Madden, J. (2011). Modelling the economic impacts of the Sydney Olympics in retrospect: Game over for the bonanza story? *Economic Papers (Economic Society of Australia), 30*(2), 218–232. doi:10.1111/j.1759-3441.2011.00109.x

Hodur, N. M., & Leistritz, F. L. (2006). Estimating the economic impact of event tourism: A review of issues and methods. *Journal of Convention & Event Tourism, 8*(4), 63–79. doi:10.1300/J452v08n04_05

Huang, H., Mao, L., Kim, S., & Zhang, J. (2014). Assessing the economic impact of three major sport events in China: The perspective of attendees. *Tourism Economics: The Business and Finance of Tourism and Recreation, 20*(6), 1277–1296. doi:10.5367/te.2013.0340

Jago, L., & Dwyer, L. (2006). *Economic evaluation of special events: A practitioner's guide*. Gold Coast, Queensland: Sustainable Tourism Cooperative Research Centre.

Jaimangal-Jones, D., Fry, J., & Haven-Tang, C. (2018). Exploring industry priorities regarding customer satisfaction and implications for event evaluation. *International Journal of Event and Festival Management, 9*(1), 51–66. doi:10.1108/IJEFM-06-2016-0044

54 Event management and leverage

Kasimati, E. (2003). Economic aspects and the Summer Olympics: A review of related research. *International Journal of Tourism Research, 5*(6), 433–444. doi:10.1002/jtr.449

Kim, H. J., Gursoy, D., & Lee, S.-B. (2006). The impact of the 2002 World Cup on South Korea: Comparisons of pre- and post-games. *Tourism Management, 27*(1), 86–96. doi:10.1016/j.tourman.2004.07.010

Kim, M. K., Kim, S.-K., Park, J.-A., Carroll, M., Yu, J.-G., & Na, K. (2017). Measuring the economic impacts of major sports events: The case of Formula One Grand Prix (F1). *Asia Pacific Journal of Tourism Research, 22*(1), 64–73. doi:10.1080/10941665.2016.1176061

Kim, W., Jun, H., Walker, M., & Drane, D. (2015). Evaluating the perceived social impacts of hosting large-scale sport tourism events: Scale development and validation. *Tourism Management, 48*, 21–32. doi:10.1016/j.tourman.2014.10.015

Kim, S. S., & Petrick, J. F. (2005). Residents' perceptions on impacts of the FIFA 2002 World Cup: The case of Seoul as host city. *Tourism Management, 26*, 25–38.

Laitila, O., & Herpen, N. V. (2018). The direct economic impact of international sport events for the hosting city. In M. Dodds, K. Heisey, & A. Ahonen (Eds.), *Routledge Handbook of International Sport Business* (1st ed., pp. 155–166). Abingdon, Oxon: Routledge.

Li, S., Blake, A., & Thomas, R. (2013). Modelling the economic impact of sports events: The case of the Beijing Olympics. *Economic Modelling, 30*(1), 235–244. doi:10.1016/j.econmod.2012.09.013

Liu, D. (2016). Social impact of major sports events perceived by host community. *International Journal of Sports Marketing & Sponsorship, 17*(1), 78–91. doi:10.1108/IJSMS-02-2016-005

Lorde, T., Greenidge, D., & Devonish, D. (2011). Local residents' perceptions of the impacts of the ICC Cricket World Cup 2007 on Barbados: Comparisons of pre- and post-games. *Tourism Management, 32*(2), 349–356. doi:10.1016/j.tourman.2010.03.004

Mahadevan, R., & Ren, C. (2019). To value or not to value the arctic winter games? *Event Management, 23*(1), 93–107.

Mair, J., & Whitford, M. (2013). An exploration of events research: Event topics, themes and emerging trends. *International Journal of Event and Festival Management, 4*(1), 6–30. doi:10.1108/17582951311307485

Mao, L. L., & Huang, H. (2016). Social impact of Formula One Chinese Grand Prix: A comparison of local residents' perceptions based on the intrinsic dimension. *Sport Management Review, 19*(3), 306–318. doi:10.1016/j.smr.2015.08.007

Nordvall, A., & Brown, S. (2020). Evaluating publicly supported periodic events: The design of credible, usable and effective evaluation. *Journal of Policy Research in Tourism, Leisure and Events, 12*(2), 152–171. doi:10.1080/19407963.2018.1556672

Ohmann, S., Jones, I., & Wilkes, K. (2006). The perceived social impacts of the 2006 Football World Cup on Munich residents. *The Journal of Sport Tourism, 11*(2), 129–152. doi:10.1080/14775080601155167

Oshimi, D., Harada, M., & Fukuhara, T. (2016). Residents' perceptions on the social impacts of an international sport event: Applying panel data design and a moderating variable. *Journal of Convention & Event Tourism, 17*(4), 294–317. doi:10.1080/15470148.2016.1142919

O'Sullivan, D., Pickernell, D., & Senyard, J. (2009). Public sector evaluation of festivals and special events. *Journal of Policy Research in Tourism, Leisure and Events, 1*(1), 19–36. doi:10.1080/19407960802703482

Event impact evaluation   55

Page, S. J., & Connell, J. (2011). Retrospect and prospect. In S. J. Page & J. Connell (Eds.), *The Routledge handbook of events* (pp. 526–533). Abingdon, Oxon: Routledge.

Pasanen, K., Taskinen, H., & Mikkonen, J. (2009). Impacts of cultural events in Eastern Finland: Development of a Finnish Event Evaluation Tool. *Scandinavian Journal of Hospitality and Tourism, 9*(2–3), 112–129. doi:10.1080/15022250903119546

Reid, S. (2004). The social consequences of rural events: The Inglewood olive festival. Paper presented at *the Creating Tourism Knowledge, Proceedings of the 2004 CAUTHE Conference*, Brisbane.

Robertson, M., Rogers, P., & Leask, A. (2009). Progressing socio-cultural impact evaluation for festivals. *Journal of Policy Research in Tourism, Leisure and Events, 1*(2), 156–169. doi:10.1080/19407960902992233

Saayman, M., & Saayman, A. (2012). The economic impact of the Comrades Marathon. *International Journal of Event and Festival Management, 3*(3), 220–235. doi:10.1108/17582951211262675

Scandizzo, P. L., & Pierleoni, M. R. (2018). Assessing the Olympic Games: The economic impact and beyond. *Journal of Economic Surveys, 32*(3), 649–682. doi:10.1111/joes.12213

Schlenker, K., Foley, C., & Getz, D. (2010). *ENCORE festival and event evaluation kit: Review and redevelopment*. Gold Coast, Queensland: CRC for Sustainable Tourism.

Sherwood, P. (2007). *A triple bottom line evaluation of the impact of special events: The development of indicators* (Unpublished Doctoral thesis). Victoria University, Melbourne, Victoria.

Singh, N., Shalender, K., & Su, C.-H. (2019). Developing impacts and indicators for sustainable event management using a triple bottom line approach: A study of Auto Expo. *Event Management, 24*, 1–16. doi:10.3727/152599519X15506259855887

Small, K. (2007). Social dimensions of community festivals: An application of factor analysis in the development of the Social Impact Perception (SIP) scale. *Event Management, 11*(F0020001), 45–55.

Small, K., Edwards, D., & Sheridan, L. (2005). A flexible framework for evaluating the socio-cultural impacts of a small festival. *International Journal of Event Management Research, 1*(1), 66–77.

Smith, A. (2012). *Events and urban regeneration the strategic use of events to revitalise cities*. Abingdon, Oxon: Routledge.

Thomson, A., Schlenker, K., & Schulenkorf, N. (2013). Conceptualizing sport event legacy. *Event Management, 17*(2), 111–122. doi:10.3727/152599513X13668224082260

Tyrrell, T. J., & Johnston, R. J. (2006). The economic impacts of tourism: A special issue. *Journal of Travel Research, 45*(1), 3–7.

Waitt, G. (2003). Social impacts of the Sydney Olympics. *Annals of Tourism Research, 30*(1), 194–215.

Wallstam, M., Ioannides, D., & Pettersson, R. (2020). Evaluating the social impacts of events: In search of unified indicators for effective policymaking. *Journal of Policy Research in Tourism, Leisure and Events, 12*(2), 122–141. doi:10.1080/19407963.2018.1515214

Walton, H., Longo, A., & Dawson, P. (2008). A Contingent Valuation of the 2012 London Olympic Games: A regional perspective. *Journal of Sports Economics, 9*(3), 304–317. doi:10.1177/1527002507308769

Wicker, P., Hallmann, K., Breuer, C., & Feiler, S. (2012). The value of Olympic success and the intangible effects of sport events: A contingent valuation approach in Germany. *European Sport Management Quarterly, 12*(4), 337–355. doi:10.1080/16184742.2012.693117

56 *Event management and leverage*

Williams, M., & Bowdin, G. A. J. (2007). Festival evaluation: An exploration of seven UK arts festivals. *Managing Leisure, 12*(2–3), 187–203. doi:10.1080/13606710701339520

Wood, E. H. (2008). An impact evaluation framework: Local government community festivals. *Event Management, 12*, 171–185.

Woosnam, K. M., Jiang, J., Van Winkle, C. M., Kim, H., & Maruyama, N. (2016). Explaining festival impacts on a hosting community through motivations to attend. *Event Management, 20*(1), 11–25. doi:10.3727/152599516X14538326024919

Woosnam, K. M., Van Winkle, C. M., & An, S. (2013). Confirming the Festival Social Impact Attitude Scale in the Context of a Rural Texas Cultural Festival. *Event Management, 17*(3), 257–270. doi:10.3727/152599513x13708863377917

Yürük, P., Akyol, A., & Şimşek, G. G. (2017). Analyzing the effects of social impacts of events on satisfaction and loyalty. *Tourism Management (1982), 60*, 367–378. doi:10.1016/j.tourman.2016.12.016

Part 2

Event management and leverage in practice

Cases, contexts, and challenges

5 Events and commercial engagement

Business and social factors

Introduction

For many events and festivals around the world, financial sustainability depends on commercial engagement and investment. This chapter discusses commercial aspects of event management, focusing on event sponsorship, leveraging commercial partnerships and tensions between authenticity and commercialisation. We explore multifarious business and social considerations associated with event commercialisation and outline industry trends and future directions.

Commercialisation is ubiquitous in the contemporary events industry. Events ranging from local and community-based events to hallmark, major, and international events engage in commercial activity to varying degrees. While ticket and merchandise sales generate revenue for event owners, it is rarely enough to break even. Moreover, reduced funding and support from governments, for regional events and festivals in particular, has seen an increase in event dependency on commercial sponsorship to provide financial backing (Shin, Lee, & Perdue, 2018). Sponsorship is defined as a dyadic business relationship between the sponsored property (e.g. event, team, athlete) and sponsoring organisation, where both parties seek benefit.

The 1984 Los Angeles Olympic Games was one of the first events to showcase the value of selling sponsorship rights. This prompted exponential growth of the sponsorship industry, with corporate branding now visible across the entire sector. With this growth, sponsorship has evolved from a philanthropic activity to a core function of marketing, with sponsors seeking an ostensible return on investment. The practice of sponsoring events now plays a pivotal role in the marketing mix of firms worldwide.

Organisations strategically invest in sponsoring a property to secure the rights to exploit the commercial value associated with the property's brand (Morgan, Taylor, & Adair, 2020). It is this commercial intent which differentiates sponsorship from pure donation (Polonsky & Speed, 2001). However, in recent years, we have seen sponsoring firms seek not only financial gain but also social benefits. Marketers have realised the potential image-related opportunities for cause-related marketing. Cause-related marketing is a popular strategy where organisations explicitly communicate their commitment to responsible business practices or

DOI: 10.4324/9781003002772-7

60   *Event management and leverage in practice*

support for social causes (Andersen & Johansen, 2016). With growing pressure on organisations to act in a socially responsible manner, sponsorship portfolios are becoming increasingly intertwined with corporate social responsibility (CSR) initiatives (Seguin, Parent, & O'Reilly, 2010). Further to commercial or altruistic drivers, social identity and tribal association can also motivate sponsor investment (Garry, Broderick, & Lahiffe, 2008). While sponsor motivations vary, one thing is clear, sponsorship is now a strategic co-marketing alliance (Morgan, Adair, Taylor, & Hermens, 2014). The management and leverage of these partnerships are critical for event managers to maximise value from existing relationships and to seek new commercial investment.

The purpose of this chapter is to expand this discussion of commercial engagement with events, assessing both business and social considerations. We provide insights into sponsorship management and debate the tensions between commercialisation and event authenticity. This chapter also looks at the influence of digital technologies and impact of global issues, such as COVID-19, on commercial activity.

Event sponsorship

The operations of events have become reliant on the strategic investments of corporate partners, with sponsorship emerging as a key marketing tool for companies and a major source of revenue for event organisations. Sponsorship presents significant commercial prospect for both the sponsoring organisation (sponsor) and the sponsored property (sponsee). As opposed to traditional forms of advertising, sponsoring an event (or any other property) allows organisations to engage in indirect marketing, where brand attitudes can be enhanced through incidental brand exposure (Meenaghan & O'Sullivan, 2013). It is well established that sponsorship presents an avenue for sponsor organisations to generate brand exposure, create brand awareness (Houlder, 2009), and in turn enhance brand image and trigger brand loyalty (Cliffe & Motion, 2005). In fact, enhancing brand image is recognised as the most cited objective for companies engaging in sponsorship (Grohs, Wagner, & Vsetecka, 2004).

The attraction of event sponsorship is linked to the potential value it brings for communication with consumers and business-to-business networks (Ko, Chang, Park, & Herbst, 2017). Sponsorship can help retain existing customers and can be effective in reaching new markets (Shank & Lyberger, 2015). As the sponsorship industry has matured, the objectives of sponsors have moved beyond brand image benefits to incorporate relational outcomes (Gillooly, Crowther, & Medway, 2017). Sponsorship is seen as a method to interact and strengthen relationships with multiple stakeholders (Farrelly, Quester, & Burton, 2006).

As well as commercially based sponsorship objectives, corporate goodwill and social responsibility often underpin sponsorship spend (Houlder, 2009). For example, sponsoring a local cultural event can be seen by attendees as supporting the community and enhancing the event experience (Alexandris, Tsaousi, & James, 2007). Corporate social responsibility (CSR) is an important consideration

Events and commercial engagement 61

for marketers, as consumers now expect companies to be responsible corporate citizens. Event sponsorship is widely used as a platform to communicate CSR (Scheinbaum, Lacey, & Liang, 2017). It has been found that sponsorship that links to CSR positively affects perceptions of the brand and increases brand credibility (Habitzreuter & Koenigstorfer, 2018; Uhrich, Koenigstorfer, & Groeppel-Klein, 2014). Sponsorship activity and policy directed towards CSR has also been found to have an impact internally on employee motivation and commitment (Miragaia, Ferreira, & Ratten, 2017). Even those companies investing in highly commercial sponsorship of mega-events, such as the Olympic Games, can achieve a variety of objectives including social or environmental interests. Commercial and community objectives are not necessarily mutually exclusive and often firms seek sponsorship to satisfy a broad range of corporate and social objectives (Morgan, 2019). Regardless of the rationale for sponsorship spend, it is critical that sponsors articulate their objectives, as one of the most frequently cited reasons for sponsorship failure is a lack of clearly defined objectives (Roy, 2010).

Sponsorship is based on the notion of brand image transfer between the sponsor and the sponsee. In exchange for financial and/or value-in-kind investment, sponsors seek to exploit commercial value through association with the sponsee's brand. This brand image transfer is a two-way process, with the brand strength of both the sponsor and the sponsee influencing one another (Westberg, Stavros, & Wilson, 2011). Thus, sponsorship partner selection is a critical decision for both parties. Olson (2010) studied both sport and cultural sponsorship and found the sincerity of the sponsors and sponsor–sponsee fit to be critical in determining sponsorship effects.

The fit between sponsor and sponsee has been recognised as an important consideration in partner selection and is one of the most prevalent factors in academic sponsorship research (Grohs & Reisinger, 2014; Henderson, Mazodier, & Sundar, 2019). Partner fit in sponsorship refers to the similarity, relatedness, or congruence between sponsor and sponsee based on consumer perceptions. Gwinner (1997) outlined that a sponsor can have a functional or image-related fit with an event. Functional fit refers to sponsoring products being directly relevant to the event, for example, the tyre brand Pirelli sponsoring the Formula 1 World Championship. Image-related fit refers to the similarity between sponsor and event brands, for example, Rolex sponsoring the US Open Championship (golf). It has been suggested that both functional similarity (Henseler, Wilson, & De Vreede, 2009) and strong brand congruence (Roy & Cornwell, 2003) intensify image transfer and improve the benefit of the association. Gwinner (1997, p. 153) proposed that this was due to similarity "more firmly anchoring the relationship in the consumer's mind". It has also been found that weak brand compatibility and strategic fit can lead to tensions developing within the sponsor–sponsee relationship (Morgan et al., 2020).

While sponsorship fit has been found to influence sponsor's brand equity constructs (Tsordia, Papadimitriou, & Parganas, 2018), there are many occasions when brands do not naturally align to the events they seek to sponsor. In these situations, low-fitting brands can improve perceptions of congruence by clearly

62   *Event management and leverage in practice*

articulating their relationship to the event (Madrigal & King, 2017). Sponsorship articulation is the act of explaining the relationship to develop meaning in the mind of consumers (Cornwell, Humphreys, Maguire, Weeks, & Tellegen, 2006). As well as strategic communication, Henderson et al. (2019) found that brands without an inherent congruence to an event can enhance their sponsorship benefits by adopting the event's branding and colour scheme in visual marketing displays.

The benefits of sponsorship are not guaranteed when the relationship is seen as dishonest or extremely incongruent (Shoffner & Koo, 2020). For example, unhealthy product sponsors at sport events have not been positively received by the public and can generate damaging consumer evaluations (Pappu & Cornwell, 2014). Shoffner and Koo (2020) found that unhealthy product sponsors are perceived as unauthentic despite any CSR initiatives accompanying the sponsorship. However, despite the potential negative impact of these sponsorship associations, events are increasingly forming partnership with sceptical sponsors. The process of image transfer can result in sponsors generating a negative effect on the event brand (Henseler et al., 2009), so these incongruent sponsors could be damaging the event brand.

As well as congruence and brand image transfer between the event and the sponsor, consideration should be given to concurrent sponsorship. It is the norm for events to be sponsored by more than one company and the image of each sponsor can impact upon the others. Gross and Wiedmann (2015) note that personality profiles of brands can transfer between concurrent sponsors. Boronczyk and Breuer (2021) examined the transfer of brand associations between an event, focal sponsor, and cosponsor and found both direct and indirect spillover effects between concurrent sponsors. This can be positive or negative, depending on whether the transferred brand personality traits enhance or dilute brand image (Carrillat, Soloman, & d'Astous, 2015). Cobbs, Groza, and Rich (2015) found that consumers assigned greater brand equity to sponsors when they appeared with other high-equity brands. Thus, it is critical for events to manage their sponsorship partners in consideration of their sponsorship portfolio and determine whether the brands complement one another. The potential rub-off affects, positive or negative, of brand image between cosponsors must be considered by event managers when negotiating with new potential partners (Gross & Wiedmann, 2015).

Sponsorship activation

The acquisition of sponsorship rights for an organisation merely signifies the commencement of the sponsorship process (Crompton, 2004a). For sponsorship to generate benefit it is critical to leverage or activate the partnership. Sponsorship activation is defined as "communications that promote the engagement, involvement, or participation of the sponsorship audience with the sponsors" (Weeks, Cornwell, & Drennan, 2008, p. 639). Successful sponsorship requires ongoing financial and resource investment to leverage the association through marketing activation means. This leveraging activity will advance sponsorship awareness and promote market differentiation (Weeks et al., 2008). A study into consumer perceptions of sponsor brand equity, at a festival in Turkey, concluded that sponsors must be actively involved and leverage their association to create perceived congruence between their brand and the event (Sözer & Vardar, 2009).

Sponsorship activation has traditionally involved a range of promotional and advertising activities, for example, competitions and product sampling. However, sponsorship activation should be innovative and provide an experience for the consumer market, as opposed to a simple logo or brand display (Cornwell, 2008). Meenaghan and O'Sullivan (2013) recognised that for the sponsorship to continue delivering value, brand experiences and active engagement are needed, rather than merely exposure opportunities.

Recently, we have seen sponsors further invest in activation by developing extensive experiential marketing campaigns. This reflects a broader shift in brand marketing towards an experience orientation. Brands are realising that to gain true customer loyalty, they need to give something more than their product offering. That is, marketing is focusing on creating memorable and valuable customer experiences, where the customer remembers the brand's marketing because it gave them an unforgettable experience (Smilansky, 2017). Gillooly et al. (2017) investigated Cisco's experiential sponsorship activations as part of its London 2012 Olympic and Paralympic Games sponsorship. It was found that effective use of brand design principles, creative marketing, and collaboration with other sponsors were beneficial in helping Cisco cut through the clutter of Olympic sponsorship (Gillooly et al., 2017). Thus, commercial leveraging opportunities should be exploited by the sponsor organisation to widen strategic potential. If this does not eventuate, then the sponsorship purchase takes on little more than a servicing role.

Advances in digital technologies have transformed marketing campaigns, offering vast leveraging potential for events and sponsors. Social media has revolutionised audience behaviour and provides a direct channel for brands to interact with consumers. Social media platforms, such as Twitter, Facebook, Instagram, and TikTok, have changed the public's role from passive receivers of advertising information to content sharers, co-creators, and opinion generators (Utz, Schultz, & Glocka, 2013). In brand marketing, it is recognised that consumers now act as brand ambassadors when sharing brand experiences and influencing prospective customers across digital networks (Yu, Tsai, Wang, Lai, & Tajvidi, 2020). Social media channels present events and their sponsors with opportunities to communicate their congruence and actively engage consumers in communication and activation (Hazari, 2018).

Digital technologies are playing an increasingly important role in sponsorship activation (Hazari, 2018). Event sponsors often launch online competitions and various promotions to generate interest and active engagement in the lead up to an event. For example, ahead of the 2015 Glastonbury festival, event sponsor EE ran a game on Twitter where users could win tickets to the event. EE, a United Kingdom mobile phone network, created a virtual treasure hunt where users had to guess where tickets were buried on the Glastonbury treasure map. Participants had to tweet @EE and use the hashtag #Glastonburied with their guess of where the tickets were buried. The campaign was a big success, reaching over 300,000 people on the first day (Digital Strategy Consulting Limited, 2021).

64   *Event management and leverage in practice*

Social media also provides leveraging opportunities during the event. At the most rudimentary level, events and their sponsors can create hashtags to encourage attendees to share content through their social channels while connecting with the event or sponsor brand. However, innovative brands are becoming much more creative in how they merge onsite activation with online engagement. This allows brands a broad reach beyond the onsite event attendees. Vans, a leading action sports and youth culture brand, provides a good example of the potential value social media presents. During their Park Series events, Vans generated US$13 million of earned media value through athletes, fans, and media sharing content on their digital channels (Hookit, 2019). This also saw the event, Park Series, increase their social media following by 90% (Hookit, 2019).

Importantly, as Farrelly et al. (2006) note, sponsees should adopt an active role in leveraging their sponsorships, with the aim of enhancing the attraction for consumers and increasing engagement with sponsors. Sponsors launching in-store promotions, digital media campaigns and/or competitions, in the lead up to an event, provide valuable exposure and generate interest in the event. Moreover, experiential onsite sponsor activations can improve the event experience and provide added value for event attendees. Sponsors add significantly more value to events than the initial investment of revenue and thus, facilitating leverage opportunities should be considered by event managers.

Sponsorship management

As events are often highly dependent on commercial investment, event managers need prioritise the servicing of their commercial partners. Referred to as sponsorship relationship management, the process of meeting the needs and expectations of partners is critical for sponsorship success. It has been suggested that for sponsorship to function well, the sponsee and their sponsors ought to have effective business relationships (Morgan et al., 2014). In that sense, sponsorship should no longer be based singularly on a discrete transaction, where capital is exchanged for branding rights. It should involve procedural exchange, characterised by dyadic collaboration and regular communication between partners (Chadwick & Thwaites, 2005). For event managers to develop long-term relationships, they need to work collaboratively with their sponsors to develop an effective strategy to maximise benefits for both parties (Ko et al., 2017).

When considering the importance of sponsorship relationships, relationship marketing theory provides an appropriate framework by which to highlight antecedents to relationships' success or failure (Morgan et al., 2020). Relationship marketing theory posits that parties receive reciprocal benefits through collaboration and the relational exchange process (Gummesson, 2008). There is notable support for this relational approach to both sponsorship management and sponsorship research (Cousens, Babiak, & Slack, 2001; Farrelly et al., 2006; Meenaghan, 1999). The relationship marketing paradigm can highlight the relationship dynamics, which "helps to further a more nuanced understanding of this unique marketing relationship" (Jensen & Cornwell, 2017, p. 402). Relationship marketing

Events and commercial engagement 65

theory has been applied in studies of various aspects of sponsorship, including: marketing orientation, trust and commitment from the sponsor perspective (Farrelly & Quester, 2003); value creation and mitigation of tension from the sponsee perspective (Morgan et al., 2020); and various factors that may jeopardise relationships (Jensen & Cornwell, 2017) or have caused discontinuation of relationships (van Rijn, Kristal, & Henseler, 2019).

While historically most of the research attention has been given to the sponsor side of the relationship, the sponsee's perspective is emerging (Dickenson & Souchon, 2020; Toscani & Prendergast, 2018; Morgan et al., 2020; van Rijn et al., 2019). Components of relationship management, including trust, mutual understanding, long-term perspective, communication, and coordination (Nufer & Bühler, 2010), are critical to longevity of sponsorship arrangements (Farrelly, 2010). Toscani and Prendergast (2018) highlight the importance of sponsee's understanding and articulating their own objectives to develop congruent relationships with their sponsors. As Morgan et al. (2020, p. 848) note, "Commercial and marketing activity is dynamic and thus in inter-organisational settings, processes should be in place to ensure effective management and dyadic satisfaction".

A critical component of sponsorship management is measurement and evaluation. However, it is well documented that despite the growth in sponsorship expenditure, a measurement deficit continues to exist in the sponsorship industry (Jensen & Cobbs, 2014; Nickell & Johnston, 2020). There is a reliance on media exposure analysis and determining advertising equivalency of publicity in sponsorship evaluation. The value of media exposure generated through sponsorship is determined by assigning an equivalent value on the exposure if the organisation had invested in rate-card advertising (Tripodi, Hirons, Bednall, & Sutherland, 2003). This can be an important visibility and exposure metric, as it enables comparison among different sponsorship properties and year-on-year comparisons. However, this is a measure of publicity rather than effects of sponsorship activation (Meenaghan & O'Sullivan, 2013).

Sponsorship awareness is another common form of evaluation. This is based on surveying consumers as to their recall and/or recognition of event sponsors. This can be effective if enhanced awareness was the primary objective underpinning the sponsorship investment and remains a critical first base in the sponsorship management process (Meenaghan & O'Sullivan, 2013). However, as concluded by Crompton (2004b), a limitation of measuring sponsorship effectiveness by recall is that consumers are likely to recognise a company based on popularity rather than on the effectiveness of the sponsorship message. Thus, awareness measures provide only the initial phase of cognition as to whether the sponsor was lodged in the survey respondent's memory. This does not indicate behavioural change or intent to purchase sponsor products.

As sponsors continue to engage in digital activations, measuring effectiveness and engagement online is increasingly important. Social media metrics allow event managers to provide hard numbers to sponsors, such as the number of "likes", "shares", and "comments" and which content performs best across different platforms. These metrics provide an indication of consumer engagement

66   *Event management and leverage in practice*

with the content. However, caution must be taken when interpreting these results, as online engagement doesn't necessarily translate to purchase behaviour or increased brand loyalty.

For a sponsor to renew a sponsorship contract, it is essential that the event has demonstrated value in the association. While the aforementioned evaluation measures of media exposure and recall/recognition may not represent all sponsorship value, it is important that event managers can report on sponsorship outcomes. Return on investment (ROI) is the common term used when evaluating the success of a marketing campaign or strategy. However, ROI focuses on the financial value of an event and not all success can be directly attributed to revenue. Increasingly, return on objectives (ROO) is being used to determine sponsorship value. ROO considers the less tangible outcomes, such as brand awareness and customer loyalty. These metrics may not have an immediate financial value but are critical for future growth. Lack of information regarding sponsorship's impact on the bottom line of business is an ongoing challenge in the industry. It is important for both events and sponsors to consider how they should best measure the strategic performance of their sponsorship, which should be directly related to their objectives.

As with any inter-organisational arrangement, sponsorship comes with a range of risks for both parties. A thorough risk assessment of sponsorship decision-making is vital. Wagner and Nissen (2015) explored perceived sponsorship risks and found that marketing managers are most concerned with a lack of cooperation, no profitability, and bad media exposure. However, risks are not just a concern of sponsors. There are two main potentially negative sponsorship outcomes event managers must consider—operational risk and reputational risk (Crompton, 2014). Operational risk occurs when sponsors use their power to insist on changing the format of the event in some way. This could be rule changes, event site layout, or location changes or event content changes. Reputational risk is associated with sponsor–sponsee brand image transfer and the potential negative public perceptions of certain sponsor brands. This can be related to the type of sponsor brand, for example, unhealthy food or sports betting brands, or can manifest as a result of a brand scandal or crisis. While not all risks can be foreseen, event managers should thoroughly investigate potential negative outcomes resulting from commercial partnerships.

Event authenticity and commercialisation

While this chapter focuses on managing and leveraging commercial partnerships, it is important for event managers to consider appropriate levels of commercialisation in the context of their event. It has been proposed that the commercialisation of events can potentially undermine its core purpose and bring into question the event's true authenticity (Rahman & Lockwood, 2011). The tension between authenticity and commercialisation is a common area of discussion in contemporary events-based research. While commercial activity can deliver notable value for events (e.g. financial investment, marketing promotion, experiential

Events and commercial engagement 67

activations), consideration needs to be given to maintaining authenticity. A challenge in the events industry is how much commercialisation is too much. This question has been raised particularly regarding cultural festivals and local events. Have they become too commodified and are the free identities and cultures at the core of the events being lost?

The concept of authenticity is discussed in myriad fields. In the marketing discipline it is recognised that "consumer's search for authenticity is one of the cornerstones of contemporary marketing" (Brown, Kozinets, & Sherry, 2003, p. 21). In the field of consumer research, brand authenticity has been defined as the perceived genuineness of a brand, consisting of four dimensions: continuity, originality, reliability, and naturalness (Bruhn, Schoenmüller, Schäfer, & Heinrich, 2012). In tourism and events scholarship, it is noted that perceived authentic experience can increase tourist or attendee satisfaction with the destination or event experience and can be considered part of the event product that organisers can partially control (Robinson, & Clifford, 2012). While there remains some ambiguity as to what authenticity incorporates, it can be defined as "a concept that encapsulates what is genuine, real, and/or true" (Castéran & Roederer, 2013, p. 153).

As discussed throughout this book, events can be leveraged for economic and social benefit. However, economic and social tensions often arise within event management and can compromise the ability to deliver multifaceted value (Ziakas, 2019). In terms of commercialisation, the event must be broadly conceptualised and event value clearly identified to ensure commercial aspirations don't overshadow the authentic social value. Antchak (2017) analysed the event portfolio of the city of Auckland, New Zealand. It was found that the city has a clear focus on bidding and hosting events that gain predominantly economic benefits, which affects the multidimensional value of the events portfolio (Antchak, 2017). Focusing solely on economic results has meant social-oriented events which are supposed to deliver the most social outcomes and represent the cultural diversity of Auckland have been ignored or become overly commercialised. As one of the interviewees in the study noted, events such as the Pasifika Festival, which celebrates Pacific Islander culture and traditions, have become "too commercialised, too regimented and very expensive" (Antchak, 2017, p. 293). This is not limited to local and regional events. Maguire, Barnard, Butler, and Golding (2008) note that the modern Olympic movement is more concerned with media, marketing, and corporate advertising than the values and ideals of "Olympism". The event industry is confronted with a serious challenge: how do you continue to grow commercial leverage opportunities while not losing event authenticity?

Ziakas (2019) highlights the challenge events face with the interference of politics and overcommercialisation that can compromise their authenticity. As event commercialisation predominantly concerns sponsorship, most discussion of overcommercialisation centres on incongruent sponsors or a clutter of sponsor advertising. Consumers' evaluation of commercial sponsorship varies depending on the type of event. In the not-for-profit sector, for example a local sport event, sincerity of sponsors is an important driver of consumer response (Ko & Kim, 2014). Regarding cultural events, McCartney and Osti (2007) highlight the risk of

68   *Event management and leverage in practice*

commercialisation impacting attendees' cultural perspective of the event, which can diminish the importance of the intrinsic meanings behind it. If authenticity is lost, events risk being less attractive and visitors less motivated to attend in the future (McCartney & Osti, 2007). Further, sponsorship that is seen as overly commercial or that with questionable association to the event brand can have negative impacts on the sponsoring brand (Fleck & Quester, 2007).

Attribution theory suggests that consumers cognitively infer a motive for sponsorship investment (Rifon, Choi, Trimble, & Li, 2004). That is, consumers make either altruistic or self-serving inferences towards event sponsors (Becker-Olsen, Cudmore, & Hill, 2006). Perceptions of altruism infer that the sponsor is involved because the event's social cause aligns with its core values, whereas self-serving rationale sees sponsorship investment based on media exposure and commercial benefit. The inferences consumers make regarding sponsors mediate the effects of the sponsorship.

Research has shown that perceived sincerity of sponsors is a key antecedent of consumer attitude towards the sponsorship (Ko et al., 2017; Rifon et al., 2004). Ko et al. (2017) found perceived sincerity to be an important characteristic in the context of not-for-profit sponsorship and thus, sponsor characteristics are important for event managers to consider. Local events and festivals can benefit from inviting local businesses to sponsor the event. However, it is critical that the sponsors communicate their sincere motivation for supporting the event. For sponsors to be perceived as sincere, they must consider their communication and promotion and ensure they are not overly commercial (Olson, 2010).

As noted by Ziakas (2019, p. 129),

> [E]vents are complex and polysemic social constructions that have a variety of roles, and therefore, they cannot be viewed merely as commercial products or assets. That would leave unexploited the opportunity to use different events for sustainable development purposes balancing their economic, social and environmental value.

This links to aspects of event sustainability and triple bottom line considerations. Scheinbaum et al. (2017) discuss event social responsibility and note that "events holding strong social responsibility associations play a pivotal role in generating greater enthusiasm for the event and its sponsors". Moreover, event social responsibility also affects consumers' perceptions of sponsors' sincerity (Scheinbaum et al., 2017). Considering event social responsibility, it is of benefit to both the event and their sponsors, if they clearly communicate the values of the event and why the sponsors support this.

Conclusions and outlook

Considering the future of events and commercial relationships, it is important to recognise the significant impact the global COVID-19 pandemic has had on the events and sponsorship sectors. With the cancellation or postponement of events many sponsors changed their planned marketing campaigns and, in many cases,

Events and commercial engagement 69

withdrew from their sponsorship commitments. Following the announcement that the Tokyo 2020 Olympic Games were postponed, many worldwide Olympic sponsors pivoted their marketing plans. For example, Visa, a worldwide partner of the International Olympic Committee since 1986, drastically changed their activation plans to better reflect the current environment. Visa launched a digital marketing campaign "Do your part like an Olympian" showcasing athletes in their own homes promoting COVID-19 related safety messages and using the hashtag #StayHome (see: https://twitter.com/nbcolympics/status/1247950378265645056?lang=en). In other situations, as marketing budgets froze, commercial sponsors ended their partnerships. For example, Qantas Airlines announced the end of its 30-year sponsorship of the Wallabies (the Australian men's rugby union team), worth approximately AU$5 million a year, due to financial struggles caused by COVID-19. While these examples represent large-scale partnerships, the effect of sponsor budget cuts may hit local and regional events even harder. At the time of writing this book, it is too early to judge the full effects and challenges events will face in securing sponsorship partners. Now more than ever, effective relationship management is critical.

Digital content creation has been on the rise for the past few years; however, the COVID-19 pandemic has accelerated engagement generating value through digital content. With no (or minimal) live events, archive footage, competitions and online challenges became key content for marketers. The ability to engage a wider audience through the virtual world is an exciting prospect for events and their sponsors. Although, as highlighted throughout this chapter, event managers need to consider how to generate exploitable commercial return, while maintaining their commercial integrity and authenticity.

Looking ahead, hybrid events that integrate physical and cyber-space will become mainstream. Virtual interaction allows events to transcend geographical boundaries and expand the scope of event delivery and attendee engagement. Augmented reality will help events synthesise their physical and virtual offerings, changing how events are experienced and consumed. The prospect of further digital advancements and virtual event experiences presents an exciting time for commercially leveraging events. Looking forward, measuring the digital customer experience will be key to driving commercial investment.

A notable trend influencing the industry is the growing popularity of behind the scenes, exclusive footage. For example, *The Last Dance*, a documentary series about Michael Jordan and his basketball career at the Chicago Bulls, was released in April 2020 and broke viewership records. In the United States, Episode 1 averaged 6.3 million viewers on ESPN and it was the number one trending topic on Twitter (NBC Sports, 2021). Across Facebook, Instagram, and Twitter, ESPN's The Last Dance-related posts generated nine million engagements (NBC Sports, 2021). Event managers and sponsors should consider the exclusive content and unique experiences they can provide, as this is clearly an avenue attracting consumer attention.

Another significant trend influencing commercial aspects of events is the growth of e-sports. In 2020, the global e-sports market was valued at over US$950 million (Gough, 2020). One of the biggest ever e-sports events, the 2018

70 *Event management and leverage in practice*

League of Legends Mid-Season Invitational, had 60 million unique viewers tune in online and a prize pool of over US$1.3 million (de la Naarre, 2020). Most of the e-sports revenue comes from sponsorship and this commercial investment will continue to rise in the coming years. The e-sports industry transcends international borders and the diverse audience is highly engaged, which creates for an enticing sponsorship property. While the popularity of e-sports has been on the incline for the past few years, COVID-19 saw new players enter the scene with traditional sport leagues, teams, and athletes engage with e-sport platforms. Celebrities and professional sport stars connected with spectators by joining the virtual game tournaments and live-streaming the content. E-sports is an industry in a state of unprecedented growth and disruption which is incredibly attractive to brands. Internationally, event managers need to consider the opportunities and competitive challenges the e-sports market presents.

The uncertainty created by the COVID-19 pandemic has raised concerns as to the value of sponsoring live events in the future. Traditionally, sponsorship contracts have been quite rigid and time specific. However, events (and other sponsored properties) need to review this approach and assess how their sponsorship contracts may need to change in the future. There is a need for more agility and flexibility in contractual agreements. While maintaining security and certainty is crucial, COVID-19 has shown the importance of being agile and adaptable. Can sponsorship contracts be designed on value generation rather than specific time commitments? That is, rather than devising a three-year contract, the length of the partnership is flexible depending on when objectives are achieved.

Event managers need to be designing and managing their sponsorship contracts individually, as a one-size-fits-all approach does not consider the nuances of each relationship. Moreover, events need to consider event cancellation clauses in their contracts and adjust contractual obligations accordingly. This will allow sponsors increased comfort with renewing or signing new sponsorship agreements. During times of uncertainty, preparedness and forethought can be beneficial in building trust within the sponsorship relationship. However, it is not just what events can do to maintain relationships, sponsors should also consider their role in the recovery process. A recent survey in the United Kingdom found that 53% of people saw sponsors as critical to helping sport teams and leagues rebuild the live experience for fans (The Nielsen Company, 2021).

There are many areas within event sponsorship that require further research attention and industry consideration. For example, how can events and their sponsors best leverage sponsorship in the online world? Further, how can digital content complement traditional advertising campaigns? How should sponsorship relationships and associated marketing campaigns be managed in times of uncertainty? What strategies should events adopt to best meet the commercial needs of their partners, while also maintaining event authenticity? Given the competitive nature of the sponsorship industry and significant growth of digital platforms and influencer marketing, there is mounting pressure on events to increase their value proposition and successfully manage their sponsorship relationships.

References

Alexandris, K., Tsaousi, E., & James, J. (2007). Predicting sponsorship outcomes from attitudinal constructs: The case of a professional basketball event. *Sport Marketing Quarterly, 16*(3), 130–139.

Andersen, S. E., & Johansen, T. S. (2016). Cause-related marketing 2.0: Connection, collaboration and commitment. *Journal of Marketing Communications, 22*(5), 524–543.

Antchak, V. (2017). Portfolio of major events in Auckland: Characteristics, perspectives and issues. *Journal of Policy Research in Tourism, Leisure and Events, 9*(3), 280–297.

Becker-Olsen, K. L., Cudmore, B. A., & Hill, R. P. (2006). The impact of perceived corporate social responsibility on consumer behavior. *Journal of Business Research, 59*(1), 46–53.

Boronczyk, F., & Breuer, C. (2021, January). The company you keep: Brand image transfer in concurrent event sponsorship. *Journal of Business Research, 124*, 739–747.

Brown, S., Kozinets, R. V., & Sherry, J. F. Jr. (2003). Teaching old brands new tricks: Retro branding and the revival of brand meaning. *Journal of Marketing, 67*(3), 19–33.

Bruhn, M., Schoenmüller, V., Schäfer, D., & Heinrich, D. (2012). Brand authenticity: Towards a deeper understanding of its conceptualization and measurement. *Advances in Consumer Research, 40*, 567–576.

Carrillat, F. A., Solomon, P. J., & d'Astous, A. (2015). Brand stereotyping and image transfer in concurrent sponsorships. *Journal of Advertising, 44*(4), 300–314.

Castéran, H., & Roederer, C. (2013). Does authenticity really affect behavior? The case of the Strasbourg Christmas market. *Tourism Management, 36*, 153–163.

Chadwick, S., & Thwaites, D. (2005). Managing sport sponsorship programs: Lessons from a critical assessment of English soccer. *Journal of Advertising Research, 45*(3), 328–338.

Cliffe, S. J., & Motion, J. (2005). Building contemporary brands: A sponsorship-based strategy. *Journal of Business Research, 58*(8), 1068–1077.

Cobbs, J., Groza, M. D., & Rich, G. (2015). Brand spillover effects within a sponsor portfolio: The interaction of image congruence and portfolio size. *The Marketing Management Journal, 25*(2), 107–122.

Cornwell, T. B. (2008). State of the art and science in sponsorship-linked marketing. *Journal of Advertising, 37*(3), 41–55.

Cornwell, T. B., Humphreys, M. S., Maguire, A. M., Weeks, C. S., & Tellegen, C. L. (2006). Sponsorship-linked marketing: The role of articulation in memory. *Journal of Consumer Research, 33*(3), 312–321.

Cousens, L., Babiak, K., & Slack, T. (2001). Adopting a relationship marketing paradigm: The case of the national basketball association. *International Journal of Sport Marketing & Sponsorship, 2*(4), 331–355.

Crompton, J. L. (2004a). Sponsorship ambushing in sport. *Managing Leisure, 9*(1), 1–12.

Crompton, J. L. (2004b). Conceptualization and alternate operationalizations of the measurement of sponsorship effectiveness in sport. *Leisure Studies, 23*(3), 267–281.

Crompton, J. L. (2014). Potential negative outcomes from sponsorship for a sport property. *Managing Leisure, 19*(6), 420–441.

de la Naarre, T. (2020, June 4). *Biggest eSports live events in history*. Retrieved from www.lineups.com/esports/biggest-esports-live-events-in-history/

Dickenson, P., & Souchon, A. L. (2020). Sponsees matter! How collective responsibility judgments of sport sponsors affect sponsee equity. *European Sport Management Quarterly, 20*(5), 537–559.

72 *Event management and leverage in practice*

Digital Strategy Consulting Limited. (2021). *Gamification case study: EE launches Glastonbury ticket treasure hunt on Twitter #Glastonburied.* Retrieved from www. digitaltrainingacademy.com/casestudies/2015/06/gamification_case_study_ee_launches_glastonbury_ticket_treasure_hunt_on_twitter_glastonburied.php

Farrelly, F. (2010). Not playing the game: Why sport sponsorship relationships break down. *Journal of Sport Management, 24*(3), 319–337.

Farrelly, F., & Quester, P. (2003). The effects of market orientation on trust and commitment. *European Journal of Marketing, 37*(3/4), 530–533.

Farrelly, F., Quester, P., & Burton, R. (2006). Changes in sponsorship value: Competencies and capabilities of successful sponsorship relationships. *Industrial Marketing Management, 35*(8), 1016–1026.

Fleck, N. D., & Quester, P. (2007). Birds of a feather flock together . . . definition, role and measure of congruence: An application to sponsorship. *Psychology & Marketing, 24*(11), 975–1000.

Garry, T., Broderick, A. J., & Lahiffe, K. (2008). Tribal motivation in sponsorship and its influence on sponsor relationship development and corporate identity. *Journal of Marketing Management, 24*(9/10), 959–977.

Gillooly, L., Crowther, P., & Medway, D. (2017). Experiential sponsorship activation at a sports mega-event: The case of Cisco at London 2012. *Sport, Business and Management: An International Journal, 7*(4), 404–425.

Gough, C. (2020, October 13). *Revenue of the global eSports market 2018–2023.* Retrieved from www.statista.com/statistics/490522/global-esports-market-revenue/#:~:text=In%202020%2C%20the%20global%20eSports,rapidly%20in%20the%20coming%20years

Grohs, R., & Reisinger, H. (2014). Sponsorship effects on brand image: The role of exposure and activity involvement. *Journal of Business Research, 67*(5), 1018–1025.

Grohs, R., Wagner, U., & Vsetecka, S. (2004). Assessing the effectiveness of sport sponsorships: An empirical examination. *Schmalenbach Business Review, 56*(2), 119–138.

Gross, P., & Wiedmann, K. P. (2015). The vigor of a disregarded ally in sponsorship: Brand image transfer effects arising from a cosponsor. *Psychology & Marketing, 32*(11), 1079–1097.

Gummesson, E. (2008). *Total relationship marketing* (3rd ed.). Amsterdam: Butterworth-Heinemann.

Gwinner, K. (1997). A model of image creation and image transfer in event sponsorship. *International Marketing Review, 14*(3), 145–158.

Habitzreuter, A. M., & Koenigstorfer, J. (2018). The impact of environmental CSR-linked sport sponsorship on attitude toward the sponsor depending on regulatory fit. *Journal of Business Research, 124*, 720–730.

Hazari, S. (2018). Investigating social media consumption, sports enthusiasm, and gender on sponsorship outcomes in the context of Rio Olympics. *International Journal of Sports Marketing and Sponsorship,* 19(4), 396–414.

Henderson, C. M., Mazodier, M., & Sundar, A. (2019). The color of support: The effect of sponsor: Team visual congruence on sponsorship performance. *Journal of Marketing, 83*(3), 50–71.

Henseler, J., Wilson, B., & De Vreede, D. (2009). Can sponsorships be harmful for events? Investigating the transfer of associations from sponsors to events. *International Journal of Sports Marketing and Sponsorship, 10*(3), 244–251.

Hookit. (2019, January 31). *Vans proves sponsorship ROI with $13M of earned media value.* Retrieved from www.hookit.com/case-studiesvans-proves-sponsorship-roi-with-13m-of-earned-media-value/

Events and commercial engagement 73

Houlder, F. (2009). *SportBusiness group report: Sponsorship measurement and evaluation.* London: SportBusiness Group.

Jensen, J. A., & Cobbs, J. B. (2014). Predicting return on investment in sport sponsorship: Modeling brand exposure, price, and ROI in Formula One automotive competition. *Journal of Advertising Research, 54*(4), 435–447.

Jensen, J. A., & Cornwell, T. B. (2017). Why do marketing relationships end? Findings from an integrated model of sport sponsorship decision-making. *Journal of Sport Management, 31*(4), 401–418.

Ko, Y. J., Chang, Y., Park, C., & Herbst, F. (2017). Determinants of consumer attitude toward corporate sponsors: A comparison between a profit and nonprofit sport event sponsorship. *Journal of Consumer Behaviour, 16*(2), 176–186.

Ko, Y. J., & Kim, Y. K. (2014). Determinants of consumers' attitudes toward a sport sponsorship: A tale from college athletics. *Journal of Nonprofit & Public Sector Marketing, 26*(3), 185–207.

Madrigal, R., & King, J. (2017). Creative analogy as a means of articulating incongruent sponsorships. *Journal of Advertising, 46*(4), 521–535.

Maguire, J., Barnard, S., Butler, K., & Golding, P. (2008). "Celebrate humanity" or "consumers"?: A critical evaluation of a brand in motion. *Social Identities, 14*(1), 63–76.

McCartney, G., & Osti, L. (2007). From cultural events to sport events: A case study of cultural authenticity in the dragon boat races. *Journal of Sport Tourism, 12*(1), 25–40.

Meenaghan, T. (1999). Commercial sponsorship: The development of understanding. *International Journal of Sports Marketing & Sponsorship, 1*(1), 11–23.

Meenaghan, T., & O'Sullivan, P. (2013). Metrics in sponsorship research: Is credibility an issue? *Psychology & Marketing, 30*(5), 408–416.

Miragaia, D. A., Ferreira, J., & Ratten, V. (2017). Corporate social responsibility and social entrepreneurship: Drivers of sports sponsorship policy. *International Journal of Sport Policy and Politics, 9*(4), 613–623.

Morgan, A. (2019). An examination of women's sport sponsorship: A case study of female Australian rules football. *Journal of Marketing Management, 35*(17–18), 1644–1666.

Morgan, A., Adair, D., Taylor, T., & Hermens, A. (2014). Sport sponsorship alliances: Relationship management for shared value. *Sport, Business and Management: An International Journal, 4*(4), 270–283.

Morgan, A., Taylor, T., & Adair, D. (2020). Sport event sponsorship management from the sponsee's perspective. *Sport Management Review, 23*(5), 838–851.

NBC Sports. (2021). *"The Last Dance" premiere smashes records, becomes most viewed ESPN documentary.* Retrieved from www.nbcsports.com/chicago/bulls/last-dance-premiere-smashes-records-becomes-most-viewed-espn-documentary

Nickell, D., & Johnston, W. J. (2020). An attitudinal approach to determining sponsorship ROI. *Marketing Intelligence & Planning, 38*(1), 61–74.

Nufer, G., & Bühler, A. (2010). Establishing and maintaining win-win relationships in the sports sponsorship business. *Journal of Sponsorship, 3*(2), 157–168.

Olson, E. L. (2010). Does sponsorship work in the same way in different sponsorship contexts? *European Journal of Marketing, 44*(1/2), 180–199.

Pappu, R., & Cornwell, T. B. (2014). Corporate sponsorship as an image platform: Understanding the roles of relationship fit and sponsor: Sponsee similarity. *Journal of the Academy of Marketing Science, 42*(5), 490–510.

Polonsky, M. J., & Speed, R. (2001). Linking sponsorship and cause related marketing. *European Journal of Marketing, 35*(11/12), 1361–1385.

74 *Event management and leverage in practice*

Rahman, M., & Lockwood, S. (2011). How to "use your Olympian": The paradox of athletic authenticity and commercialization in the contemporary Olympic Games. *Sociology, 45*(5), 815–829.

Rifon, N. J., Choi, S. M., Trimble, C. S., & Li, H. (2004). Congruence effects in sponsorship: The mediating role of sponsor credibility and consumer attributions of sponsor motive. *Journal of Advertising, 33*(1), 30–42.

Robinson, R. N., & Clifford, C. (2012). Authenticity and festival foodservice experiences. *Annals of Tourism Research, 39*(2), 571–600.

Roy, D. (2010, February 10). *Selling sponsorship ROO in an ROI world*. Retrieved from https://donaldproy.com/selling-sponsorship-roo-in-an-roi-world/

Roy, D. P., & Cornwell, T. B. (2003). Brand equity's influence on responses to event sponsorships. *Journal of Product & Brand Management, 12*(6), 377–393.

Scheinbaum, A. C., Lacey, R., & Liang, M. C. (2017). Communicating corporate responsibility to fit consumer perceptions: How sincerity drives event and sponsor outcomes. *Journal of Advertising Research, 57*(4), 410–421.

Seguin, B., Parent, M. M., & O'Reilly, N. (2010). Corporate support: A corporate social responsibility alternative to traditional event sponsorship. *International Journal of Sport Management and Marketing, 7*(3/4), 202–222.

Shank, M. D., & Lyberger, M. R. (2015). Sports marketing: A strategic perspective. New York, NY: Routledge.

Shin, H., Lee, H., & Perdue, R. R. (2018). The congruity effects of commercial brand sponsorship in a regional event. *Tourism Management, 67*, 168–179.

Shoffner, S., & Koo, G. Y. (2020). Examining the effects of unhealthy product sponsors and CSR on sport sponsorship authenticity and the sporting event. *Journal of Global Sport Management*, 1–20.

Smilansky, S. (2017). *Experiential marketing: A practical guide to interactive brand experiences*. Philadelphia, ND: Kogan Page Publishers.

Sözer, E. G., & Vardar, N. (2009). How does event sponsorship help in leveraging brand equity? *Journal of Sponsorship, 3*(1), 35–42.

The Nielsen Company. (2021). *Study: 53% of UK fans say sponsors key in rebuilding live sports experience*. Retrieved from https://nielsensports.com/study-53-of-uk-fans-say-sponsors-key-in-rebuilding-live-sports-experience/

Toscani, G., & Prendergast, G. (2018). Sponsees: The silent side of sponsorship research. *Marketing Intelligence & Planning, 36*(3), 396–408.

Tripodi, J. A., Hirons, M., Bednall, D., & Sutherland, M. (2003). Cognitive evaluation: Prompts used to measure sponsorship awareness. *International Journal of Market Research, 45*(4), 435–455.

Tsordia, C., Papadimitriou, D., & Parganas, P. (2018). The influence of sport sponsorship on brand equity and purchase behavior. *Journal of Strategic Marketing, 26*(1), 85–105.

Uhrich, S., Koenigstorfer, J., & Groeppel-Klein, A. (2014). Leveraging sponsorship with corporate social responsibility. *Journal of Business Research, 67*(9), 2023–2029.

Utz, S., Schultz, F., & Glocka, S. (2013). Crisis communication online: How medium, crisis type and emotions affected public reactions in the Fukushima Daiichi nuclear disaster. *Public Relations Review, 39*(1), 40–46.

van Rijn, M., Kristal, S., & Henseler, J. (2019). Why do all good things come to an end? An inquiry into the discontinuation of sport sponsor: Sponsee relationships. *International Journal of Sports Marketing and Sponsorship, 20*(2), 224–241.

Wagner, U., & Nissen, R. (2015). Enacted ambiguity and risk perceptions: Making sense of national elite sport sponsorships. *Sport in Society, 18*(10), 1179–1198.

Weeks, C. S., Cornwell, T. B., & Drennan, J. C. (2008). Leveraging sponsorship on the internet: Activation, congruence, and articulation. *Psychology of Marketing Communications, 25*(7), 637–654.

Westberg, K., Stavros, C., & Wilson, B. (2011). The impact of degenerative episodes on the sponsorship B2B relationship: Implications for brand management. *Industrial Marketing Management, 40*(4), 603–611.

Yu, C.-H., Tsai, C.-C., Wang, Y., Lai, K.-K., & Tajvidi, M. (2020). Towards building a value co-creation circle in social commerce. *Computers in Human Behavior, 108*, 1–10.

Ziakas, V. (2019). Issues, patterns and strategies in the development of event portfolios: Configuring models, design and policy. *Journal of Policy Research in Tourism, Leisure and Events, 11*(1), 121–158.

6 Events and international business opportunities

Introduction

The falling barriers to the movement of goods and people are distinct features of the globalisation phenomenon, which has increased since the early 1980s. A critical driver of globalisation has been the development and increased use of information technology worldwide. As a result, even some products and services meant for the domestic market can be accessed by international consumers. Despite the increasing use of e-commerce, the physical interaction between buyers and sellers in business-to-business (B2B) and for high-value business-to-consumer (B2C) products and services remains the preferred option (Sainaghi, Mauri Aurelio, Ivanov, & d'Angella, 2019).

Business events allow interactions that lead to economic activities, including training, product promotion and sale, and collaboration (Business Events Council of Australia, 2020). Deery, Jago, Fredline, and Dwyer (2005) categorise business events into meetings, incentives, conventions, and exhibitions. The decision about where these events are held is critical and influences the event's success or failure. This is especially true in special events, such as large international exhibitions that are dubbed as mega-events. Event organisers have to address several related questions before deciding on the location of an event, especially those that are international:

- Is the host location globally connected by air transport to cater to international visitors?
- Is the infrastructure appropriate for hosting the event?
- Is the institutional environment (both formal and informal) conducive for hosting events of a specific nature?
- What investments are required to host these events and how can the host-city achieve long-term benefits (legacy)?

In this chapter, we address the influence of the geographic location, the infrastructure, the cultural environment, and the host government's support on the selection, and potential benefits of hosting mega-events. Using the World Expos example, we highlight the potential advantages and challenges a city may face when hosting such a special event. We discuss the long-term benefit of these

DOI: 10.4324/9781003002772-8

Events and international business 77

events for the host "global cities" and use the example of Dubai as the host city of the 2020 World Expo to discuss how it can sustain these advantages.

Mega-events and their legacy

Mega-events are characterised by extensive budget demands and include multiple subprojects whose interrelationships require sound management. Hosting such events demands in-depth planning for the long-term economic and social development of the destination country and a massive amount of capital investment (Li, Lu, Ma, & Kwak, 2018). Mega-events are distinct from other events due to their scale and impact on the host city (external characteristics). The Olympics, the Fédération Internationale de Football Association (FIFA) World Cup, and World Expos are some of the mega-events held every few years and boast a large number of participants and spectators and require a complex system to manage them. Media coverage and tourism attractiveness are some of the external characteristics that one could consider to evaluate the event's impact (Malfas, Theodoraki, & Houlihan, 2004).

The high cost of organising mega-events requires careful evaluation of short- and long-term benefits. This involves identifying the key stakeholders and highlighting how the perceived economic and other hosting outcomes align with their interests. Perhaps, the most important stakeholder group is the citizens of the host city and broadly the country. Smith, Ritchie, and Chien (2019) suggest that the citizens' support for the event would depend on their willingness to accept the ongoing financial liabilities and disruption and inconvenience that the hosting of the event would cause in return for the potential benefits the event may bring (including, urban regeneration and creating an event environment).

The extant literature highlights a shifting trend towards the use of computable general equilibrium (CGE) models to assess the economic benefits of events (Massiani, 2018). CGE modelling uses economic data to estimate how an economy might react to external factors (including hosting events). It does not have the limitations found in other modelling tools such as input–output multipliers, which assume no supply-side constraints (Massiani, 2018). A more recent input in mega-events' cost–benefit analyses involves assessing sustainable development and the environmental impacts, especially in mega sport events (Collins, Jones, & Munday, 2009). However, despite claims by organisations and sponsors, the events' general assessment is undertaken in terms of direct economic benefits, which consider only the short-term returns.

Hiller (1998) suggests that there is little attention paid to the non-economic impact of events and proposes a political economy model that distinguishes three types of linkages: (1) forward linkages – the direct effects caused by the event; (2) backward linkages – the background objectives that are used to justify hosting the event; and (3) parallel linkages – side-effects that occur due to the event but are neither planned nor controlled by the organisers.

Hence, this model facilitates evaluation of the pre-event, event, and post-event impact longitudinally over time (Hiller, 1998). Historically, the lack of

78   *Event management and leverage in practice*

an appropriate template was blamed for organisations not undertaking environmental and sustainable reporting. However, today the Global Reporting Initiative (GRI) and other relevant sustainability reporting systems provide organisers opportunities to communicate to the community the environmental, sustainable, and sociocultural impacts of the event (GRI, 2020).

To understand the return on investment in the long run, the government has to plan how it will use the mega-event infrastructure in the future. Will there be enough demand for the hotels and accommodation options to remain sustainable once the event is over? How will the stadia and exhibition centres continue to be used? The construction of these and other infrastructure projects are costly and can be justified by the legacies that they create (Grix, Brannagan, Wood, & Wynne, 2017). This can include a sustained long-term increase in the number of international tourists' arrivals or multinational enterprises (MNEs) moving their operations to the country to take advantage of the regulatory environment and developed infrastructure. The evidence about the long-term benefits is mixed. While studies found the 2012 Summer Olympics held in London provided a boom to the tourism sector with return travellers visiting the city (Brown, Smith, & Assaker, 2016), other examples of mega-events paint a bleak picture. For example, the tourism sector in Norway did not experience the growth predicted in the aftermath of the 1994 Winter Olympic Games in Lillehammer, with 40% of the hotels in the area going bankrupt (Teigland, 1999). This despite the approximately US$ 2.0 billion investment and operating cost for the 16-day event being deemed a success at the time based on the sales of 1.2 million tickets, 12,000 people employed by the organisers, and a daily worldwide audience of 669 million (Teigland, 1999).

Solberg (2017) evaluated the impact of the Nagano Winter Olympic Games of 1998 on Japan's Hakuba village. The long-term evaluation of the Games showed that while the infrastructure, such as the transportation network, was improved, the village attracted fewer users and events than expected and resulted in financial burdens on the municipality (Solberg, 2017). However, a legacy of the event is that the tourism sector in Hakuba has developed a better understanding of foreign tourists' needs and the value of working collaboratively with the village office to make the destination more enjoyable. The study observed increased volunteerism and improved knowledge of environmental protection among the local population (Solberg, 2017).

We conclude that the mega-event projects' legacy is debatable and host governments and organisations need to use more accurate predictive modelling to ensure optimal use of their assets and appropriate returns.

Global cities as host locations

Global cities are attractive locations to host special events. Their advanced infrastructure, global connectivity, and ability to accommodate the large volume of inbound travellers fit a host city's criteria. Wild (2019) described global cities as networked societies, where economic activities and societal trends are centred and concentrated. Some leading global cities act as interconnected hubs

Events and international business 79

and host many MNEs' head offices (Wild, 2019). The international business literature states that when firms enter an international market, they face the liability of foreignness. Being outsiders, they are at a disadvantage as far as local business knowledge and networks are concerned (Johanson & Vahlne, 2009). In contrast, due to the international networks, these global cities are more welcoming of foreign firms and individuals and provide access to contextual knowledge about the target country, thus limiting the liability of foreignness (Belderbos, Du, & Slangen, 2020).

Building on this notion of networked societies, Goerzen, Asmussen, and Nielsen (2013) identified three attributes of global cities: a high degree of interconnectedness to local and international markets; a cosmopolitan environment; and high levels of advanced producer services. These characteristics make global cities distinct from megacities (cities with more than 10 million inhabitants) or industrial clusters (cities that specifically focus on a particular industry, such as Silicon Valley in San Francisco, known for high-technology goods and services). Global cities are critical governance nodes in global production networks (Parnreiter, 2019). The broader international linkages, high information velocity, and leading business service firms make these global cities an attractive destination for MNEs' foreign direct investment (FDI). For these MNEs, the global cities provide a base in the region from which they can use to service their customers (Goerzen et al., 2013).

Many global cities are also smart cities, which use information and communication technologies (ICT) to deploy sustainable solutions to urbanisation challenges. Other cities that do not meet these criteria still can promote smart action (De Falco, 2019). Global cities' digital infrastructure capacity provides the impetus for firms, especially small- and medium-sized enterprises (SMEs), to venture into international markets using the digital platform (Wild, 2019).

ATKearney (2020) publishes the annual Global Cities Index (GCI), which assesses how globally engaged cities are using five dimensions:

- business activity,
- human capital,
- information exchange,
- cultural experience, and
- political engagement.

The index includes 30 cities ranked high on these dimensions and are categorised as the top global cities (see Table 6.1). These cities tend to undertake large-scale investment in developing human capital through education and training, have more open and liberal policies that help attract MNEs and global talent, invest in building landmarks to attract international visitors, are considered to be economically stable, and have fewer international political conflicts.

All the cities in the list have hosted mega-events, which supports the view that these locations are appealing sites for such activities.

80 *Event management and leverage in practice*

Table 6.1 2020 Global Cities Index

Rank	City	Rank	City
1	New York	16	Madrid
2	London	17	Seoul
3	Paris	18	Melbourne
4	Tokyo	19	Toronto
5	Beijing	20	Moscow
6	Hong Kong	21	Boston
7	Los Angeles	22	Vienna
8	Chicago	23	Amsterdam
9	Singapore	24	Munich
10	Washington	25	Buenos Aires
11	Sydney	26	Barcelona
12	Shanghai	27	Dubai
13	San Francisco	28	Frankfurt
14	Brussels	29	Montreal
15	Berlin	30	Miami

Source: ATKearney (2020)

World Expos

We use the example of World Expos to illustrate the regulatory and infrastructure challenges that global cities face as hosts. Using knowledge gained from previous expos, we highlight these events' legacy and the sociocultural, political, and sustainability issues in hosting such mega-events. Known officially as International Registered Exhibitions, the World Expo is organised every five years by the Paris-based Bureau International des Expositions (BIE). These expos are a global gathering of nations where countries have their dedicated pavilion where they can showcase goods and services to tens of millions of visitors worldwide (Bureau International des Expositions, 2021a).

The first World Expo, known as the Great Exhibition, was held in London in 1851. Since the end of World War II, the universal Expos have been hosted by Port-au-Prince (1949), Brussels (1958), Seattle (1962), Montreal (1967), Osaka (1970), Seville (1992), Hanover (2000), Aichi (2005), Shanghai (2010), and Milan (2015). As a result of the COVID-19 pandemic, the 2020 World Expo in Dubai was rescheduled for 2021, and Osaka Kansai will host the 2025 expo (Bureau International des Expositions, 2020). In addition to the World Expo, three other types of Expos are organised by the BIE: Specialised Expos, Horticultural Expos, and the Triennale di Milano.

A difference between the World Expo and mega sport events is the level of media coverage that is generated. Sport events can promise billions of viewers on electronic media. However, these events showcase only the venue (football ground, swimming arena, etc.). These stadia have limited use for the general population after the event. On the other hand, expos have been found to generate legacy-led urban development planned for long-term use by the host city's population. For example, advanced planning ensured that the Shanghai subway stations' construction for Expo 2010 was integrated into the city's rail network and continue to be used by commuters. The World Expos are also distinct in terms of the landmarks they create (Wilson, 2018). Perhaps, the most recognised Expo landmark is the Eiffel Tower in Paris. The Tower was built as the 1889 World Fair entrance and remains a symbol of Paris and attracts international tourists. In contrast, sport mega-events tend not to develop landmarks. What is similar across all mega-events is the intangible benefit they create. For example, the hospitality industry benefits from exposure to international tourists, and restaurants can adapt their menus to suit the customers' palates better and offer menus in multiple languages (Wilson, 2018).

So how did the recent World Expos fare when it comes to the benefits they generate and their legacy? We evaluate the two recent Expos held in Shanghai in 2010 and Milan in 2015. One of the Shanghai World Expo aims was to further a positive view as a global city. The public relations exercise relied on global news reporting of the event and the city. A content analysis of English language newspapers in ten countries between November 2009 and April 2011 by Xue, Chen, and Yu (2012) showed that the Shanghai Expo was the topic of most stories on Shanghai during this period. The authors observed a significant positive change in the news content and attitudes towards the city (Xue et al., 2012).

As highlighted earlier, one of the key stakeholders is the local population. Lv, Mosoni, Wang, Zheng, and Sun (2017) sought the residents' perceptions of the Shanghai World Expo and found a positive response to it. Specifically, the residents believed that the Expo positively influenced developing Shanghai into a multicultural city, enhanced the local economy's strength, and resulted in innovation in science and technology (Lv et al., 2017). The event was significant also in changing sociocultural attitudes as community discussions around the Expo's organisation, and the related tourism activities helped develop participative decision-making. This community participation is not common in China and highlights how this mega-event influenced attitudes (Lamberti, Noci, Guo, & Zhu, 2011).

The sustainable development and green city campaign were one of the elements identified during the Shanghai Expo. Green technologies were used during the event, highlighting a shift in urban planning and building design and further applying these ideas (Zhang, 2013). Here, we again see a change in urban development that was prompted by the World Expo.

The analysis of the Milan Expo 2015 highlighted a significant reduction in seasonality in the hotel sector since the event, resulting in better occupancy rate throughout the year. As a result, the hotel rates improved, providing significant financial benefits to the industry (Sainaghi & Mauri, 2018). Magno and Dossena (2020) advanced that the residents view the Expo's advantages as a collective outcome for the community rather than for individuals. Finally, the Milan residents perceived the Expo to be beneficial for its environmental impact. However, few were aware of the event's environmental certification (Guizzardi, Mariani, & Prayag, 2017).

Our analysis of the World Expos and the two recent events shows a positive legacy of these events. The Expos have also been economically viable, which suggests better long-term planning than many other mega-events. We explore these

82 *Event management and leverage in practice*

issues further by discussing how Dubai has prepared as the host of Expo 2020 and what economic outcomes and legacy are predicted from this event.

Expo 2020 Dubai

Dubai is the only city in the Middle East, Africa, and South Asia (MEASA) region named in the top 30 global cities list for 2020. Dubai's geographic location makes it an ideal hub and a gateway between the East and the West. The city can be accessed by two-thirds of the world's population within an eight-hour flight. Modern-day Dubai has few similarities with the old Dubai. Initially a fishing village, Dubai's efforts to modernise its society and economy commenced in the 1950s. Unlike neighbouring Abu Dhabi, Dubai did not have large oil reserves (Taher, 2016), and the City State's rulers relied on trading activities to develop its infrastructure.

In the 1970s, Dubai invested heavily in developing the deep-water seaport and a free trade cone (Jebel Ali Free Zone) to start building its claim as a regional hub (Jebel Ali Free Zone, 2021). The long-term vision for Dubai was to become a global hub that helped connect firms and buyers. The development of the Dubai airport, Emirates airlines, theme parks, and luxury hotels was part of this vision. In line with developing a future knowledge-based economy, Dubai has invested in higher education and hosts international universities' campuses. Today, Dubai is home to people of 200 nationalities and boasts a skilled and youthful population. Dubai airport is the third busiest airport globally (International Airport Review, 2020), and the city welcomed 16.7 million visitors in 2019.

Tourism is a critical economic sector for Dubai, with the city known for its landmarks. These include the Burj Khalifa (the tallest building in the world), the Burj Al Arab hotel, the Dubai Fountain, and the Dubai Mall, the world's largest shopping arena (Dubai Expo News, 2020). This investment in the infrastructure follows Porter's (1990) suggestion that nations need to invest in both basic and advanced factors to have a national competitive advantage. Basic factors include those features and elements in an economy, such as geographic location and natural resources. Advanced factors help countries take advantage of the basic factors (Porter, 1990). For example, investment in the higher education sector to upskill the population and infrastructure development facilitates supply and value chains. Today, the United Arab Emirates (UAE) ranks sixteenth in the Ease of Doing Business ranking published by the World Bank (The World Bank, 2020), and thirteenth in the Market Potential Index of countries that are seen as attractive markets for US firms to invest and sell in (globalEDGE, 2020).

In November 2013, BIE Member States voted for the UAE to host World Expo 2020 in Dubai. This is the first-ever World Expo to be held in the MEASA region. The Expo theme *Connecting Minds, Creating the Future – Opportunity, Mobility and Sustainability* fits well with Dubai's vision for its knowledge-intensive economy and society (Bureau International des Expositions, 2021b). Over 200 exhibitors, including countries, MNEs, and non-government organisations have signed up for the event, and 25 million visits are expected at the Expo.

Events and international business   83

According to a report published by EY (2019), Expo 2020 Dubai's benefits are expected in the pre-, during-, and post-event legacy phases. The event is expected to contribute $33.4 billion to the economy between 2013, when the announcement about Dubai as the host city was made, through 2031. The pre-Expo share of the total gross value (GVA) to Gross Domestic Product (GDP) is $10.3 billion, the during-Expo share is $6.2 billion, and the post-Event share is $16.9 billion (EY, 2019). About 68% of the investment in the pre-Expo phase will be channelled to the construction sector, while 20% (approximately $1.28 billion) will be for Dubai's small- and medium-sized enterprise (SME) sector. The during-Expo period's contribution will be primarily from visitor expenditure, including the onsite purchase of entry tickets and food, and off-site expenses such as flights to Dubai, accommodation, retail, and local transportation (ArabianBusiness, 2019). The hospitality sector will absorb the majority of visitors' spending.

The Expo is expected to create 905,200 full-time jobs, equivalent to approximately 49,700 jobs being generated each year. Additionally, the event will allow 30,000 volunteers to participate and gain experience (EY, 2019), thereby, addressing the capacity-building aims of such events.

The legacy plans for Expo 2020 focus on sustainable urban development, with long-term goals for using the infrastructure built for the event. The Expo site will be rebadged as District 2020, which will be occupied by various tenant companies and an expanded Dubai Exhibition Centre. Roughly 80% of the Expo's construction will be retained for this new district, with plans for further development to expand it into another city (EY, 2019). This city will be a planned smart city with an emphasis on technology and innovation. Some leading MNEs, including Siemens and Accenture, have signed up to become part of this long-term vision (EY, 2019).

Additionally, the UAE expects to use the Expo 2020 platform to enhance bilateral political and economic relations with other countries in the region and beyond (ArabianBusiness, 2019). It is also hoped that Dubai's high profile would entice those international travellers who use the Dubai airport while transiting to consider taking a short city break in Dubai before travelling to their destination. These potential short-breaks are expected to generate significant economic benefits and international visitor goodwill for the city. The 2020 Expo has been cited as one of the critical reasons for Dubai's inclusion in the Lonely Planet's ten must-visit destinations (Bureau International des Expositions, 2021b). Responding to the COVID-19 pandemic, the BIE Member States in May 2020 approved Expo 2020 Dubai's postponement to 1 October 2021–31 March 2022. The event will keep the name "Expo 2020 Dubai".

The UAE has taken several steps to enhance the country's sociocultural and political environment to maximise the benefit of hosting the Expo and entice first-time and repeat international visitors to the country, specifically Dubai. As discussed earlier, the overwhelming majority of people residing in the city are expatriates. While many of them are unskilled workers, a large number of people are knowledge workers, who chose Dubai as their home while they work. As Dubai looks at developing an economic future that aligns with Industry 4.0,

84 *Event management and leverage in practice*

Table 6.2 Projected Outcomes of the Expo 2020 Dubai

Pre-Expo	During-Expo	Post-Expo (Legacy)
Job Creation	*Job Creation*	*Job Creation*
Economic Contribution $10.3 billion	**Economic Contribution** $6.2 billion	**Economic Contribution** $16.9 billion
Industry Focus • *Construction*	**Industry Focus** • *Hospitality* • *Transport*	**Industry Focus** • *High-Tech Business Services*
Government Policies • *Change in laws regarding women's protection, consumption of alcohol, etc.* • *Relaxed entry visa* • *Recognition of Israel*	**Expo 2020 Dubai** 1 Oct 2021–31 March 2022	**Expected Outcomes** • *Convert Expo area and infrastructure into new city* • *Urban redevelopment* • *Enhanced bilateral trade*

Source: Data sourced from EY (2019)

selecting from and attracting global talent to work in the city is a priority. However, some of the country's laws have been called archaic and need to be updated to respond to society's changes (Tlozek, 2020). In November 2020, the UAE announced changes to laws aimed at improving protection for women, relaxing regulations on alcohol consumption, and permitting non-citizens to follow foreign laws for inheritance and divorce. Touted as promoting tolerance, one should see the changes in the 2020 World Expo context, which is expected to draw millions of visitors (Hubbard, 2020).

Regarding political relations, the UAE has good bilateral relations with many countries. The only exception was Israel, as the UAE did not recognise the country. This meant that Emiratis and Israelis could not visit each other's countries, and official bilateral trade was negligible. However, this changed in the year 2020 when UAE became the first Gulf State in 72 years to recognise Israel (Bowen, 2020; The Economist, 2020). This shift has opened up the movement of people between the two countries with Israelis able to avail themselves of the visa-free travel entry into Dubai (Times of Israel, 2021). Israeli firms have the option of opening representative and sale offices in the city to take advantage of Dubai's location and international networks.

The various decisions made by the UAE government and the expected benefits generated from the Expo 2020 are illustrated in Table 6.2.

Conclusion and managerial implications

This chapter details the challenges and benefits of hosting a special mega-event like the World Expo. Such mega-events require a long-term vision and careful planning to maximise the returns for the host location. Using the example of Expo 2020 Dubai, we show how global cities can be considered ideal places for hosting special events. In the case of the Dubai Expo, we see that planning for sustainable use of the event resources can help generate long-term employment opportunities and urban development. However, there are many challenges beyond economic concerns that require government interventions and regulatory responses. A large event that attracts millions of visitors allows the host city to showcase the very best of what it can offer to entice international visitors to return. In the Dubai example, we see that the government-initiated adjustments to the formal and informal institutional environment (through laws prompting sociocultural change) attracts more visitors. Similarly, by becoming the first Gulf country to recognise Israel, the UAE is signalling the openness of its economy and society and hoping to attract the Israeli government, MNEs, and visitors to attend and participate in the Expo.

The issues covered in this chapter suggest several implications for managers. Recent examples of mega sport events have been marred by inefficiencies, delays, and failed legacy. However, our analysis of the previous two World Expos in Shanghai and Milan, and the next one scheduled in Dubai, suggests that it is desirable for organising committees to select global cities for mega-events. These cities boast modern infrastructure, geographic and virtual connectivity, and in most cases are set up for smart actions that are based on big data analysis. For the local host city, the expected returns need to be articulated in terms of legacy. Short-term emphasis and return are unlikely to sustain the economic growth achieved during the event. As we demonstrate in Table 6.2, by clearly demarking the expected benefits and returns in three phases of the event (pre-, during, and post-), managers can make strategic choices about investments in specific industries. Failure to appropriately plan for these mega-events can result in the host city being remembered for the wrong reasons.

References

ArabianBusiness. (2019, April 18). The economic impact of Expo 2020 Dubai. Retrieved from www.arabianbusiness.com/politics-economics/418105-the-economic-impact-of-dubai-expo-2020

ATKearney. (2020). *2020 Global Cities Index: New priorities for a new world*. Retrieved December 20 from www.kearney.com/global-cities/2020

Belderbos, R., Du, H. S., & Slangen, A. (2020). When do firms choose global cities as foreign investment locations within countries? The roles of contextual distance, knowledge intensity, and target-country experience. *Journal of World Business*, *55*(1), 101022. https://doi.org/10.1016/j.jwb.2019.101022

Bowen, J. (2020, September 14). Five reasons why Israel's peace deals with the UAE and Bahrain matter. *BBC News*. Retrieved from www.bbc.com/news/world-middle-east-54151712

Brown, G., Smith, A., & Assaker, G. (2016, January 8). Revisiting the host city: An empirical examination of sport involvement, place attachment, event satisfaction and spectator intentions at the London Olympics. *Tourism Management*, *55*, 160–172. https://doi.org/10.1016/j.tourman.2016.02.010

Bureau International des Expositions. (2020). *All world expos*. Retrieved October 15 from www.bie-paris.org/site/en/all-world-expos

86 *Event management and leverage in practice*

Bureau International des Expositions. (2021a). *About world expos*. Retrieved January 5 from www.bie-paris.org/site/en/about-world-expos

Bureau International des Expositions. (2021b). *Expo 2020 Dubai*. Retrieved January 10 from www.bie-paris.org/site/en/2020-dubai

Business Events Council of Australia. (2020). *What is a business event?* Retrieved May 21 from www.businesseventscouncil.org.au/page/about_business_events.html

Collins, A., Jones, C., & Munday, M. (2009). Assessing the environmental impacts of mega sporting events: Two options? *Tourism Management, 30*(6), 828–837. https://doi.org/10.1016/j.tourman.2008.12.006

Deery, M., Jago, L. K., Fredline, L., & Dwyer, L. (2005). *The national business events study: An evaluation of the Australian Business Events sector*. Altona, VIC, Australia: Common Ground Publishing.

De Falco, S. (2019). Are smart cities global cities? A European perspective. *European Planning Studies, 27*(4), 759–783. https://doi.org/10.1080/09654313.2019.1568396

Dubai Expo News. (2020, 11 September). 5 of Dubai's best landmarks to visit during Expo 2020. Retrieved from www.dubaiexponews.com/5-of-dubais-best-landmarks-to-visit-during-expo-2020/

The Economist. (2020, September 11). Bahrain joins the UAE in recognising Israel. Retrieved from www.economist.com/middle-east-and-africa/2020/09/11/bahrain-joins-the-uae-in-recognising-israel

EY. (2019, April 15). The economic impact of Expo 2020 Dubai. Retrieved from www.ey.com/en_ae/news/2019/04/expo-2020-dubai-expected-to-contribute-aed122-6b-to-uae-economy-from-2013-2031

globalEDGE. (2020). *Market Potential Index (MPI): 2020*. Retrieved September 18 from https://globaledge.msu.edu/mpi

Goerzen, A., Asmussen, C. G., & Nielsen, B. B. (2013). Global cities and multinational enterprise location strategy. *Journal of International Business Studies, 44*, 427–450. https://doi.org/10.1057/jibs.2013.11

GRI. (2020). *Global reporting initiative-sustainability disclosure database*. Retrieved August 20 from http://database.globalreporting.org/

Grix, J., Brannagan, P. M., Wood, H., & Wynne, C. (2017). State strategies for leveraging sports mega-events: Unpacking the concept of "legacy". *International Journal of Sport Policy and Politics, 9*(2), 203–218. https://doi.org/10.1080/19406940.2017.1316761

Guizzardi, A., Mariani, M., & Prayag, G. (2017). Environmental impacts and certification: Evidence from the Milan World Expo 2015. *International Journal of ContemporaryHospitalityManagement,29*(3),1052–1071.https://doi.org/10.1108/IJCHM-09-2015-0491

Hiller, H. H. (1998). Assessing the impact of mega-events: A linkage model. *Current Issues in Tourism, 1*(1), 47–57. https://doi.org/10.1080/13683509808667832

Hubbard, B. (2020, November 9). U.A.E. changes laws to attract foreign tourists and investment. *The New York Times*. Retrieved from www.nytimes.com/2020/11/09/world/middleeast/united-arab-emirates-laws-tourists.html

International Airport Review. (2020). *The top 20 busiest airports in the world by aircraft movements*. Retrieved September 8 from www.internationalairportreview.com/article/110871/top-20-busiest-airports-world-aircraft-movements/

Jebel Ali Free Zone. (2021). *About us*. Retrieved January 4 from https://jafza.ae

Johanson, J., & Vahlne, J.-E. (2009). The Uppsala internationalization process model revisited: From liability of foreignness to liability of outsidership. *Journal of International Business Studies, 40*(9), 1411–1431. https://doi.org/10.1057/jibs.2009.24

Lamberti, L., Noci, G., Guo, J., & Zhu, S. (2011). Mega-events as drivers of community participation in developing countries: The case of Shanghai World Expo. *Tourism Management, 32*(6), 1474–1483. https://doi.org/10.1016/j.tourman.2010.12.008

Li, Y., Lu, Y., Ma, L., & Kwak, Y. H. (2018). Evolutionary governance for Mega-Event Projects (Meps): A case study of the World Expo 2010 in China. *Project Management Journal, 49*(1), 57–78. https://doi.org/10.1177/875697281804900105

Lv, K., Mosoni, G., Wang, M., Zheng, X., & Sun, Y. (2017). The image of the 2010 World Expo: Residents' perspective. *Engineering Economics, 28*(2), 217–214. https://doi.org/10.5755/j01.ee.28.2.3048

Magno, F., & Dossena, G. (2020). Pride of being part of a host community? Medium-term effects of mega-events on citizen quality of life: The case of the World Expo 2015 in Milan. *Journal of Destination Marketing & Management, 15*, 100410. https://doi.org/10.1016/j.jdmm.2020.100410

Malfas, M., Theodoraki, E., & Houlihan, B. (2004). Impacts of the Olympic Games as mega-events. *Proceedings of the Institution of Civil Engineers: Municipal Engineer, 157*(3), 209–220. https://doi.org/10.1680/muen.2004.157.3.209

Massiani, J. (2018). Assessing the economic impact of mega-events using Computable General Equilibrium models: Promises and compromises. *Economic Modelling, 75*, 1–9. https://doi.org/10.1016/j.econmod.2018.05.021

Parnreiter, C. (2019). Global cities and the geographical transfer of value. *Urban Studies, 56*(1), 81–96. https://doi.org/10.1177/0042098017722739

Porter, M. E. (1990). The competitive advantage of nations: (Cover story) [Article]. *Harvard Business Review, 68*(2), 73–93.

Sainaghi, R., & Mauri, A. (2018). The Milan World Expo 2015: Hospitality operating performance and seasonality effects. *International Journal of Hospitality Management, 72*, 32–46. https://doi.org/10.1016/j.ijhm.2017.12.009

Sainaghi, R., Mauri Aurelio, G., Ivanov, S., & d'Angella, F. (2019). Mega-events and seasonality: The case of the Milan World Expo 2015. *International Journal of Contemporary Hospitality Management, 31*(1), 61–86. https://doi.org/10.1108/IJCHM-10-2017-0644

Smith, A., Ritchie, B. W., & Chien, P. M. (2019). Citizens' attitudes towards mega-events: A new framework. *Annals of Tourism Research, 74*, 218–210. https://doi.org/10.1016/j.annals.2018.07.006

Solberg, H. A. (2017). Mega-events: Why cities are willing to host them, despite the lack of economic benefits. In I. Brittain, J. Bocarro, T. Byers, & K. Swart (Eds.), *Legacies and Mega-Events: Fact or Fairy Tales?* Abingdon, UK: Routledge. https://doi.org/10.4324/9781315558981

Taher, R. (2016, May 20). Dubai and its notable advancement. *globalEDGE*. Retrieved from https://globaledge.msu.edu/blog/post/41170/dubai-and-its-notable-advancement

Teigland, J. (1999). Mega-events and impacts on tourism; the predictions and realities of the Lillehammer Olympics. *Impact Assessment and Project Appraisal, 17*(4), 305–317. https://doi.org/10.3152/147154699781767738

Times of Israel. (2021, January 13). UAE approves visa exemption agreement with Israel, Foreign Ministry says. Retrieved from www.timesofisrael.com/uae-approves-visa-exemption-agreement-with-israel-foreign-ministry-says/

Tlozek, E. (2020, December 28). The United Arab Emirates is trying to rebrand its image by making changes to its "antiquated" legal system. *ABC News*. Retrieved from www.abc.net.au/news/2020-12-28/uae-is-trying-to-rebrand-its-image-by-making-changes-to-its-laws/12984988

88 *Event management and leverage in practice*

Wild, P. O. (2019). *Firm internationalization and global cities: Exploring the role of Singapore for Swiss SMEs in Southeast Asia Université de Genève.* Switzerland. Retrieved from https://archive-ouverte.unige.ch/unige:120462

Wilson, M. (2018). *Expos: Temporary events with lasting impacts.* Retrieved September 8 from https://bie-paris.org/site/en/focus/entry/expos-temporary-events-with-lasting-impacts

The World Bank. (2020). *Doing business: United Arab Emirates.* Retrieved December 20 from www.doingbusiness.org/en/data/exploreeconomies/united-arab-emirates

Xue, K., Chen, X., & Yu, M. (2012). Can the World Expo change a city's image through foreign media reports? *Public Relations Review, 38*(5), 746–754. https://doi.org/10.1016/j.pubrev.2012.06.013

Zhang, X. (2013). Going green: Initiatives and technologies in Shanghai World Expo. *Renewable and Sustainable Energy Reviews, 25,* 78–88. https://doi.org/10.1016/j.rser.2013.04.011

7 Events, strategic alliance, and network management

Introduction

A critical factor in leveraging events is the successful management of stakeholder relationships and the formation of strategically beneficial alliances. In this chapter we introduce the principles of strategic alliance governance as they relate to the events industry. The purpose is to convey key considerations, benefits, and challenges of managing event-based alliances. We provide insight into intra-organisational and inter-organisational characteristics that influence the governance of alliances and the value creation within them. The aim is to highlight how event managers can most effectively develop strategy and govern their alliance portfolios.

Inter-organisational alliances are ubiquitous in the international business marketplace. The proliferation of alliances has impacted virtually every industry sector (Ring, Doz, & Olk, 2005), with the events industry being no exception. Alliances are formed not only for manufacturing and production purposes but also for co-branding; joint marketing; and research and development. Partnering up with other entities presents adept opportunities to attain and perpetuate market competitiveness.

Strategic alliances are relationships between two or more organisations that are formed to generate individual and common benefit (Hansen, Hoskisson, & Barney, 2008). The underlying rationale of inter-organisational alliance formation is the generation and sustainability of competitive advantage (Mamédio, Rocha, Szczepanik, & Kato, 2019). Focusing on gaining a competitive advantage and achieving common goals within a specific time frame differentiates strategic alliances from other forms of relationships (Parmigiani & Rivera-Santos, 2011). Alliances are a vehicle to enhance performance by providing complementary capabilities that would ordinarily exceed the capacities of a singular organisation (Dyer & Singh, 1998).

Strategic alliances have become a cornerstone in many event organisations' attempts to achieve market advantage. There are various forms of alliances involved in event planning, management, and delivery. Public–private partnerships are important for event delivery and funding, commercial partnerships are critical to event marketing, and in a not-for-profit voluntary context, partnerships

DOI: 10.4324/9781003002772-9

90 *Event management and leverage in practice*

are vital for accessing resources and networking. By engaging in strategic alliances, events can access resources and capabilities beyond their stand-alone capacities.

Alliances play a central role in business strategy development and implementation (Ko, Kim, Lee, & Song, 2020). When discussing competitiveness and strategic success, this not only refers to the value of events from a purely economic perspective but also relates to social and environmental considerations. Even for events not specifically profit driven, forming strategic alliances presents vast opportunities.

As has been highlighted throughout this book, events are no longer just about entertainment, they are also leveraged for significant economic and social gain (Beesley & Chalip, 2011). Thus, a strategic approach to event planning and management is required to ensure benefits are maximised. Developing inter-organisational alliances can assist in generating both economic (O'Brien, 2006) and social benefit (Kellett, Hede, & Chalip, 2008). However, the events industry is unique in that it cuts across the public, private, and not-for-profit sectors, which adds to the complexity of alliance and network formation and governance.

The aim of this chapter is to contribute to our understanding of alliance portfolios and networks by drawing on insights from strategic alliance and marketing literature. To understand and unpack how collaborative relations in events are best governed, we draw on strategic alliance scholarship. The discussion then turns to service-dominant logic to consider how events can best co-create value for both business and social impact.

Strategic alliances

Strategic alliances are collaborative relationships between organisations that involve the pooling of resources and aim to achieve mutually compatible goals. Amongst strategic alliance literature, a commonly cited definition is that alliances are "voluntary arrangements between firms involving exchange, sharing, or codevelopment of products, technologies, or service" (Gulati, 1998, p. 293). Culpan (2009) refined this and highlighted the importance of long-term commitment of resources in the pursuit of mutual benefit. Mutual benefit refers to partner organisations seeking strategic objectives by exchanging and combining resources and capabilities to the reward of all involved (Hansen et al., 2008). The term *strategic* implies that alliance partners have developed planned objectives, with the dominant focus on improved product/service market combination (Duysters & Hagedoorn, 2000).

There are various types of strategic alliances, typically categorised into: joint ventures; minority equity alliances; and, non-equity (or contractual) alliances (Das & Rahman, 2010). Despite the various alliance formations, Mowla (2012, p. 5) pinpointed five common features: (1) defined scope and objectives, (2) interdependent contractual arrangements, (3) specifically defined responsibilities and commitments, (4) organisational independence outside the alliance, and (5) a fixed time period in which to achieve set goals. While there are variations in alliances

Strategic alliance and network management 91

pertaining to events, they generally fit within the non-equity category. Non-equity alliances have the lowest degree of structural amalgamation; an integrated entity as such is not created to manage the alliance (Teng & Das, 2008). They are based on agreements stipulated contractually, where partnering entities work together to create both private and common benefits. These contractual alliances include dyadic relationships (between two parties) and multiple network arrangements (Culpan, 2009).

Strategic alliance governance

As the configuration of strategic alliances continues to gain popularity within the events sector, it is imperative that event managers develop skills in alliance governance to manage these dynamic inter-organisational relationships efficiently. Alliance governance is an umbrella term that incorporates structures and processes directing internal organisational activity and dyadic inter-organisational exchange.

Alliance governance is categorised into structural and relational divisions. It is thought that the degree of influence of each is contingent on the specific alliance context and the nature of partaking organisations (Hansen et al., 2008). Structural variables include alliance design, partner selection, strategic compatibility, and contractual stipulations. Relational governance is predominantly concerned with social exchange post-alliance formation; for example, mutual information sharing and partner communication. Relational capabilities in this context are perceived as the proficiency of organisations to interact with others, assisting in knowledge transfer and innovative alliance growth (Lorenzoni & Lipparini, 1999).

There are numerous factors that influence alliance governance and impact alliance performance. Decision-making is influential in determining alliance direction, performance, and ultimately success. There are numerous ways that decisions are made within one organisation and within the scope of an inter-organisational alliance. It has been suggested that as partnering organisations in alliances do not give up their autonomy (Albers, 2010), bargaining becomes an integral part of alliance decision-making processes and governance (Garette & Dussauge, 2000).

Alliance performance-based research can be broadly categorised into two streams; inter-organisational and intra-organisational. These two branches of research seek to identify factors critical to performance; however, attention is drawn to different units of analysis. Scholars adopting an inter-organisational focus draw on dyadic or exchange-based constituents, such as partner trust and cooperation. Trust has been found to be a key factor in alliance success as it reduces transaction costs, including those associated with inter-partner conflict (Dyer & Chu, 2003; Zaheer, McEvily, & Perrone, 1998). In the context of sport sponsorship alliances, trust and commitment have been found to be critical for the satisfaction of the sponsor (Farrelly & Quester, 2005a) and the sponsored event (Morgan, Taylor, & Adair, 2020). However, Robson, Katsikeas, Schlegelmilch, and Pramböck (2019) note that when trust builds to high levels, inter-partner familiarity can breed relational inertia. Thus, alliance managers should note that

92   *Event management and leverage in practice*

the nature of the inverted U-shaped relationship of trust with alliance performance depends on the level of resource complementarity (Robson et al., 2019).

Research investigating the intra-organisational antecedents to alliance performance is fundamentally concerned with alliance capabilities or internal mechanisms of an organisation. The primary focus is on exploring the complexity of alliance capability development (Heimeriks, Klijn, & Reuer, 2009; Kale, Dyer, & Singh, 2002). For example, scholars have explored the internal influence of organisational structure and culture (Cheung & Rowlinson, 2007), the creation of a dedicated alliance function (Kale et al., 2002), previous alliance experience (Simonin, 1997), the process of learning (Kale & Singh, 2007), and the associated development of collaborative know-how (Zollo & Winter, 2002). When attention shifts from the inter-organisational contingencies to the intra-organisational functions, the unit of analysis broadens to the entire alliance portfolio rather than one specific alliance exchange relationship. Events have multiple alliances operating concurrently, often referred to as an alliance portfolio (Ko et al., 2020), and, as such, it is critical that a network-based perspective is considered. When negotiating strategic alliances, it is important to consider your and your potential partner's broader portfolio of alliances. Alliance portfolio management requires a holistic approach, which includes: partner selection based on needs and opportunities of the portfolio; exploitation of synergies within the portfolio; and, conflict management across the entire portfolio (da Costa, Junior, Porto, & Martinez, 2018).

It is evident that both inter- and intra-organisational structures and processes play a critical role in alliance governance. An organisation must understand dyadic issues in light of internal processes and structures in order to optimise partner satisfaction and alliance performance. It has been argued that alliance governance must be flexible and adaptive in order to match dynamic business requirements in the market (Reuer & Arino, 2007). As inter-organisational relationships between alliance partners develop, the governance structure may change as new opportunities for collaboration become apparent (de Man, Roijakkers, & de Graauw, 2010).

Another important consideration in alliance governance is partner legitimacy. Legitimacy relates to the alliance partners' perceptions of one another, which helps to build reputational capital, cooperation, and lower transaction costs (Kumar & Das, 2007). These perceptions subsequently influence how collaboration unfolds within the alliance. While legitimacy influences governance, organisations will seek out alliance partnerships to improve their legitimacy. Drayer and Martin (2010) found that when the National Football League (NFL) formed alliances with legitimate ticketing providers, the market gained legitimacy.

Sino Weibo's Spider Web of strategic alliances

Sino Weibo is China's top social media platform with over 550 million active monthly users (Cortese, 2020). In 2014, Weibo launched Weibo Sports, a platform for sport fans to interact with sport events, clubs, and athletes. The Operations Manager at Weibo Sports, Zhou Tianyi, noted that "Our ultimate goal is to bring sports organisations together, in order to deliver the highest quality content to the largest possible audience" (cited in Collins, 2016). Since launching, Weibo Sports has formed strategic partnerships with sport and event organisations internationally. Through their developed network, Weibo often acts as the conduit between users and their partnering organisations.

During the 2016 Rio Olympic Games, Weibo held a "Social Olympics" for users. Through the formation of various partnerships with organisations associated with the delivery of the Games, they provided real-time news to users. It also led to the Brazilian President, Dilma Rousseff, opening a Weibo account in a marketing effort to raise the popularity of the global event in China. Weibo developed a comprehensive network of partners in Brazil and China to generate organic and original Olympic news coverage. Domestically, strategic alliances were formed with China's most influential sports media, CCTV5 and China Sports Daily. Drawing on the resources of each party, Weibo users were provided with a more mobile and social Olympic spectator experience (Collins, 2016).

In 2017, Weibo Sports announced its first domestic strategic alliance with sports digital consultancy, Mailman Group. The two brands work together on content promotion, commercial promotion and provide data insights to sport organisations globally (Srivastav, 2017). This partnership has changed the digital sports market in China and has opened up the Chinese consumer market to events, leagues, and clubs internationally.

Weibo Sports has also formed strategic partnerships with many sports events and clubs globally. For example, in 2017, the National Basketball Association (NBA) announced a long-term strategic alliance with Weibo and in 2019, Weibo became UFC's "Official Social Media Platform" in China. This partnership provides Weibo users with access to UFC live event content and highlights (UFC, 2019). They also joined forces with English football club Wolverhampton Wanderers to launch an eSports team, the Wolves Weibo eSports.

Event alliances

Within sport and event management scholarship, most alliance-based discussion has focused on marketing partnerships, specifically sponsorship alliances (e.g. Farrelly & Quester, 2005b; Morgan, Adair, Taylor, & Hermens, 2014; van Rijn, Kristal, & Henseler, 2019). A review of sponsorship literature was provided in Chapter 5 of this book. While sponsorship alliances may have dominated research, alliances are formed across various industry sectors to facilitate event planning, management, and delivery.

Recently, we have seen a rise in alliances formed during the event bidding process. For numerous major and mega-events, joint event bids between multiple countries or regions have emerged. This is the result of escalating costs of

Event management and leverage in practice

hosting these large-scale events, including the provision of stadiums and related infrastructure (Maennig & Vierhaus, 2017). In the context of sport events, Byun, Leopkey, and Ellis (2020) examine how the formation of joint bidding alliances can influence the creation of organisational legitimacy. Similarly, in the context of bidding to host sport events, Byun, Ellis, and Leopkey (2020) examined joint bid alliances and the impact of such alliances on the success of the bid. They found that when countries form an alliance and present a joint bid to host an event, they build wider and stronger networks for pooling resources (Byun, Ellis et al., 2020). Legacies of presenting joint bids can include economic, sport development, and political impact.

In 2019, the International Olympic Committee (IOC) announced significant reform to the Olympic Games' bidding and hosting parameters. While previously the Games were held in one city and its surrounding region, the IOC extended the definition of a "host" to allow multiple cities, regions, and/or countries to generate joint bids. IOC President, Thomas Bach, stated that "Flexibility is a necessity to ensure good governance and to have sustainable Olympic Games in the future" (IOC, 2019). This could see the increased use of existing facilities and sharing of associated hosting costs. Potentially, this will minimise negative impacts associated with building new infrastructure for each Games.

The Trans-Tasman World Cup alliance

In June 2020, it was announced that Australia and New Zealand's joint bid to host the 2023 FIFA Women's World Cup was successful. The alliance developed between Football Federation Australia (FFA) and New Zealand Football Federation has the potential to generate positive outcomes for both countries. FFA chairman, Chris Nikou, stated the successful bid presents a great opportunity to grow football in the region, "FIFA today has made not one, but two countries very happy" (cited in Howard, 2020). This is not the first time these two countries have formed a hosting partnership. In 1987, they co-hosted the Rugby World Cup, in 2015 the Cricket World Cup, and in 2017 the Rugby League World Cup.

The FFA forecasts the social and economic benefit of hosting the tournament at AU$460 million (ABC, 2020). It is also expected to result in the significant celebration of, and benefit for, women's sport in both countries. Hosting large sport events can generate a trickle-down effect in grassroots participation. The global media spotlight on elite women's sport not only should increase public interest but will potentially entice further commercial investment. While in recent years, public and commercial interest in women's professional sport has been increasing in both Australia and New Zealand, there remain numerous areas of gender inequality on and off the pitch. A key theme of the successful joint bid document for the 2023 tournament was women's empowerment and gender equality (FIFA, 2020).

This is the first time in a major FIFA tournament that there has been a successful bid split over two Confederations (Asia and Oceania). FIFA Council President, Gianni Infantino, discussed the expanded tournament, noting that "It will be even more global and have much positive impact on the development of women's football" (cited in, Howard, 2020). Given the scale of the World Cup, effective alliance governance will be critical for the co-host football federations. Both structural and relational considerations will be key, as the two entities plan for and deliver the tournament.

Opportunities and challenges within strategic alliances

Academics and practitioners have recognised a multitude of potential benefits with respect to entering strategic alliances; for example, access to new resources and networks (Das & Teng, 2000) and the possibilities to enter new markets (Cousens & Bradish, 2018). There is also vast potential for knowledge acquisition and exploitation (Yli-Renko, Autio, & Sapienza, 2001). It has been recognised that alliances provide opportunities for organisations to learn skills, knowledge, and technologies from their alliance partners (Chen & Chen, 2002). As asserted by Teng and Das (2008), organisations that have developed "collaborative know-how" are better equipped to manage alliances in the longer-term.

Diversity between events-based alliance partners is inevitable due to the unique nature of events and their partnering organisations. Events' inter-organisational alliances will often be cross-sectoral arrangements. Thus, structural and cultural differences can affect behaviour and alliance processes, presenting notable challenges (Babiak & Thibault, 2008). There can be variation across the specification of resources, capabilities, structures, processes, and internal cultures. This diversity can either be harnessed to the advantage of the alliance or instigate instabilities to the detriment of the alliance. It has been recognised that strategic, organisational, and cultural diversity can be potentially damaging in strategic alliances (Das & Kumar, 2011).

Differences in organisational priorities, cultures, and strengths must be considered by management involved in all strategic alliances. An organisation's intangible personal and cultural attributes may impact the governance of its inter-organisational relations (Anand & Khanna, 2000). Cultural differences – referring to organisational culture and/or national culture – present potential complexities in terms of managing inter-organisational alliances. This is a particularly pertinent consideration for global events, where partner arrangements often transcend national and cultural boundaries. In a study exploring inter-partner sensemaking in alliances, Das and Kumar (2010) conclude that cultural diversity between partners can be detrimental to overall alliance performance.

The complexity of alliances can lead to conflict between partners and alliance instability is common. Moreover, the duality of inter-organisational alliances causes discrepancies in expectations, motivations and can instigate inter-partner conflict. Alliance studies have identified numerous reasons for alliance

96 *Event management and leverage in practice*

breakdown, including lack of commitment and trust (Ariño & de la Torre, 1998), absence of a defined common goal and understanding of value (Doz & Hamel, 1998), lack of experience (Anand & Khanna, 2000), and changes in bargaining power (Inkpen & Beamish, 1997). As noted by Das and Kumar (2010), the common theme is disparity among partner expectations associated with various failure variables, which consequently inhibit inter-organisational coordination.

Scholars have averred that the two key problems experienced by failing alliance partners are coordination and appropriation. Coordination problems arise when a partner is not effectively managing the integration of the inter-organisational alliance, while the latter concerns the appropriate value generated for both parties (Das & Kumar, 2010). Thus, in an event sponsorship alliance, for example, it is critical that co-branding and leveraging activity is well planned and coordinated between sponsorship partners. Moreover, both parties must be receiving the expected value from the partnership.

Research acknowledges that partner selection and appropriate organisational fit are crucial to alliance success (Duisters, Duysters, & de Man, 2011). It is important to recognise that the strategic direction of organisations is dynamic, and partners must be cognisant of change in one another's expectations and perceptions of value (Koza & Lewin, 2000). For event managers, a critical consideration is their underlying strategy. It is pertinent to understand what the event wants to achieve through a partnership before prospecting the market for alliance opportunities. As the co-creation of value is critical in alliance situations, expectations and outcomes must be explicitly outlined. The true advantage of a strategic alliance is that it is mutually beneficial.

Farrelly and Quester (2005b), in the context of sport sponsorship alliances, highlight the importance of strategic compatibility, goal congruence, commitment, trust, and satisfaction between partners. Similarly, Morgan et al. (2014) examined sponsorship alliances and highlight the interdependencies between structural and relational governance mechanisms. It is recognised that while contractual stipulations are critical, informal processes also played a key role in generating value and mitigating tension between alliance partners (Morgan et al., 2014).

All events will have a unique alliance ecosystem. The idiosyncrasies of each relationship will generate unique opportunities and challenges. The following case study box provides a brief overview of a tri-alliance between a sport event (Spartan Race), a broadcast network (NBC), and an apparel company (Reebok).

The power of 3: Spartan Race, NBC & Reebok join forces

In 2014, a multi-year strategic alliance was formed between three parties: Spartan Race; NBC Sports Ventures; and, Reebok. Spartan Race is the global leader in obstacle racing, with over 250 annual events across 42+ countries (Spartan Race Inc, 2020). The alliance generated unprecedented media coverage of the Spartan Race series across all NBC platforms, including live-streaming and encore presentations, and Reebok became the headline sponsor for the series. The alliance saw cooperation between the three entities in terms of joint marketing, promotional and sales efforts. NBC Sports Ventures led the Spartan Race's sponsorship and international television sales efforts, as well as providing the event with marketing and promotional support. The Senior Vice President, NBC Sports Ventures, stated that "We are thrilled to launch this strategic alliance with Spartan Race and join them as pioneers in bringing this new sport category to television" (NBC Universal, 2014). Reebok similarly noted their enthusiasm in bringing this sport to a wider audience. As the Vice President, Global Brand Communications, stated, "This partnership will not only raise the sport's profile, but will inspire people watching at home to get out and challenge themselves – and have a great time doing it" (NBC Universal, 2014).

Service-dominant logic and event management

Applying a marketing lens to event management by considering perspectives such as Service-Dominant logic (S-D logic) can improve stakeholder relationships and maximise leverage potential. S-D logic introduces a new viewpoint of exchange and value, by embracing the concept of co-created value. S-D logic was first introduced as a new way to conceptualise economic exchange (Vargo & Lusch, 2004). Vargo and colleagues have since extended and evolved the perspective (Vargo, 2009; Vargo & Lusch, 2016; Vargo, Akaka, & Wieland, 2020). Value co-creation and S-D logic research spans various areas of management and marketing. For example, it has been applied to supply chain management (Vural, 2017), innovation management (Harengel, Clauß, & Laudien, 2016), knowledge management (Tregua, D'Auria, & Brozovic, 2020), and brand extensions (Brown, Sichtmann, & Musante, 2011). It has also become a leading approach to the service-industry, attracting attention in sport (Gerke, Woratschek, & Dickson, 2020; Woratschek, Horbel, & Popp, 2014), tourism (Wang, Li, & Li, 2013), and event (Werner, Griese, & Hogg, 2017) management literature.

S-D logic proposes an alternative view to the traditional goods-dominant logic by offering a broad view of social and economic exchange. Focus is given to the integration of resources, exchange of service for service, and co-creation of value among actors. From this perspective, actor-to-actor (A2A) exchange replaces the traditionally discussed business-to-business (B2B) and business-to-consumer (B2C) perspectives (Vargo & Lusch, 2016). This A2A view presents a more comprehensive outlook of actors and suggests value-in-(social and cultural) context. The locus of value is no longer restricted to the producer of the value proposition, as it is a collaborative process between all actors (Woratschek et al., 2014). In business networks co-creation of value is seen as essential for business survival (Chowdhury, Gruber, & Zolkiewski, 2016).

As the generation of co-created value is critical in strategic alliance function, S-D logic is an important perspective for event managers to consider during alliance portfolio governance. Werner et al. (2017) discuss the value of applying an

98   *Event management and leverage in practice*

S-D logic framework to explain the complexity of event sustainability. They note that S-D logic is applicable to the events sector due to the importance of operant resources, co-created value, and relationships for event managers (Werner et al., 2017). Moreover, S-D logic considers the importance of social norms, values, and culture specific for each event network actor (Werner et al., 2017).

Woratschek et al. (2014) applied S-D logic to sport management and presented the Sport Value Framework (SVF). The SVF suggests that the entire value co-creation system be considered, as opposed to individual actors. Woratschek et al. (2014, p. 21) note that sport events are a platform "that actors can use to co-create value in their business and leisure activities". In terms of leveraging events, these actors include a range of stakeholders, such as attendees, performers, sponsors and licensees, and the media. Gerke et al. (2020) also apply an S-D logic lens to sport management, investigating sport B2B networks. However, as these scholars note, this relatively new perspective requires further research and justification (Gerke et al., 2020).

Conclusions and outlook

Inter-organisational alliances present numerous opportunities for events of all size and scope. As illustrated through this chapter, events form alliances with a range of organisations across various industry sectors. While the context of each alliance will vary, as discussed earlier, there are common inter- and intra-organisational considerations that events (and their partners) should be aware of. The effective governance of strategic alliances is critical for event managers to generate maximum value from their partnerships.

While strategic alliance literature has proliferated over the past three decades, further research is needed in the role of alliances in leveraging events. An enticing area for future research is the impact of co-hosting events (for example, Australia and New Zealand co-hosting the 2023 Women's FIFA World Cup) on leverageable opportunities and event legacies. How are these international host alliances managed, and do cultural and structural differences impact on economic and social leverage? This would advance scholarly understanding and provide valuable insight for practitioners.

It would be remiss to discuss the outlook of the events industry without considering the impacts of the COVID-19 global pandemic. While undoubtedly, managing cash flow is an immediate challenge, event managers should be considering how various cross-sectoral partnerships can help in their recovery and future sustainability. During the pandemic we have seen live events shift to the digital world. While this has encouraged the creative delivery of content and maintenance of relationships, the financial return is insubstantial. As we look ahead, there are opportunities for events to adopt a hybrid approach, where live events and digital delivery are integrated. However, while technology can help address logistics issues, save expenditure and promote digital interactions, stronger infrastructure is required. This is where relationships with business service providers, event technology partners, and channel partners will be critical. Some key questions will arise as to how events can maintain continuity and avoid supply chain

Strategic alliance and network management 99

disruption. Events will benefit from adopting an S-D logic perspective, where value is co-created with their partners.

While COVID-19 has generated unprecedented challenges for the events sector, opportunities have also emerged. We have seen new and strengthened collaboration between various stakeholders, which has resulted in revised contracts, particularly force majeure clauses and insurance policy improvements. Creative and innovative solutions to cancelled or postponed events have appeared, benefits of which can be carried forward to the industry post-pandemic. Technology will continue to play an increasing role in event delivery. For example, live-streaming, integration with online video platforms, and lead capture and engagement tools will be important for event managers to leverage.

There is no doubt that the digitalisation of events and wider use of technology present ongoing opportunity for the industry. However, will the heightened interest in digital and virtual content extend post-pandemic? And what are the associated revenue opportunities that event managers should be leveraging? This is where strategically formed alliances with service providers may be essential for event managers to balance two main priorities; ensuring the safety of all stakeholders and meeting financial obligations.

In today's dynamic, complex, and interconnected environment, inter-organisational partnerships and networks are becoming increasingly important for events to improve their competitive position. Event managers must consider how they can generate alliance portfolio value through complementary resources, capabilities, and access to innovation. Relationship management, effective alliance governance, and the co-creation of value have never been more critical for the planning, management, and delivery of events.

References

Albers, S. (2010, July). Configurations of alliance governance systems. *Schmalenbach Business Review, 62*, 204–233.

Anand, B. N., & Khanna, T. (2000). Do firms learn to create value? the case of alliances. *Strategic Management Journal, 21*(3, Special Issue: Strategic Networks), 295–315.

Ariño, A., & de la Torre, J. (1998). Learning from failure: Towards an evolutionary model of collaborative ventures. *Organization Science, 9*(3), 306–325.

Australian Broadcasting Corporation. (2020, June 10). *FFA CEO says Australia's joint bid for Women's World Cup still going strong, following Brazil's withdrawal.* Retrieved from www.abc.net.au/news/2020-06-10/ffa-ceo-says-australia-committed-to-wwc2023-bid/12338136

Babiak, K., & Thibault, L. (2008). Managing inter-organisational relationships: The art of plate spinning. *International Journal of Sport Management and Marketing, 3*(3), 281–302.

Beesley, L. G., & Chalip, L. (2011). Seeking (and not seeking) to leverage mega-sport events in non-host destinations: The case of Shanghai and the Beijing Olympics. *Journal of Sport & Tourism, 16*(4), 323–344.

Brown, B., Sichtmann, C., & Musante, M. (2011). A model of product-to-service brand extension success factors in B2B buying contexts. *Journal of Business & Industrial Marketing, 26*(3), 202–210.

100 *Event management and leverage in practice*

Byun, J., Ellis, D., & Leopkey, B. (2020). The pursuit of legitimacy through strategic alliances: The examination of international joint sport event bidding. *European Sport Management Quarterly*, 1–20.

Byun, J., Leopkey, B., & Ellis, D. (2020). Understanding joint bids for international large-scale sport events as strategic alliances. *Sport, Business and Management: An International Journal, 10*(1), 39–57.

Chen, H., & Chen, T. (2002). Asymmetric strategic alliances: A network view. *Journal of Business Research, 55*(12), 1007–1013.

Cheung, Y. K. F., & Rowlinson, S. (2007). Supply chain engagement through relationship management? *Symposium: Building across Borders Built Environment Procurement CIB W092 Procurement Systems*, Newcastle, NSW, pp. 119–126.

Chowdhury, I. N., Gruber, T., & Zolkiewski, J. (2016). Every cloud has a silver lining: Exploring the dark side of value co-creation in B2B service networks. *Industrial Marketing Management, 55*, 97–109.

Collins, A. (2016, May 31). *Weibo sports Q&A*. Retrieved from www.mailmangroup.com/post/weibo-sports-q-a

Cortese, A. J. (2020, May 20). *Weibo reports record user growth in Q1, targets livestreaming and video content in 2020*. Retrieved from https://kr-asia.com/weibo-reports-record-user-growth-in-q1-targets-livestream-and-video-content-in-2020

Cousens, L., & Bradish, C. L. (2018). Sport and corporate partnerships. In D. Hassan (Ed.), *Managing sport business* (pp. 421–439). Abingdon, UK: Routledge.

Culpan, R. (2009). A fresh look at strategic alliances: Research issues and future directions. *International Journal of Strategic Business Alliances, 1*(1), 4–23.

da Costa, P. R., Junior, S. S. B., Porto, G. S., & Martinez, M. P. (2018). Relational capability and strategic alliance portfolio configuration. *International Journal of Emerging Markets, 13*(5), 1026–1049.

Das, T. K., & Kumar, R. (2010). Interpartner sensemaking in strategic alliances: Managing cultural differences and internal tensions. *Management Decision, 48*(1), 17–36.

Das, T. K., & Kumar, R. (2011). Regulatory focus and opportunism in the alliance development process. *Journal of Management, 37*(3), 682–708.

Das, T. K., & Rahman, N. (2010). Determinants of partner opportunism in strategic alliances: A conceptual framework. *Journal of Business and Psychology, 25*(1), 55–74.

Das, T. K., & Teng, B. S. (2000). A resource-based theory of strategic alliances. *Journal of Management, 26*(1), 31–62.

de Man, A., Roijakkers, N., & de Graauw, H. (2010). Managing dynamics through robust alliance governance structures: The case of KLM and northwest airlines. *European Management Journal, 28*(3), 171–181.

Doz, Y. L., & Hamel, G. (1998). *Alliance advantage: The art of creating value through partnering*. Boston, MA: Harvard Business School Press.

Drayer, J., & Martin, N. T. (2010). Establishing legitimacy in the secondary ticket market: A case study of an NFL market. *Sport Management Review, 13*(1), 39–49.

Duisters, D., Duysters, G., & de Man, A. (2011). The partner selection process: Steps, effectiveness, governance. *International Journal of Strategic Business Alliances, 2*(1/2), 7–25.

Duysters, G., & Hagedoorn, J. (2000, August–September). Organizational modes of strategic technology partnering. *Journal of Scientific & Industrial Research, 59*, 640–649.

Dyer, J. H., & Chu, W. (2003). The role of trustworthiness in reducing transaction costs and improving performance: Empirical evidence from the United States, Japan, and Korea. *Organization Science, 14*(1), 57–68.

Strategic alliance and network management 101

Dyer, J. H., & Singh, H. (1998). The relational view: Cooperative strategy and sources of inter-organizational competitive advantage. *The Academy of Management Review, 23*(4), 660–679.

Farrelly, F., & Quester, P. (2005a). Examining important relationship quality constructs of the focal sponsorship exchange. *Industrial Marketing Management, 34*(3), 211–219.

Farrelly, F., & Quester, P. (2005b). Investigating large-scale sponsorship relationships as co-marketing alliances. *Business Horizons, 48*(1), 55–62.

FIFA. (2020). *FIFA Women's World Cup 2023 bid evaluation report.* Retrieved from https://img.fifa.com/image/upload/hygmh1hhjpg30lbd6ppe.pdf

Garette, B., & Dussauge, P. (2000). Alliances versus acquisitions: Choosing the right option. *European Management Journal, 18*(1), 63–69.

Gerke, A., Woratschek, H., & Dickson, G. (2020). The sport cluster concept as middle-range theory for the sport value framework. *Sport Management Review, 23*(2), 200–214.

Gulati, R. (1998). Alliances and networks. *Strategic Management Journal, 19*(4), 293–317.

Hansen, M. H., Hoskisson, R. E., & Barney, J. B. (2008). Competitive advantage in alliance governance: Resolving the opportunism minimization-gain maximization paradox. *Managerial and Decision Economics, 29*(2–3), 191–208.

Harengel, P., Clauß, T., & Laudien, S. M. (2016, June). Perspectives of service-dominant logic for innovation management: A bibliometric analysis. *ISPIM Innovation Symposium*, The International Society for Professional Innovation Management (ISPIM), Manchester, pp. 1–24.

Heimeriks, K. H., Klijn, E., & Reuer, J. J. (2009). Building capabilities for alliance portfolios. *Long Range Planning, 42*(1), 96–114.

Howard, J. (2020, June 26). *Australia and New Zealand to host 2023 FIFA Women's World Cup.* Retrieved from www.abc.net.au/news/2020-06-26/australia-and-new-zealand-to-host-2023-fifa-womens-world-cup/12394688

Inkpen, A. C., & Beamish, P. W. (1997). Knowledge, bargaining power, and the instability of international joint ventures. *Academy of Management Review*, 177–202.

International Olympic Committee. (2019, June 26). *Evolution of the revolution: IOC transforms future Olympics Games elections.* Retrieved from www.olympic.org/news/evolution-of-the-revolution-ioc-transforms-future-olympic-games-elections

Kale, P., Dyer, J. H., & Singh, H. (2002). Alliance capability, stock market response, and long-term alliance success: The role of the alliance function. *Strategic Management Journal, 23*(8), 747–767.

Kale, P., & Singh, H. (2007). Building firm capabilities through learning: The role of the alliance learning process in alliance capability and firm-level alliance success. *Strategic Management Journal, 28*(10), 981–1000.

Kellett, P., Hede, A.-M., & Chalip, L. (2008). Social policy for sport events: Leveraging (relationships with) teams from other nations for community benefit. *European Sport Management Quarterly, 8*(2), 101–122.

Ko, W. L., Kim, S. Y., Lee, J. H., & Song, T. H. (2020). The effects of strategic alliance emphasis and marketing efficiency on firm value under different technological environments. *Journal of Business Research, 120*, 453–461.

Koza, M., & Lewin, A. (2000). Managing partnerships and strategic alliances: Raising the odds of success. *European Management Journal, 18*(2), 146–151.

Kumar, R., & Das, T. K. (2007). Interpartner legitimacy in the alliance development process. *Journal of Management Studies, 44*(8), 1425–1453.

Lorenzoni, G., & Lipparini, A. (1999). The leveraging of interfirm relationships as a distinctive organizational capability: A longitudinal study. *Strategic Management Journal, 20*(4), 317–338.

102 *Event management and leverage in practice*

Maennig, W., & Vierhaus, C. (2017). Winning the Olympic host city election: Key success factors. *Applied Economics, 49*(31), 3086–3099.

Mamédio, D., Rocha, C., Szczepanik, D., & Kato, H. (2019). Strategic alliances and dynamic capabilities: A systematic review. *Journal of Strategy and Management, 12*(1), 83–102.

Morgan, A., Adair, D., Taylor, T., & Hermens, A. (2014). Sport sponsorship alliances: Relationship management for shared value. *Sport, Business and Management, 4*(4), 270–283.

Morgan, A., Taylor, T., & Adair, D. (2020). Sport event sponsorship management from the sponsee's perspective. *Sport Management Review, 23*(5), 838–851.

Mowla, M. A. (2012). An overview of strategic alliance: Competitive advantages in alliance constellations. *Journal of Business Management and Corporate Affairs, 1*(1), 1–10.

NBC Universal. (2014, July 14). *NBC sports ventures announces strategic alliance with spartan race.* Retrieved from https://nbcsportsgrouppressbox.com/2014/07/14/nbc-sports-ventures-announces-strategic-alliance-with-spartan-race/

O'Brien, D. (2006). Event business leveraging: The Sydney 2000 Olympic Games. *Annals of Tourism Research, 33*(1), 240–261. doi:10.1016/j.annals.2005.10.011

Parmigiani, A., & Rivera-Santos, M. (2011). Clearing a path through the forest: A meta-review of interorganizational relationships. *Journal of Management, 37*(4), 1108–1136.

Reuer, J. J., & Arino, A. (2007). Strategic alliance contracts: Dimensions and determinants of contractual complexity. *Strategic Management Journal, 28*(3), 313–330.

Ring, P. S., Doz, Y., & Olk, P. (2005). Managing formation processes in R&D alliances. *California Management Review, 47*(4), 137–156.

Robson, M. J., Katsikeas, C. S., Schlegelmilch, B. B., & Pramböck, B. (2019). Alliance capabilities, interpartner attributes, and performance outcomes in international strategic alliances. *Journal of World Business, 54*(2), 137–153.

Simonin, B. L. (1997). The importance of collaborative know-how: An empirical test of the learning organization. *Academy of Management Journal, 40*(5), 1150–1174.

Spartan Race Inc. (2020). *What is Spartan.* Retrieved from https://race.spartan.com/en/what-is-spartan

Srivastav, T. (2017, December 7). *Weibo Sports forges strategic alliances with Mailman Group.* Retrieved from www.thedrum.com/news/2017/12/07/weibo-sports-forges-strategic-alliances-with-mailman-group

Teng, B. S., & Das, T. K. (2008). Governance structure choice in strategic alliances: The roles of alliance objectives, alliance management experience, and international partners. *Management Decision, 46*(5), 725–742.

Tregua, M., D'Auria, A., & Brozovic, D. (2020). Value-oriented knowledge management: Insights from theory and practice. *Knowledge Management Research & Practice,* 1–11.

UFC. (2019, May 14). *UFC partners with Weibo.* Retrieved from www.ufc.com/news/ufc-partners-weibo

van Rijn, M., Kristal, S., & Henseler, J. (2019). Why do all good things come to an end? An inquiry into the discontinuation of sport sponsor: Sponsee relationships. *International Journal of Sports Marketing and Sponsorship, 20*(2), 224–241.

Vargo, S. L. (2009). Toward a transcending conceptualization of relationship: A service-dominant logic perspective. *Journal of Business & Industrial Marketing, 24*(5/6), 373–379.

Vargo, S. L., Akaka, M. A., & Wieland, H. (2020). Rethinking the process of diffusion in innovation: A service-ecosystems and institutional perspective. *Journal of Business Research, 160,* 526–534.

Vargo, S. L., & Lusch, R. F. (2004). Evolving to a new dominant logic for marketing. *Journal of Marketing, 68*(1), 1–17.

Vargo, S. L., & Lusch, R. F. (2016). Institutions and axioms: An extension and update of service-dominant logic. *Journal of the Academy of Marketing Science, 44*(1), 5–23.

Vural, C. A. (2017). Service-dominant logic and supply chain management: A systematic literature review. *Journal of Business & Industrial Marketing, 32*(8), 1109–1124.

Wang, D., Li, X. R., & Li, Y. (2013). China's "smart tourism destination" initiative: A taste of the service-dominant logic. *Journal of Destination Marketing & Management, 2*(2), 59–61.

Werner, K., Griese, K.-M., & Hogg, J. (2017). Service dominant logic as a new fundamental framework for analyzing event sustainability: A case study from the German meetings industry. *Journal of Convention & Event Tourism, 18*(4), 318–343.

Woratschek, H., Horbel, C., & Popp, B. (2014). The sport value framework: A new fundamental logic for analyses in sport management. *European Sport Management Quarterly, 14*(1), 6–24.

Yli-Renko, H., Autio, E., & Sapienza, H. J. (2001). Social capital, knowledge acquisition, and knowledge exploitation in young technology-based firms. *Strategic Management Journal, 22*(6), 587–613.

Zaheer, A., McEvily, B., & Perrone, V. (1998). Does trust matter? Exploring the effects of interorganizational and interpersonal trust on performance. *Organization Science, 9*(2), 141–159.

Zollo, M., & Winter, S. G. (2002). Deliberate learning and the evolution of dynamic capabilities. *Organization Science, 13*(3), 339–351.

8 Business events, knowledge management, and strategic responses

Introduction

As discussed in Chapter 6, business events cover any public or private activity that involves at least 15 persons with a common interest held in a specific venue and hosted by an organisation (Business Events Council of Australia, 2020). The success of business events involves both immediate and long-term outcomes. The long-term benefits or legacies include how physical assets are leveraged, the continued stream of tourists and travellers after the event has concluded, and intangible outcomes, such as increased organisational learning and knowledge acquisition (Kaplanidou, Giannoulakis, Odio, & Chalip, 2019). While it is possible to measure the physical assets' benefits, assessing learning and knowledge acquisition from business events can be challenging. One option to assess the knowledge transfer and management process's effectiveness is to evaluate whether subsequent events learn from the past and adopt best practices while avoiding previous mistakes. This requires the transfer of both the explicit and tacit knowledge after each event concludes.

While the successful transfer of knowledge and its management has been highlighted as difficult, the issue becomes more complex when these activities are attempted across national boundaries. Cultural and national institutional differences add to the complexity of efficient knowledge transfer (Falahat, Lee, Ramayah, & Soto-Acosta, 2020). This chapter highlights the business events' knowledge acquisition, management, and transfer processes across national boundaries. We discuss the challenges that business events face in accessing and transferring existing knowledge and identify strategies used to facilitate the effective management of knowledge worldwide.

Organisational learning and knowledge management

Organisational learning is a broad term that encompasses the way firms "*build, supplement and organize knowledge and routines around their activities and within their cultures, and adapt and develop organizational efficiency by improving the use of the broad skills of their workforces*" (Dodgson, 1993, p. 377). There is a consensus that learning involves understanding how an organisation's

DOI: 10.4324/9781003002772-10

Knowledge management & strategic responses   105

operations align with the local business environment. This learning is translated into knowledge and successfully managing, monitoring, and communicating it can have a positive influence on an organisation's outcomes (Lombardi, 2019).

Organisations hold business events, and one of the primary functions of organisations is to convert the learning to generate new knowledge (Baumard, 1999). Business event organisations and managers need to consider some questions when planning future events. For example, what were the reasons for success in the previous event? What challenges were faced? How were these challenges addressed? The knowledge management activity requires learning from previous business events and implementing processes that support the identification, generation, and leveraging of new and existing knowledge sources. But where does this learning and knowledge lie? While previous studies have emphasised the explicit knowledge at the organisational level (Jiménez-Jiménez & Sanz-Valle, 2011), much of the knowledge that provides a competitive advantage is tacit and resides in the individuals or groups (Pokharel & Choi, 2015).

Explicit knowledge includes information made available in a physical form and transferred through various media, such as written documents or audiovisual means. Hence, explicit knowledge is considered to be easier to transfer, understand, and replicate. Tacit knowledge is held by individuals in organisations in an implicit form and is more challenging to transfer. Business events are inherently service-based activities even though there may be a physical output, that is, hosting the event itself. Tacit knowledge management requires interaction between individuals and creating organisational cultures and norms where communication is fluid and exchange of ideas and experiences encouraged (Zhong & Luo, 2018).

Nonaka and Takeuchi (1995) studied the systems that Japanese organisations follow to convert tacit knowledge into an explicit form and then transfer it to other individuals. According to the authors, the transfer of tacit knowledge is possible through physical interaction between individuals. This interaction is introduced in a model, representing the four stages of *Socialisation*, *Externalisation*, *Combination*, and *Internalisation* (SECI). The socialisation process is facilitated through the direct interactions of individuals in the organisation, such as formal and informal discussions, working together in groups, or other social engagements and interactions. By observing and discussing how individuals work, others can learn and attempt to replicate the steps and processes they follow. The knowledge gained during the socialisation process needs to be transformed into an explicit form. This is achieved in the externalisation step, where the new knowledge is articulated into words and presented in documents (Nonaka & Takeuchi, 1995).

The next step, combination, requires combining the documents created during the externalisation process and combining them with existing explicit knowledge in the organisation. This step results in creating new knowledge that is distributed in an explicit form to members within the organisation. The final step of the process involves ensuring that the new explicit knowledge available to individuals in the organisation is understood and applied in the processes they follow. Hence, this explicit knowledge now takes on a tacit form through the step known as internalisation (Nonaka & Takeuchi, 1995). This process involves transferring the explicit

106 *Event management and leverage in practice*

knowledge to the individual, who transforms it into an implicit form and utilises it in the future.

Rammal and Rose (2014) argue that since service firms do not use physical assets for production, they rely heavily on managing tacit knowledge, its acquisition, and transfer. While achieving such norms can be a challenge in any organisation, it is more difficult in cross-border situations where national cultural beliefs and values may influence the communication patterns and accepted hierarchical systems in organisations. Organising international business events requires appropriate strategies to manage these challenges and transfer the learning and tacit knowledge across different formal (regulations) and informal (cultures, norms, etc.) institutional systems.

Challenges in cross-border knowledge transfer

The cross-border knowledge transfer process is complex and involves diverse processes and procedures involved in the international environment due to the legal frameworks, nature of regulations, cultural and linguistic differences (Easterby Smith, Lyles, & Tsang, 2008). Organisations seek sources of knowledge to sustain their international competitive advantage, and external stakeholders can play a significant role in the acquisition of new knowledge (Lopez & Esteves, 2013). This is achieved by developing an effective and efficient knowledge transfer process, including generating internal capabilities to integrate and functionalise new knowledge effectively and efficiently (Jensen & Szulanski, 2004). The transferred knowledge is effective only if comprehended by the recipients (Spraggon & Bodolica, 2012).

Organisations should conduct knowledge transfer in a usable and explicable manner (Zahra, Ireland, & Hitt, 2000). This is especially relevant in business events where the transferred knowledge is tacit and intangible. The challenges include the abilities of the knowledge holder and the absorptive capacity of the receiver (Camisón & Forés, 2010; Chang, Gong, & Peng, 2012; Song, 2014). An individual who holds the relevant knowledge about how to organise and host successful business events may not articulate this knowledge in a form that the recipients easily understand. Similarly, the knowledge recipient may lack the absorptive capacity (ability to grasp the learning being shared) to apply the new knowledge (Cohen & Levinthal, 1990; Khan, Lew, & Marinova, 2019; Tseng, Chang Pai, & Hung, 2011). The experience of the knowledge holder and the receiver, their skill levels and their educational experiences are influenced by the informal and formal institutional systems.

Informal institutional challenges

The knowledge management literature highlights key challenges in cross-border transfer, including the receivers' ability to grasp the knowledge and apply it in the way intended by the individuals from whom the knowledge originated. The difficulties associated with the knowledge transfer process is called knowledge stickiness (Jensen & Szulanski, 2004; Szulanski, Ringov, & Jensen, 2016), and one of the most significant contributors to this is national culture differences (Hofstede, 1994).

Geert Hofstede's study on cultures identified cultural dimensions and is regarded as the seminal work in cross-cultural business. Using data collected from middle managers from IBM's worldwide subsidiaries, Hofstede classified cultures along various dimensions (Hofstede, 1980). According to Hofstede, cultures can be classified along six dimensions[1] labelled as power distance, uncertainty avoidance, individualism, masculinity, long-term orientation, and indulgence (Hofstede, Hofstede, & Minkov, 2010; Minkov & Hofstede, 2011). Of these, the dimensions of power distance, uncertainty avoidance, and individualism have a significant bearing on the cross-border tacit knowledge transfer process.

Power distance refers to the acceptance of higher power held by superiors in organisations. Cultures classified as high power distance tend to have a strong hierarchy of power with top-down, one-way communication and decision-making. The opposite is true of cultures with a low power distance that have less emphasis on titles of power and authority and a more egalitarian structure. In such societies communication is two-way, and decision-making involves the inclusion of diverse views and ideas. The dimension of *uncertainty avoidance* considers how comfortable people are in a culture with ambiguity (Venaik & Brewer, 2010). The higher the level of uncertainty avoidance, the more people in that society would want clear directions and processes, whereas societies with low uncertainty avoidance have a certain level of comfort with ambiguous situations and can manage their affairs even during unusual times. *Individualism* looks at whether a culture displays individualistic or collectivist behaviour (Brewer & Venaik, 2011). Cultures classified as demonstrating high individualism tend to have a smaller inner circle of influence that tends to include the immediate family and select friends and colleagues. The tasks and rewards in such societies are focused on the individual's skill sets and motivation. In collectivist societies, the circle of influence is wider, with extended families and work colleagues and friends seen as legitimate stakeholders in an individual's decision-making process. In these societies, tasks and rewards are developed while considering the interests of the team rather than that of an individual.

The influence of these cultural dimensions on tacit knowledge transfer relates to the stickiness that differences between societies create (Li & Hsieh, 2009). For example, an individual from Australia, a low power distance society, may find it challenging to get individuals in a country like Malaysia, which is classified as high power distance culture, to interact and exchange ideas. The communication process that people from the high power distance country expect would be in a one-way direction from the superior rather than a two-way exchange of ideas. Therefore, it would be difficult for the individual from Australia to ascertain whether the knowledge has been transferred and understood how it was intended and would be appropriately applied when required. Similarly, how knowledge would be understood and applied would be influenced by whether the knowledge receivers have a high or low uncertainty avoidance preference. Those with

108 *Event management and leverage in practice*

high uncertainty avoidance would need clear instructions about when the learnt knowledge should be applied and how. This makes it a challenge to attempt to transfer the knowledge between individuals. On the other hand, individuals in low uncertainty avoidance cultures may not understand the limitations of when an appropriate strategy should be applied and could be more risk-taking and indulgent in how they use the knowledge to respond to various situations. Finally, who the knowledge is transferred to also varies across cultures (Chen, Sun Peter, & McQueen Robert, 2010). In societies that rate high on individualism, the transfer of knowledge would be between individuals. However, the knowledge transfer in collectivist societies would require teams to work with other teams to exchange ideas and share their learning.

As highlighted earlier, business events are held worldwide, and their success depends on how the knowledge from one event is transferred to the next. This learning and the subsequent knowledge creation are some of the legacies that successful business events create. The cultural dimensions suggested by Hofstede can guide organisations in identifying the potential challenges associated with knowledge transfer. These broader cultural differences also have implications for the patterns of communication prevalent in society. Cultures can be classified as following a high-context or low-context pattern of communication. High-context societies such as Japan tend to follow an implicit form of communication, and feelings and ideas are not clearly expressed. In low-context societies, people express their feelings and communicate explicitly (Hall, 1981). The sharing of ideas between individuals using different communication patterns can pose a challenge to effective knowledge sharing and absorption (Wang, Clegg, Gajewska-De Mattos, & Buckley, 2020).

Formal institutional challenges

In addition to these informal institutional challenges (cultural differences), the hosting of business events worldwide also faces the challenge of different formal institutional systems and regulations (Dang, Jasovska, & Rammal, 2020). As Nonaka and Takeuchi (1995) suggested, the first step of converting tacit knowledge into an explicit form requires the interaction between individuals. In cross-border settings, this is achieved by the individual (or talent worker) moving to the location of where the business activity will be undertaken. Thus, the talent worker (expatriate) takes on a boundary spanning role to ensure diffusion of organisational learning and consistency in the way tasks are managed (Au & Fukuda, 2002; Brymer, Boss, Uhlenbruck, & Bierman, 2020). Japanese multinational enterprises (MNEs) applied this principle to diffuse knowledge within their global intra-organisational network, with Japanese expatriates from head office managing the host-country operations and imparting their organisational and individual knowledge to the local employees (Dang & Rammal, 2020).

The movement of these knowledge workers was previously not regulated, and organisations could post individuals in their international subsidiaries with few restrictions. However, the formation of the General Agreement on Trade in

Knowledge management & strategic responses 109

Services (GATS) under the World Trade Organization (WTO) in 1991 has changed this (Dowlah, 2014). The GATS covers four modes of supplies that organisations use to service their customers worldwide (WTO, 2018). The four modes include:

- Mode 1 – Cross-border trade: This mode covers services provided to customers in another territory without the need for the service provider or the customer to leave their own territory. Such activities are provided virtually and can include back-office services, including customer services helpline.
- Mode 2 – Consumption abroad: The second mode covers activities that involve the consumer of the service travelling to the provider's territory. Therefore, the service provider becomes involved in international business activities without having to leave their territory. International tourism is included in this mode of supply.
- Mode 3 – Commercial presence: Under this mode, service firms establish a representative office in the customers' territory. This mode resembles the traditional international subsidiary model and is used by professional services organisations such as accounting, law, etc.
- Mode 4 – Presence of natural persons: The final mode of supply covers the movement of people who provide services and transfer their knowledge in the customers' territory. This covers the traditional expatriation and short-term travel of knowledge workers.

Regardless of whether organisations' activities fall under the manufacturing or service category, the movement of individuals covered under Mode 4 applies to all. Each country commits to allow or restrict the presence of a natural person from another territory. If a country does permit foreign knowledge workers to operate within their territory, it then decides on the length of the stay for corporate-assigned expatriates and self-initiated expatriates. These decisions vary for individuals in various sectors. For business events, the transfer of the knowledge legacy developed requires individuals from one completed event to work closely with individuals organising the next event for a substantial amount of time. The restriction on the movement of individuals or the time available in the host country can influence this process and cause inefficiencies in the learning and applying knowledge in future business events (Rammal & Rose, 2014). However, even if a country permits natural persons' presence, there may be other requirements that restrict the ability of the individual to undertake their tasks.

The most common restrictions relate to the mutual recognition of the qualification and experience of the individuals (Nordås, 2016). The role of professional bodies is prominent at this stage as they set the eligibility criteria for assessing the suitability of international knowledge workers to operate in the country (Borchert, Gootiiz, & Mattoo, 2014). The qualification criteria can require attaining a certain education level for the individual to work in the country. However, even if the knowledge worker has that qualification, it may not be recognised by the host country's associated professional bodies. Further, in some sectors, such as professional services, individuals may be required to complete local examination

110　*Event management and leverage in practice*

to be eligible to enter the country under Mode 4. Temporary work permits can be provided for individuals in certain industries where the country does not have the local talent to undertake the tasks. But in case local talent exists, it can be difficult to justify the presence of foreign knowledge workers.

Finally, recognising the prior experience of knowledge workers is another consideration in the presence of natural persons. If the individual is senior manager or organiser of events in their home territory, they are unlikely to accept a lower-ranked role in the host country. However, individual countries may see the previous experience to be insufficient or unrelated to the host country's activities. This could translate to the individual not qualifying as a senior-level employee in the organisation and could affect their license to operate in the country. Such scenarios have been identified in functional areas and knowledge-intensive areas, including professional services (Bai, Chen, & He, 2019; Dowlah, 2014). Business events that have a specialised functional or technical focus fall under this category, and these restrictions would affect the ability of the organisation to host their events.

Strategic response to knowledge transfer challenges

Various strategies can be implemented to address the informal and formal institutional barriers faced by business events organisations. The response to informal institutional barriers require developing a strong organisational culture that can reduce the effects of varied norms and processes found across countries internationally (Al Saifi Said, 2015). Organisations that host business events internationally should create strong processes through documentation (explicit knowledge) that articulates their values, mission, vision, and aims. Doing so allows the organisation to have clear expectations of how the events are managed and what activities are undertaken.

The documentation needs to be produced in a manner that individuals easily understand in low- and high-context societies. To further encourage communication aimed at sharing knowledge gained by successfully hosting business events, organisations could consider creating a succession plan with the rotation of members every 3–5 years on the organising committee (Durst & Wilhelm, 2012). Such a plan facilitates the interaction between individuals over an extended period of time, can reinforce the organisational culture, and provide the opportunity for individuals to share their tacit knowledge. Learning by observing (Zozimo, Jack, & Hamilton, 2017) and learning by doing (Jin, Hewitt, & Thomas, 2018) are key elements of tacit knowledge transfer, and business event organisations can emphasise and preserve the knowledge legacy they create over time. This strategy addresses the patterns of communication differences as individuals working together learn to use verbal and non-verbal cues to ensure that their message is effectively transferred and provide the opportunity to apply a feedback loop to correct any translation issues caused by cultural differences, known as "noise" (Ghauri, Ott, & Rammal, 2020).

The organising committee membership provides a practical solution to implement the SECI model and to address the informal institutional differences in the process. However, these activities can still be limited through formal restrictions on

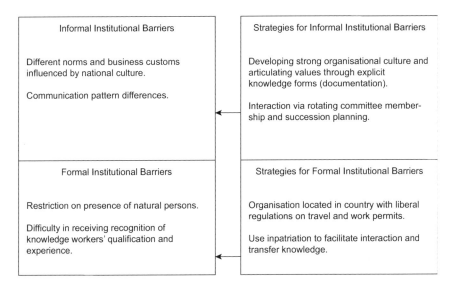

Figure 8.1 Institutional Barriers to Knowledge Transfer in Business Events and Strategic Response

the movement of individuals across national boundaries. Guo, Jasovska, Rammal, and Rose (2020) studied the challenges faced by knowledge-intensive service MNEs and found that the movement of knowledge workers was limited by governments to protect its local workforce's interests. Using a case of an Indian management consulting firm, the authors found that the MNE overcame this issue by using the inpatriate training method, where individuals from the host country would travel to the organisation's head office and work with the knowledge workers over a period of six months to one year (Guo et al., 2020). This time frame was sufficient for the new employees to learn about the organisational culture and learn from the knowledge workers in the firm. While the Indian government facilitated this by providing travel and work permits for the inpatriates, other countries may not necessarily do the same. Therefore, business event organisations would need to be strategic in their choice of which territory they are registered. Locating in a country with liberal travel and work regulations would allow the organisation to implement the inpatriate mode in instances where the host country may restrict foreign knowledge workers' presence and individuals from the host locations can travel to the organisation's territory to gain the required knowledge. Figure 8.1 summarises the key barriers and the suggested strategic response to them.

Conclusion and managerial implications

This chapter highlights some of the major challenges in the knowledge management process faced by organisations involved in hosting business events. Using the SECI model, we highlight how tacit knowledge can be transferred through

112 *Event management and leverage in practice*

steps that involve the translation from tacit to the explicit form of knowledge and then internationalised by the knowledge recipients to make it part of their individual tacit knowledge (Lievre & Tang, 2015). The success of business events is measured, among other things, by the legacy of knowledge it creates regarding best practices to follow and pitfalls to avoid. Transferring this knowledge can be a challenge, especially when the knowledge is tacit in nature and needs to be transferred internationally (Ling, Yen, & Yen, 2016; Park, Vertinsky, & Becerra, 2015). These challenges are further complicated in cross-cultural settings where the norms and customs related to how business activities are conducted vary. We highlight how cultural dimensions such as power distance, uncertainty avoidance, and individualism, along with the high- and low-context patterns of communication, influence the knowledge transfer process. Also, formal institutional requirements regarding the presence of international knowledge workers, the time span permitted to remain in the country, and recognition of their qualifications and experience all impact the successful cross-border transfer and application of the knowledge (Boehe, 2016).

We identify several strategies that can be applied to address these limitations and maximise knowledge acquisition, transfer, and management in business event organisations. This includes setting up members of organising committees on a 3–5 year rotational basis to ensure that incoming members get the opportunity to work with existing members and can learn by observing how tasks are undertaken. The new knowledge acquired by the committee members can be added to the existing explicit knowledge documents, and new knowledge is generated. The rotation policy means that knowledge workers remain involved (Tsai, 2018), and knowledge is retained from one event to the next. This process presents a practical way of applying the SECI model.

Regarding the limitations on the movement of natural persons across national boundaries, we suggest that organisations consider inpatriation as an option in situations where the knowledge workers' expatriation is restricted (Reiche, 2011). Such strategies are employed by leading MNEs to manage intra-organisational knowledge and could be applied in business events.

Note

1 Hofstede initially identified four dimensions: power distance, uncertainty avoidance, individualism, and masculinity. Two further dimensions, long-term orientation and indulgence, were added in subsequent studies with Michael Bond and Michael Minkov.

References

Al Saifi Said, A. (2015). Positioning organisational culture in knowledge management research. *Journal of Knowledge Management, 19*(2), 164–189. https://doi.org/10.1108/JKM-07-2014-0287

Au, K. Y., & Fukuda, J. (2002). Boundary spanning behaviors of expatriates. *Journal of World Business, 37*(4), 285–296. https://doi.org/10.1016/S1090-9516(02)00095-0

Knowledge management & strategic responses 113

Bai, T., Chen, S., & He, X. (2019). How home-country political connections influence the internationalization of service firms. *Management International Review, 59*, 541–560. https://doi.org/doi.org/10.1007/s11575-019-00386-7

Baumard, P. (1999). *Tacit knowledge in organizations.* Thousand Oaks, CA: Sage Publications.

Boehe, D. M. (2016). The internationalization of service firms from emerging economies: An internalization perspective. *Long Range Planning, 49*(5), 559–569. https://doi.org/10.1016/j.lrp.2015.09.006

Borchert, I., Gootiiz, B., & Mattoo, A. (2014). Policy barriers to international trade in services: Evidence from a new database. *The World Bank Economic Review, 28*(1), 162–188. https://doi.org/10.1093/wber/lht017

Brewer, P., & Venaik, S. (2011). Individualism: Collectivism in Hofstede and GLOBE. *Journal of International Business Studies, 42*, 436–445. https://doi.org/10.1057/jibs.2010.62

Brymer, R. A., Boss, D. S., Uhlenbruck, K., & Bierman, L. (2020). Internationalization's effect on mobility and firms' employee-based resources. *Academy of Management Perspectives, 34*(1), 114–134. https://doi.org/10.5465/amp.2016.0179

Business Events Council of Australia. (2020). *What is a business event?* Retrieved May 21 from www.businesseventscouncil.org.au/page/about_business_events.html

Camisón, C., & Forés, B. (2010). Knowledge absorptive capacity: New insights for its conceptualization and measurement. *Journal of Business Research, 63*(7), 707–715. https://doi.org/10.1016/j.jbusres.2009.04.022

Chang, Y.-Y., Gong, Y., & Peng, M. W. (2012). Expatriate knowledge transfer, subsidiary absorptive capacity, and subsidiary performance. *Academy of Management Journal, 55*(4), 927–948. https://doi.org/10.5465/amj.2010.0985

Chen, J., Sun Peter, Y. T., & McQueen Robert, J. (2010). The impact of national cultures on structured knowledge transfer. *Journal of Knowledge Management, 14*(2), 228–242. https://doi.org/10.1108/13673271011032373

Cohen, W. M., & Levinthal, D. A. (1990). Absorptive capacity: A new perspective on learning and innovation. *Administrative Science Quarterly, 35*(1), 128–152. https://doi.org/10.2307/2393553

Dang, Q. T., Jasovska, P., & Rammal, H. G. (2020). International business-government relations: The risk management strategies of MNEs in emerging economies. *Journal of World Business, 55*(1), 101042. https://doi.org/10.1016/j.jwb.2019.101042

Dang, Q. T., & Rammal, H. G. (2020). Japanese expatriates' management in global assignments: A review and research agenda. *Thunderbird International Business Review, 62*(6), 689–705. https://doi.org/10.1002/tie.22140

Dodgson, M. (1993). Organizational learning: A review of some literatures. *Organization Studies, 14*(3), 375–394. https://doi.org/10.1177/017084069301400303

Dowlah, C. (2014). Cross-border labor mobility: A critical assessment of WTO's GATS Mode 4 vis-à-vis regional trade agreements. *Journal of International Trade Law and Policy, 13*(1), 2–18. https://doi.org/10.1108/JITLP-12-2012-0020

Durst, S., & Wilhelm, S. (2012). Knowledge management and succession planning in SMEs. *Journal of Knowledge Management, 16*(4), 637–649. https://doi.org/10.1108/13673271211246194

Easterby-Smith, M., Lyles, M. A., & Tsang, E. W. (2008). Inter-organizational knowledge transfer: Current themes and future prospects. *Journal of Management Studies, 45*(4), 677–690. https://doi.org/10.1111/j.1467-6486.2008.00773.x

Falahat, M., Lee, Y. Y., Ramayah, T., & Soto-Acosta, P. (2020). Modelling the effects of institutional support and international knowledge on competitive capabilities and

114 *Event management and leverage in practice*

international performance: Evidence from an emerging economy. *Journal of International Management, 26*(4), 100779. https://doi.org/10.1016/j.intman.2020.100779

Ghauri, P. N., Ott, U. F., & Rammal, H. G. (2020). *International business negotiations: Theory and practice.* Cheltenham, UK: Edward Elgar.

Guo, Y., Jasovska, P., Rammal, H. G., & Rose, E. L. (2020). Global mobility of professionals and the transfer of tacit knowledge in multinational service firms. *Journal of Knowledge Management, 24*(3), 553–567. https://doi.org/10.1108/JKM-09-2017-0399

Hall, E. T. (1981). *Beyond culture.* Garden City, NY: Anchor Press/Doubleday.

Hofstede, G. (1980). *Culture's consequences: International differences in work-related values.* Thousand Oaks, CA: Sage Publications.

Hofstede, G. (1994). The business of international business is culture. *International Business Review, 3*(1), 1–14. https://doi.org/10.1016/0969-5931(94)90011-6

Hofstede, G., Hofstede, G. J., & Minkov, M. (2010). *Cultures and organizations: Software of the mind* (3rd ed.). New York, USA: McGraw-Hill.

Jensen, R., & Szulanski, G. (2004). Stickiness and the adaptation of organizational practices in cross-border knowledge transfers. *Journal of International Business Studies, 35*(6), 508–523. https://doi.org/10.1057/palgrave.jibs.8400107

Jiménez-Jiménez, D., & Sanz-Valle, R. (2011). Innovation, organizational learning, and performance. *Journal of Business Research, 64*(4), 408–417. https://doi.org/10.1016/j.jbusres.2010.09.010

Jin, H., Hewitt, M., & Thomas, B. W. (2018). Workforce grouping and assignment with learning-by-doing and knowledge transfer. *International Journal of Production Research, 56*(14), 4968–4982. https://doi.org/10.1080/00207543.2018.1424366

Kaplanidou, K., Giannoulakis, C., Odio, M., & Chalip, L. (2019). Types of human capital as a legacy from Olympic Games hosting. *Journal of Global Sport Management,* 1–19. https://doi.org/10.1080/24704067.2019.1674180

Khan, Z., Lew, Y. K., & Marinova, S. (2019). Exploitative and exploratory innovations in emerging economies: The role of realized absorptive capacity and learning intent. *International Business Review, 28*(3), 499–512. https://doi.org/10.1016/j.ibusrev.2018.11.007

Li, C.-Y., & Hsieh, C.-T. (2009). The impact of knowledge stickiness on knowledge transfer implementation, internalization, and satisfaction for multinational corporations. *International Journal of Information Management, 29*(6), 425–435. https://doi.org/10.1016/j.ijinfomgt.2009.06.004

Lievre, P., & Tang, J. (2015). SECI and inter-organizational and intercultural knowledge transfer: A case-study of controversies around a project of co-operation between France and China in the health sector. *Journal of Knowledge Management, 19*(5), 1069–1086. https://doi.org/10.1108/JKM-02-2015-0054

Ling, C. M., Yen, Y. Y., & Yen, W. T. M. (2016). Framework for effective cross-border knowledge transfer. *International Review of Management and Marketing, 6*(4S), 132–137.

Lombardi, R. (2019). Knowledge transfer and organizational performance and business process: Past, present and future researches. *Business Process Management Journal, 25*(1), 2–9. https://doi.org/10.1108/BPMJ-02-2019-368

Lopez, V. W. B., & Esteves, J. (2013). Acquiring external knowledge to avoid wheel re-invention. *Journal of Knowledge Management, 17*(1), 87–105. https://doi.org/10.1108/13673271311300787

Minkov, M., & Hofstede, G. (2011). The evolution of Hofstede's doctrine. *Cross Cultural Management: An International Journal, 18*(1), 10–20. https://doi.org/10.1108/13527601111104269

Nonaka, I., & Takeuchi, H. (1995). *The knowledge creating company: How Japanese companies create the dynamics of innovation.* Oxford: Oxford University Press.

Nordås, H. K. (2016). Does mutual recognition of qualifications stimulate services trade? The case of the European Union. *Applied Economics, 48*(20), 1852–1865. https://doi.org/10.1080/00036846.2015.1109042

Park, C., Vertinsky, I., & Becerra, M. (2015). Transfer of tacit vs. explicit knowledge and performance in international joint ventures: The role of age. *International Business Review, 24*(1), 89–101. https://doi.org/10.1016/j.ibusrev.2014.06.004

Pokharel, M. P., & Choi, S. O. (2015). Exploring the relationships between the learning organization and organizational performance. *Management Research Review, 38*(2), 126–148. https://doi.org/10.1108/MRR-02-2013-0033

Rammal, H. G., & Rose, E. L. (2014). New perspectives on the internationalization of service firms. *International Marketing Review, 31*(6), 550–556. https://doi.org/10.1108/IMR-09-2014-0309

Reiche, B. S. (2011). Knowledge transfer in multinationals: The role of inpatriates' boundary spanning. *Human Resource Management, 50*(3), 365–389. https://doi.org/10.1002/hrm.20423

Song, J. (2014). Subsidiary absorptive capacity and knowledge transfer within multinational corporations. *Journal of International Business Studies, 45*(1), 73–84. https://doi.org/10.1057/jibs.2013.55

Spraggon, M., & Bodolica, V. (2012). A multidimensional taxonomy of intra-firm knowledge transfer processes. *Journal of Business Research, 65*(9), 1273–1282. https://doi.org/10.1016/j.jbusres.2011.10.043

Szulanski, G., Ringov, D., & Jensen, R. J. (2016). Overcoming stickiness: How the timing of knowledge transfer methods affects transfer difficulty. *Organization Science, 27*(2), 304–322. https://doi.org/10.1287/orsc.2016.1049

Tsai, S.-P. (2018). Innovative behaviour of knowledge workers and social exchange attributes of financial incentive: Implications for knowledge management. *Journal of Knowledge Management, 22*(8), 1712–1735. https://doi.org/10.1108/JKM-07-2017-0293

Tseng, C., Chang Pai, D., & Hung, C. (2011). Knowledge absorptive capacity and innovation performance in KIBS. *Journal of Knowledge Management, 15*(6), 971–983. https://doi.org/10.1108/13673271111179316

Venaik, S., & Brewer, P. (2010). Avoiding uncertainty in Hofstede and GLOBE. *Journal of International Business Studies, 41,* 1294–1315. https://doi.org/10.1057/jibs.2009.96

Wang, Q., Clegg, J., Gajewska-De Mattos, H., & Buckley, P. (2020). The role of emotions in intercultural business communication: Language standardization in the context of international knowledge transfer. *Journal of World Business, 55*(6), 100973. https://doi.org/10.1016/j.jwb.2018.11.003

WTO. (2018). *I-TIP services: GATS: World Trade Organization, New York NY.* Retrieved from http://i-tip.wto.org/services/default.aspx

Zahra, S. A., Ireland, R. D., & Hitt, M. A. (2000). International expansion by new venture firms: International diversity, mode of market entry, technological learning, and performance. *Academy of Management Journal, 43*(5), 925–950. https://doi.org/10.5465/1556420

Zhong, D., & Luo, Q. (2018). Knowledge diffusion at business events: The mechanism. *International Journal of Hospitality Management, 71,* 111–119. https://doi.org/10.1016/j.ijhm.2017.12.003

Zozimo, R., Jack, S., & Hamilton, E. (2017). Entrepreneurial learning from observing role models. *Entrepreneurship & Regional Development, 29*(9–10), 889–911. https://doi.org/10.1080/08985626.2017.1376518

9 Social dimensions of community events

Introduction

The term "event" covers a large spectrum, from mega-events such as the Olympic Games taking place on an international stage down to small-scale, community events and festivals that originate from within a particular community, designed primarily to celebrate features of its way of life, culture, traditions, or history (Allen, Harris, & Jago, 2021). While events play important roles, serving to position a destination, attract visitation, and support specific tourism or economic goals for a destination (Allen et al., 2021), the purpose of events and festivals – particularly at the community end of the scale – is often primarily social (Mair & Duffy, 2015; Sharpley & Stone, 2011). This is understandable when we consider that regardless of size, "all events share a common characteristic: people" (Sharpley & Stone, 2011, p. 349). As such, events have a social dimension that comes from the interaction of people and place within a host community.

From a social perspective, we recognise events as an opportunity to bring people together to share experiences, celebrate, and be entertained. Recognising that these social aspects are shared by event attendees, we also note the significant potential for social benefits to accrue specifically to members of a host community arising from involvement and participation in a community event or festival. This includes opportunities for social interaction with other members of the community or with visitors to the community (Allen et al., 2021) noting that "festivals have the potential to strengthen communities through shared experience and collective celebration" (Finkel, 2010, p. 284). By providing the environment in which these shared experiences and interactions can occur, a community event encourages the formation of new relationships and social networks and plays an important role in contributing to the well-being and quality of life of its community (Yolal, Gursoy, Uysal, Kim, & Karacaoglu, 2016). Community events can also play an important role in strengthening the traditions and values held by residents, due in part to an increased sense of community spirit and pride that may result from the hosting of a successful festival (Baptista Alves & Ferreira Martins, 2010; Getz, Andersson, Armbrecht, & Lundberg, 2018; Yürük, Akyol, & Şimşek, 2017). Particularly, when an event is run by the local community, benefits to be gained by involved residents include the development of new skills, such as in

DOI: 10.4324/9781003002772-11

Social dimensions of community events   117

leadership, human resources, or hospitality (Laing & Mair, 2015), in addition to increased levels of volunteerism within a community and the development of networks between volunteers and community groups (Arcodia & Whitford, 2007).

In this chapter, our focus is on community events and festivals, which are those demonstrating strong links to their host community, whose members are not only involved in the organisation of the festival, but who attend it as a community celebration. We explore the importance of the social dimension and the significant social benefits that festivals offer to their communities. We first introduce the category of community events and festivals and then discuss the social dimensions and ways in which these events enhance their communities – by contributing to social connectedness, social capital, sense of place, and belonging. We then provide examples of specific strategies that can be used to encourage community involvement in events as a way of enhancing the social dimensions of community events. We end the chapter with a discussion of the challenges associated with the social dimension of community events and festivals.

Community events and festivals

Events range in size and scale, from mega-events taking place on an international stage attracting global media attention, down to local/community events, which are those produced by communities, targeted mostly at local audiences, and primarily staged for social and entertainment purposes (Allen et al., 2021). Of focus in this chapter is the category of local/community events. Community events originate from within a particular segment of a community wishing to celebrate particular features of its way of life or history (Dimmock & Tiyce, 2001), thus reflecting the community's culture and sense of itself (Brown & James, 2004; Derrett, 2004). These events are usually small in scale and size, and as Derrett (2000) explains, represent the point "where community and its outward manifestations of image and identity collide" (p. 120).

Many community events take the form of a festival, defined by Hall and Sharples (2008) as a "celebration of something the local community wishes to share and which involves the wider public as participants in the experience" (pp. 9–10). Adding to this, the definition from Jepson and Clarke (2013) highlights the involvement of the community in the planning process. They defined community festivals as a

> themed and inclusive community event or series of events which have been created as the result of an inclusive community planning process to celebrate the particular way of life of people and groups in the local community with emphasis on particular space and time.
>
> (Jepson & Clarke, 2013, p. 7)

Noting the multitude of definitions that exist, what stands out is that festivals tend to reflect what is distinctive about a particular community (Derrett, 2004); serve to celebrate community values and identity (Getz, Andersson, & Carlsen, 2010); and foster feelings of belonging, connection, and cohesion (Mair, 2018).

118   *Event management and leverage in practice*

While recognising that festivals are designed as a celebration of a community, its traditions, culture, or way of life, their success also depends greatly on that community "to provide the support, input and critical mass necessary for the event" (van der Zee & Olders, 2016, p. 120). Thus, a further distinguishing feature of community festivals is that they are typically organised by the host community, using local volunteers and organising committees (Finkel, 2010; Jordan, 2019), further reinforcing the linkages that these festivals have to their host community. Some consider community events as "owned" by a community, as they draw on not only local resources as volunteers and members of organising committees, but take place in public venues such as streets, parks, and community facilities (Janiskee, 1996). Community events are also usually well supported by the local community through donations and also via local participation in various forms including as artists and participants (Finkel, 2010).

It should be noted here that the terms "community events" and "community festivals" will be used interchangeably throughout the remainder of this chapter to refer to events and festivals of the type described earlier. It is also important then to provide a brief discussion of the concept of "community" in the context of community events and festivals. Given the several decades over which the term "community" has been subject to research, definition, and debate, it is not surprising that there is no one single definition of the term. However, three characteristics have been identified in a number of definitions of community that warrant further discussion. The first is geographic location, whereby a community refers to a group of people living within a specific geographic area (Poplin, 1979). The second defining characteristic of community is social interaction (Willmott, 1986). Such interaction is typically structured around a set of common interests held by members of a community (Green & Haines, 2012) and is the basis for social relationships between community members. Finally, beyond the geographic location and social interactions, a third defining characteristic is that a community represents a set of common ties or bonds between people (Poplin, 1979). Common ties are those aspects of a community, such as shared goals, values, or norms, through which people can identify with each other and develop a sense of belonging in their community (Willmott, 1986).

The term community – as used in the context of this chapter to refer to community events and festivals – describes a geographic host community in which an event is held; who come together around common interests to organise an event and attend it as a community celebration; and who identify with each other through shared values to realise a common goal of staging a festival in their community. In the next section, we discuss the significant potential for social benefits to accrue to members of a host community arising from such involvement and participation in a community event or festival.

Social dimensions of community events and festivals

The hosting of a community event or festival provides opportunities for a wide range of contributions to a host community and its members in terms of

Social dimensions of community events 119

the social dimension. The social dimension is considered quite broadly to include the variety of ways in which a festival contributes to changes to a community's way of life, encompassing changes in the values, attitudes, traditions, and quality of life because of hosting an event (Sharpley & Stone, 2011). As a celebration of the uniqueness and identity of a community, and as a provider of opportunities for social transactions and relationship building, "the socially empowering possibilities of community events are multiple" (Stevenson, 2020, p. 436). They offer important occasions to build social cohesion and strengthen community identity (Bakas, Duxbury, Remoaldo, & Matos, 2019; Finkel, 2010), enhance well-being and quality of life (Yolal et al., 2016), develop community networks and social capital (Arcodia & Whitford, 2007), and contribute to sense of place and community pride (De Bres & Davis, 2001; Derrett, 2003). These are interrelated and often overlapping concepts, and it is noted that these, amongst other concepts such as social cohesion, inclusion, community building, and connectivity are often used interchangeably and attributed varied meanings (Quinn, 2018). This section will now focus on an exploration of some of the key contributions that festivals make to host communities, including to social connectedness, the development of social capital, and a sense of place and belonging.

Social connectedness

By providing an opportunity to bring people together to share experiences, celebrate, and be entertained, community festivals are seen as activities that facilitate social interactions and connectedness (Bakas et al., 2019). They contribute to positive social engagements such as opportunities for meeting new people, social interaction, and personal connections (Laing & Mair, 2015; Taks, 2013), as well as relationship building (Yolal et al., 2016). Community festivals provide a sense of togetherness within the community as community members come together around a common social purpose (Arcodia & Whitford, 2007; Attanasi, Casoria, Centorrino, & Urso, 2013), hosting an event to celebrate particular features of its way of life, values, or history.

In a study of small-scale community festivals in the United Kingdom, Black (2016) described community festivals as enablers of connectivity. She found that festivals were viewed overwhelmingly as social occasions. They were consistently regarded as social hubs – a place for socialising and social connectivity. Festival participation was mainly driven by social rationales; in fact "the opportunity to interact with other members of the festival community was stated as most important" (Black, 2016, p. 183). It was further explained that the spatial and temporal consistency of a festival – being held in the same place at the same time each year – contributes to the perception of it as a social occasion. There was even anticipation of this occasion, with people noting they look forward to it as a time and place for "meeting up with friends, neighbours and new acquaintances" (Black, 2016, p. 181).

Themes of social connectedness were also found in the research of Wilks and Quinn (2016), who in their study of two long-standing community folk festivals

120 *Event management and leverage in practice*

in the United Kingdom and Ireland, found that community members "appreciated the opportunities to socialise, reconnect with friends and family, and enjoy the liveliness engendered by the festival activities" (Wilks & Quinn, 2016, p. 30). The spatial layout of the festivals, both of which are held in small communities and staged across public spaces and community venues, seemed to contribute to the opportunities for social connectedness. This layout, with the festivals essentially taking place in the centre of town, meant the "presence of the festivals was all pervasive" (Wilks & Quinn, 2016, p. 29). Community members reported that during the festival, they increased their use of community spaces for socialising, including attending cafes and restaurants more frequently, as well as visiting specially constructed festival spaces throughout the town. These findings suggest that a community festival encourages members of the community to come together and connect socially in and around the festival offerings.

Social capital

Another social dimension that has received attention from researchers is the potential of community events and festivals to contribute to the development of social capital (Arcodia & Whitford, 2007; Finkel, 2010; Quinn & Wilks, 2013; Schulenkorf, Thomson, & Schlenker, 2011). Early research into the concept of social capital was led by Pierre Bourdieu and James Coleman, although Robert Putnam can be credited with popularising the concept (Schuller, Baron, & Field, 2000), and his conceptualisation remains one of the most commonly used in the events literature (Arcodia & Whitford, 2007; Mair & Duffy, 2018). Putnam defines social capital as the "features of social organization such as networks, norms, and social trust that facilitate coordination and cooperation for mutual benefit" (Putnam, 1995, p. 66). Similar to the ways in which physical and human capital can provide value, social networks can also add value to both individuals and groups within a community. The value to a community is expressed as the resources and other benefits which become available as a result of the networks, bonds, other social ties, and trust that exist within a community (Putnam, 2000).

Community events provide wide-ranging opportunities for individuals to participate in the life of a community. These opportunities come in the form of positions on the organising committee and volunteering at or attending a festival. By providing the environment in which social interactions and relationship building can occur, community festivals play an important role in contributing to the development of social capital. Events generate social capital by building community resources, for example, skills and knowledge, as well as relationships and networks between volunteers and community groups that can be of ongoing benefit to the community (Arcodia & Whitford, 2007).

It has been noted by many authors that participation in the organising of a festival within a community is important to social capital development. Ongoing interactions, collaboration, and negotiations between organisers, volunteers, community groups, and other local stakeholders strengthen social bonds and the development of networks (Arcodia & Whitford, 2007; Brownett, 2018; Stevenson,

Social dimensions of community events 121

2016). In a case study of the "Up Helly Aa" festival in Scotland, Finkel (2010) found that the year-round involvement of local community volunteers was a significant contributor to developing social capital among residents. Involvement in a festival's organisation provides "opportunities for discussion and interaction and develops connections that outlast the event itself" (Stevenson, 2020, p. 441). Moreover, these connections and social bonds that develop serve to further stimulate the development of trust and reciprocity, which are also key ingredients in the development of social capital (Brownett, 2018).

Two main types of social capital are discussed in the literature: bonding and bridging. Bonding social capital represents ties that bind a homogenous group together, providing them with a strong sense of identity, trust, and belonging (Leonard & Onyx, 2004; Putnam, 2000). Bonding social capital can be built by bringing together people who hold similar interests, such as occurs when hosting a community festival. In the case of the Clunes Booktown Festival in Victoria, Australia, Mair and Duffy (2018) found that the development of bonding social capital was in fact an important driver in the creation of the festival. Expressed as "a desire for like-minded people to find leisure opportunities within the town" (Mair & Duffy, 2018, p. 884), the festival was found to develop bonding social capital. Stevenson (2016) reported the development of bonding social capital in the context of two local annual festivals in the United Kingdom. This was achieved via the organisation of stalls, projects, and event activities arranged around specific communities of interest that brought like-minded people together and allowed them to interact and develop bonding social relations.

In contrast, bridging social capital serves to create links between heterogeneous groups (Putnam, 2000) and can be built by bringing together people from diverse backgrounds around a common cause. Community festivals can encourage the development of bridging social capital by connecting people of different ages, genders, or religions, or from different groups within a community, who work together to successfully help stage a festival (Leonard & Onyx, 2004). In her study of local festivals in the United Kingdom, Stevenson (2016) found that it was amongst the festival organisers where bridging capital was developed. Coming together to develop, organise, and host a festival, the organisers came to know each other and "have developed increasingly intersecting networks and relationships" (2016, p. 1000). Outside of the creation of bridging social capital amongst event organisers, Mair and Duffy (2018) found that the local Booktown Festival was able to provide "common ground" for those groups within the community who may have otherwise had little in common. This also suggests the development of bridging social capital amongst residents with diverse backgrounds.

Sense of place and belonging

In this section, we will discuss the interrelated concepts of sense of place and belonging. To begin with, we examine the concept of sense of place, which has been defined by Williams and Stewart (1998) as "the collection of meanings, beliefs, symbols, values, and feelings that individuals or groups associate with

122 *Event management and leverage in practice*

a particular locality" (p. 19). Sense of place can therefore be thought of as our tendency to develop an emotional bond or connection to a place (Quinn & Wilks, 2013). This sense of place is "actively and continuously constructed and reconstructed within individual minds, shared cultures, and social practices" (Williams & Stewart, 1998, p. 19). Festivals are one mechanism through which communities can construct a sense of place (De Bres & Davis, 2001). This potential is further enhanced when the festival is clearly representative of the shared values and way of life of a community and thus becomes an expression of a place (Attanasi et al., 2013; Derrett, 2003).

Lau and Li (2015) found this in the context of the Cheung Chau Bun Festival, a community-based local festival in Hong Kong. The festival is regarded by locals as a "home-grown festival", and one that "allows the community to narrate its history, present the people's way of life, and share local beliefs" (Lau & Li, 2015, p. 74). It is because of these factors that the festival is perceived as playing an important role in developing a sense of place for the destination and its community.

Having a strong sense of place gives locals something to connect to, and thus sense of place can be viewed as the basis for developing a sense of belonging. The concept of belonging has been expressed in many ways. Yuval-Davis (2006) describes it as reflecting a "desire for attachment" (p. 202). Hammitt, Backlund, and Bixler (2006) suggest belonging is about affiliation and connection to place. Duffy and Waitt (2011) advance that belonging ranges from "an abstract feeling about what we may think of as our place or community to a much more concrete notion of belonging in which we participate in activities that display our allegiances and affiliations" (p. 55). Research has shown that festivals operate as an environment in which feelings of belonging can be enhanced (Black, 2016; Jaeger & Mykletun, 2013). Community festivals provide a space where "participants negotiate their identification with and sense of belonging to, a place and/or community" (Mair & Duffy, 2015, p. 286). As is the case for developing a sense of place, studies reinforce that it is the display of shared local values, culture, or way of life that also strengthens sense of belonging (Attanasi et al., 2013). Black (2016) refers to this as demonstrating *localness*. He notes however, that for this to be effective in developing a sense of belonging, "the individuals which make up that community must share a sense of affinity in recognising what is local culture . . . and share a sense of its accessibility" (p. 175).

Mykletun (2009) provided the example of an annual extreme sports festival in Voss, Norway, and he used this to explore the factors that connect a festival to a place. The festival was initiated from within the community and drew on the natural landscape and resources which are a perfect fit for the theme of the event. The festival was considered to be a representation of community interests, and "is rooted in local values" (Mykletun, 2009, p. 172). As such, the festival contributed to a sense of place and associated sense of belonging for the host community. Beyond this, residents were able to reflect on the success of the festival and how this has resulted in attention from those outside the community. This is viewed as a positive and has "bolstered locals' self-esteem" (Mykletun, 2009, p. 169). Therefore, by clearly articulating values of the community and of a distinctive

Social dimensions of community events 123

place, the festival has helped create for locals a sense of pride of belonging to that place. Black (2016) also found that the sense of place and belonging created by a festival can be accompanied by feelings of pride. Explained as pride associated with belonging to a certain place, host community members expressed this pride by wanting to "show off" their town and the uniqueness of their community festival to visitors.

Community engagement strategies

The previous section has discussed the wide range of contributions the hosting of an event can offer to a community in terms of the social dimension, including improvements to community residents' social connectedness, their sense of place and belonging, and to the development of social capital. However, the ability of a community festival to deliver on these types of social outcomes relies heavily on the involvement of the community and on inclusive community planning (Jepson & Clarke, 2013; Mair & Duffy, 2015). Thus, in this section, we discuss strategies for achieving community involvement and in turn, enhancing the social dimensions of community events.

Laing and Mair (2015), in their study of music festivals in Australia and the United Kingdom, suggested ways in which festivals and their organisers can further community engagement and thus contribute towards building strong and cohesive communities. Their findings showed that communities should be able to participate in both the consumption and production of a festival. Consumption focuses on the accessibility of the festival and the ease in which people can access the event (including both financial and physical barriers). Specific strategies to encourage ease of consumption by local residents include the running of free events and discounted tickets for disadvantaged members of the community. For example, one event organiser collaborated with cultural regeneration offices, the local council, and local partners to offer such discounted tickets. The same event also made one-third of the festival programme free of charge. Another strategy to facilitate local consumption is the opening up of community spaces, such as local historic halls, which the general public do not usually access. Consumption strategies also revolve around outreach programmes that target the local community, such as educational and skills workshops for children.

In addition to being able to participate in the consumption of a community festival, Laing and Mair (2015) highlighted that involving the host community in the production of a festival contributes towards building strong and cohesive communities. Strategies to involve the host community in the production of a festival revolve around collaborating with local suppliers, engaging in community-based partnerships, and sourcing local volunteers. For example, local artists and musicians were commissioned to bring forward ethnic diversity, multiculturalism, and localised artistic talent. The use of volunteers in the production of the event not only involves the local community but also contributes to the development of social networks and the development of social capital. Furthermore, having event organisers regularly attending community meetings was noted as a key strategy for

124 *Event management and leverage in practice*

inclusive event production "to maintain a connection with their geographic local community and develop the festival in line with community wishes" (Laing & Mair, 2015, p. 263).

In a study of the relationship between community festivals and their local residents, Rogers and Anastasiadou (2011) undertook interviews and focus groups with festival organisers and participants with an interest or role in community activities. Recognising the importance of community involvement in the long-term viability of festivals, they proposed a Community Involvement Framework to encourage local participation in festivals. It features specific strategies to involve the local community based around the five principles of community involvement, which are: involvement of schools, volunteering opportunities, participation in decision-making, accessibility, and business cooperation.

In line with the first principle of involvement of schools, Rogers and Anastasiadou (2011) suggested involving schools in festival participation is a significant way to encourage community participation and repeat engagement. Strategies include facilitating festival performances and activities within schools themselves and running field trips for children to participate in the festival. The second principle of the Community Involvement Framework is creating volunteer opportunities. Encouraging local volunteers to participate in the event is noted as being fundamental in connecting with the community. Not only do local volunteers benefit in terms of skill development and confidence building, they also benefit from the social interactions and sense of togetherness that volunteering in a community festival offers. Third, is the suggestion to encourage participation in decision-making. Importantly, this should widen the membership of those involved in decision-making to ensure a local festival reflects broad community views. One suggested strategy is to form a cross-festival liaison committee (involving community groups and local authorities) as a way to bridge the gap between festival organisers and the local community. Furthermore, actively seeking the views of the host community about festival programming and direction is important in giving locals a stake in the festival. The fourth principle is ensuring accessibility of the festival to the local community. Accessibility can be improved through designing targeted incentives, with festival organisers adopting strategies such as discounted tickets, vouchers for local council tax payers, providing concessions for public transport, the distribution of excess tickets to both students and to members of the community who are unemployed, as well as distributing rebated (government) tickets to encourage youth participation. The final principle of the Community Involvement Framework is business cooperation. It is suggested that increasing the involvement of local businesses is a means to promoting higher levels of community participation. For example, having local businesses sponsor the event or specific activities within it and display festival branding and promotional materials can help raise awareness of the festival across the host community. Another strategy is to provide local businesses with free tickets to encourage their staff to attend the event.

The Community Involvement Framework (Rogers & Anastasiadou, 2011) aligns with the recommendations of Laing and Mair (2015), who highlighted that

Social dimensions of community events 125

communities should be able to participate in both the consumption and production of a festival. The involvement of schools, business cooperation, and accessibility strategies speak of involving locals in the consumption of the festival, whereas strategies around involving volunteers and encouraging participation in decision-making address the involvement of locals in festival production. The more we can encourage these varied types of involvement by locals in a community event or festival, the more likely that host community will be exposed to and benefit from the social dimensions of events, such as social interactions and connectedness, sense of place and belonging, and the development of social capital.

In the next section, we discuss challenges associated with community festivals; the issues related to involving the local community and in enhancing the social dimensions of community events.

Challenges and issues

Although we recognise community events and festivals as "predominantly a social phenomenon with the potential to provide a variety of social outcomes" (Mair & Duffy, 2015, p. 284), this is not always easily achieved. Decisions made about an event may inadvertently prioritise some members of a community, leave others feeling excluded, and some community members may feel a lack of ownership of the festival taking place in their own backyard. Rather than promoting social connectedness, belonging, and pride, underlying inequalities in a community might be magnified, and some people may end up feeling alienated from others in their community. These and other challenges to the social dimensions of community events are discussed in this section.

As Duffy and Waitt (2011) have observed, "the festival is, in fact, a paradoxical thing; festival events function as a form of social integration and cohesion, while simultaneously they are sites of subversion, protest or exclusion and alienation" (p. 55). After lengthy discussion throughout this chapter about the "socially empowering possibilities of community events" (Stevenson, 2020, p. 436), it seems at odds now to be referring to them as sites for exclusion or alienation. Revisiting the definition and purpose of community events and festivals, we said they reflect what is distinctive about a particular community (Derrett, 2004); celebrate community values and identity (Getz et al., 2010); and foster feelings of belonging, connection, and cohesion (Mair, 2018). However, the extent to which a community can come together around a shared community identity and values – and in turn, the extent to which an event can foster feelings of belonging and connectedness – depends on how widely these values are held.

Mair and Duffy (2015) explain that "the festival activates and is activated by ideas and issues about 'community identity' and 'place' that are already in circulation. However, there is inequality in any constitution of community and place" (p. 286). Thus we cannot assume that all members of a community will necessarily subscribe to the ideas of community and community values put on display by a festival and must acknowledge that some parts of a community might experience feelings of alienation or exclusion.

126 *Event management and leverage in practice*

Rogers and Anastasiadou (2011) recognise the potential for such community alienation to contribute to festival failure. Thus, the principles that inform their Community Involvement Framework are designed to engage host communities so that positive social outcomes are realised. Other researchers recognise the importance of involving the host community, especially in the decision-making and planning processes, as a factor influencing the long-term success and viability of a festival (Derrett, 2003; Jepson & Clarke, 2016; Small, Edwards, & Sheridan, 2005; Stadler, 2013). Importantly, involvement in the initial design and development stages of a festival is crucial (Yeoman, Robertson, Ali-Knight, Drummond, & McMahon-Beattie, 2004) and can alleviate the sense that the community has been ignored or stem off feelings of exclusion or alienation.

Also at play here, in the context of potential alienation or exclusion of certain parts of a host community, are existing power dynamics within a community. Whilst typically formed of volunteers, and made up of individual community members or community organisations (Reid, 2011), community event organising committees are often viewed as "gatekeepers" and holders of power (Derrett, 2003). The specific make-up of an organising committee may contribute to a perception that certain individuals either belong or not (Mair & Duffy, 2015) and may therefore be responsible for feelings of exclusion by some members of the host community (Brownett, 2018).

A further challenge is around the development of social capital. While studies have shown that both bonding and bridging social capital can result from community involvement in festivals (Finkel, 2010; Stevenson, 2016), it is also recognised that the accrual of social capital might be uneven, and not all community members will benefit equally (Mair & Duffy, 2018). For example, Stevenson (2016) found that social capital tended to accrue most to those members of a community who were involved in the organisation of the festival. This is understandable, as members of the organising committee are involved in negotiations, collaboration, and interactions between volunteers, community groups, and other local stakeholders throughout the organisation of a festival (Arcodia & Whitford, 2007; Brownett, 2018). However, it was also found that these members of the organising committee tended to be those who had the most social capital already (Stevenson, 2016). Whilst this still represents a positive for the community in terms of growing social capital resources, it may serve to reinforce underlying inequalities whereby not all community members are able to participate evenly in community life (Mair & Duffy, 2018). This can also contribute to feelings of exclusion or alienation amongst some community members. Thus, strategies are needed to widen the membership of those involved in the organisation of a festival to include marginalised or minority groups – or those less involved in a community – such that they can "participate in community networks and also empower them to reap more of the rewards arising" (Stevenson, 2016, p. 1003).

Conclusion and outlook

In this chapter, we have explored the social dimension of community events and festivals. We have placed particular focus on the contributions these types of

Social dimensions of community events 127

events make to social connectedness, social capital, sense of place, and belonging. There are many other areas that could be explored, and indeed there is a growing social agenda for events, as facilitators of social transactions between people and as vital contributors to the well-being and quality of life of communities (Bakas et al., 2019; Stevenson, 2020; Yolal et al., 2016).

Throughout this chapter, the focus has been placed on community events and festivals. Staged primarily for social and entertainment purposes, and to celebrate features of a host community's way of life, values, or traditions, the social dimensions of community events cannot be understated. Nor can the central role the community plays in such events – not only as the host, often the organiser, and in many cases, the participant or audience.

Noting that the overall longevity and success of an event is likely to be influenced by the social contributions it makes to the host community, it is vitally important for event organisers to engage the local community. From input into the community values or local theme the festival will display, through to opportunities to participate in decision-making and staging of the event, the specific strategies and tactics for involving communities in both the consumption and production of a festival (Laing & Mair, 2015; Rogers & Anastasiadou, 2011) are important to future festival management.

The discussion presented in this chapter has illustrated significant opportunities for community events and festivals to make valuable social contributions to the communities which host them, but also that challenges exist in ensuring a broad cross-section of the community can benefit from them. What about those members of a community who feel excluded rather than socially connected? How can we ensure the stock of social capital is increased not only for those who already have access to it? The need for further research into these and other areas regarding the social dimensions of community events will be discussed in the concluding chapter of this book.

References

Allen, J., Harris, R., & Jago, L. (2021). *Festival and special event management essentials.* Milton, Queensland, Australia: John Wiley and Sons.

Arcodia, C., & Whitford, M. (2007). Festival attendance and the development of social capital. *Journal of Convention and Event Tourism, 8*(2), 1–18. doi:10.1300/J452v0 8n02_01

Attanasi, G., Casoria, F., Centorrino, S., & Urso, G. (2013). Cultural investment, local development and instantaneous social capital: A case study of a gathering festival in the South of Italy. *Journal of Socio-Economics, 47,* 228.

Bakas, F., Duxbury, N., Remoaldo, P., & Matos, O. (2019). The social utility of small-scale art festivals with creative tourism in Portugal. *International Journal of Event and Festival Management, 10*(3), 248–266. doi:10.1108/IJEFM-02-2019-0009

Baptista Alves, H., & Ferreira Martins, A. (2010). Impacts of small tourism events on rural places. *Journal of Place Management and Development, 3*(1), 22–37. doi:10.1108/17538331011030257

Black, N. (2016). Festival connections: How consistent and innovative connections enable small-scale rural festivals to contribute to socially sustainable communities.

128 *Event management and leverage in practice*

International Journal of Event and Festival Management, 7(3), 172–187. doi:10.1108/IJEFM-04-2016-0026

Brown, S., & James, J. (2004). Event design and management: Ritual sacrifice? In I. Yeoman, M. Robertson, J. Ali-Knight, S. Drummond, & U. McMahon-Beattie (Eds.), *Festival and events management: An international arts and culture perspective* (pp. 53–64). Oxford: Elsevier Butterworth-Heinemann.

Brownett, T. (2018). Social capital and participation: The role of community arts festivals for generating well-being. *Journal of Applied Arts and Health, 9*(1), 71–84. doi:10.1386/jaah.9.1.71_1

De Bres, K., & Davis, J. (2001). Celebrating group and place identity: A case study of a new regional festival. *Tourism Geographies, 3*(3), 326–337.

Derrett, R. (2000). Can festivals brand community cultural development and cultural tourism simultaneously? Paper presented at *the Events Beyond 2000: Setting the Agenda, Proceedings of Conference on Event Evaluation, Research and Education,* Sydney.

Derrett, R. (2003). Making sense of how festivals demonstrate a community's sense of place. *Event Management, 8,* 49–58.

Derrett, R. (2004). Festivals, events and the destination. In I. Yeoman, M. Robertson, J. Ali-Knight, S. Drummond, & U. McMahon-Beattie (Eds.), *Festival and events management: An international arts and culture perspective* (pp. 32–50). Oxford: Elsevier Butterworth-Heinemann.

Dimmock, K., & Tiyce, M. (2001). Festivals and events: Celebrating special interest tourism. In N. Douglas, N. Douglas, & R. Derrett (Eds.), *Special interest tourism* (pp. 355–383). Milton, Queensland, Australia: John Wiley and Sons.

Duffy, M., & Waitt, G. (2011). Rural festivals and processes of belonging. In C. Gibson & J. Connell (Eds.), *Festival places: Revitalising rural Australia* (pp. 44–60). Bristol: Channel View.

Finkel, R. (2010). "Dancing around the ring of fire": Social capital, tourism resistance, and gender dichotomies at up Helly Aa in Lerwick, Shetland. *Event Management, 14*(4), 275–285. doi:10.3727/152599510X12901814778023

Getz, D., Andersson, T. D., Armbrecht, J., & Lundberg, E. (2018). The value of festivals. In J. Mair (Ed.), *The Routledge handbook of festivals* (pp. 22–30). Abingdon, UK: Routledge.

Getz, D., Andersson, T. D., & Carlsen, J. (2010). Festival management studies. *International Journal of Event and Festival Management, 1,* 29–59.

Green, G. P., & Haines, A. (2012). *Asset building & community development* (3rd ed.). Thousand Oaks, CA: Sage Publications.

Hall, C. M., & Sharples, L. (2008). *Food and wine festivals and events around the world: Development, management and markets.* Oxford, UK: Elsevier.

Hammitt, W. E., Backlund, E. A., & Bixler, R. D. (2006). Place bonding for recreation places: Conceptual and empirical development. *Leisure Studies, 25*(1), 17–41. doi:10.1080/02614360500098100

Jaeger, K., & Mykletun, R. J. (2013). Festivals, identities, and belonging. *Event Management, 17*(3), 213–226. doi:10.3727/152599513X13708863377791

Janiskee, R. L. (1996). Historic houses and special events. *Annals of Tourism Research, 23*(2), 398–414. doi:10.1016/0160-7383(95)00069-0

Jepson, A., & Clarke, A. (2013). Events and community development. In R. Finkel, D. McGillivray, G. McPherson, & P. Robinson (Eds.), *Research themes for events* (pp. 6–17). Wallingford, UK: CABI.

Social dimensions of community events 129

Jepson, A., & Clarke, A. (2016). *Managing and developing communities, festivals and events*. London, UK: Palgrave Macmillan.

Jordan, J. (2019). Festival leadership, structures and roles In C. Newbold, J. Jordan, P. Kelly, & K. Diaz (Eds.), *Principles of festival management* (pp. 1–21). Oxford: Goodfellow Publishers.

Laing, J., & Mair, J. (2015). Music festivals and social inclusion: The festival organizers' perspective. *Leisure Sciences, 37*(3), 252–268. doi:10.1080/01490400.2014.991009

Lau, C. Y. L., & Li, Y. (2015). Producing a sense of meaningful place: Evidence from a cultural festival in Hong Kong. *Journal of Tourism and Cultural Change, 13*(1), 56–77. doi:10.1080/14766825.2014.892506

Leonard, R., & Onyx, J. (2004). *Social capital and community building: Spinning straw into gold*. London: Janus Publishing Company.

Mair, J. (Ed.). (2018). *The Routledge handbook of festivals*. Abingdon, UK: Routledge.

Mair, J., & Duffy, M. (2015). Community events and social justice in urban growth areas. *Journal of Policy Research in Tourism, Leisure and Events, 7*(3), 282–298. doi:10.1080/19407963.2014.997438

Mair, J., & Duffy, M. (2018). The role of festivals in strengthening social capital in rural communities. *Event Management, 22*(6), 875–889. doi:10.3727/152599518X15346132863229

Mykletun, R. J. (2009). Celebration of extreme playfulness: Ekstremsportveko at Voss. *Scandinavian Journal of Hospitality and Tourism, 9*(2–3), 146–176. doi:10.1080/15022250903119512

Poplin, D. E. (1979). *Communities: A survey of theories and methods of research* (2nd ed.). New York: Macmillan Publishing Company.

Putnam, R. D. (1995). Bowling alone: America's declining social capital. *Journal of Democracy, 6*(1), 65–78. doi:10.1353/jod.1995.0002

Putnam, R. D. (2000). *Bowling alone: The collapse and revival of American community*. New York: Simon and Schuster.

Quinn, B. (2018). Festivals and social sustainability. In J. Mair (Ed.), *The Routledge handbook of festivals* (pp. 53–61). Abingdon, UK: Routledge.

Quinn, B., & Wilks, L. (2013). People, place and social capital. In G. Richards, M. de Brito, & L. Wilks (Eds.), *Exploring the social impacts of events* (pp. 15–30). Abingdon, UK: Routledge.

Reid, S. (2011). Event stakeholder management: Developing sustainable rural event practices. *International Journal of Event and Festival Management, 2*(1), 20–36. doi:10.1108/17582951111116597

Rogers, P., & Anastasiadou, C. (2011). Community involvement in festivals: Exploring ways of increasing local participation. *Event Management, 15*(4), 387–399. doi:10.3727/152599511X13175676722681

Schulenkorf, N., Thomson, A., & Schlenker, K. (2011). Intercommunity sport events: Vehicles and catalysts for social capital in divided societies. *Event Management, 15*(2), 105–119. doi:10.3727/152599511X13082349958316

Schuller, T., Baron, S., & Field, J. (2000). Social capital: A review and critique. In S. Baron, J. Field, & T. Schuller (Eds.), *Social capital: Critical perspectives* (pp. 1–38). Oxford: Oxford University Press.

Sharpley, R., & Stone, P. R. (2011). Socio-cultural impacts of events: Meanings, authorized transgression and social capital. In S. J. Page & J. Connell (Eds.), *The Routledge handbook of events* (pp. 347–361). Abingdon, UK: Routledge.

130 *Event management and leverage in practice*

Small, K., Edwards, D., & Sheridan, L. (2005). A flexible framework for evaluating the socio-cultural impacts of a small festival. *International Journal of Event Management Research, 1*(1), 66–77.

Stadler, R. (2013). Power relations and the production of new knowledge within a Queensland Music Festival community cultural development project. *Annals of Leisure Research, 16*(1), 87–102. doi:10.1080/11745398.2013.767220

Stevenson, N. (2016). Local festivals, social capital and sustainable destination development: Experiences in East London. *Journal of Sustainable Tourism, 24*(7), 990–1006. doi:10.1080/09669582.2015.1128943

Stevenson, N. (2020). Having a say? The potential of local events as a tool for community engagement. *Event Management, 24*(4), 435–445. doi:10.3727/152599519X1550625 9855940

Taks, M. (2013). Social sustainability of non-mega sport events in a global world. *European Journal for Sport and Society, 10*(2), 121–141. doi:10.1080/16138171.2013.11687915

van der Zee, E., & Olders, P. (2016). Events: Cause or consequence of community involvement. In A. Jepson & A. Clarke (Eds.), *Managing and developing communities, festivals and events* (pp. 120–132). Houndmills, Basingstoke, Hampshire: Palgrave Macmillan.

Wilks, L., & Quinn, B. (2016). Linking social capital, cultural capital and heterotopia at the folk festival. *Journal of Comparative Research in Anthropology and Sociology, 7*(1), 23–39.

Williams, D. R., & Stewart, S. I. (1998). Sense of place: An elusive concept that is finding a home in ecosystem management. *Journal of Forestry, 96*(5), 18–23.

Willmott, P. (1986). *Social networks, informal care and public policy.* London: Policy Studies Institute.

Yeoman, I., Robertson, M., Ali-Knight, J., Drummond, S., & McMahon-Beattie, U. (Eds.). (2004). *Festivals and events management: An international arts and culture perspective.* Oxford: Elsevier Butterworth-Heinemann.

Yolal, M., Gursoy, D., Uysal, M., Kim, H., & Karacaoglu, S. (2016). Impacts of festivals and events on residents' well-being. *Annals of Tourism Research, 61*, 1.

Yürük, P., Akyol, A., & Şimşek, G. G. (2017). Analyzing the effects of social impacts of events on satisfaction and loyalty. *Tourism Management (1982), 60*, 367–378. doi:10.1016/j.tourman.2016.12.016

Yuval-Davis, N. (2006). Belonging and the politics of belonging. *Patterns of Prejudice, 40*(3), 197–214. doi:10.1080/00313220600769331

10 A new social field

Events-for-development

Introduction

Events of all shapes and sizes figure prominently in every society, culture, and nation.

There is not a community, village, city, or nation that does not host events, from small-scale, community-led events such as music and arts festivals, parades, and football tournaments to the biggest and grandest stage of the Olympic Games and other sport World Championship events. Niche events have emerged targeting interest groups and social, political, or other agendas, such as the Burning Man festival in the dessert of Nevada in the United States designed to showcase alternative perspectives on social life and novel art forms. Indigenous and tribal villages in the wilds of Alaska or on the Serengeti in Africa hold rites of passage ceremonies to celebrate the transition of youth into adulthood. Professional sport events have embraced a sport as entertainment mind-set and draw millions of fans to their stadia and arenas to escape from everyday lives and enjoy a spectacle of distraction. All of these events, whether small or grand, can create a transcendent, liminoid space (Turner, 1979), where those in attendance are in temporary communion with others as they bond within a shared and lived experience. The importance and value of events to society have become critically apparent at the time of this writing during the COVID-19 pandemic sweeping across the globe, which has forced the cancellation or postponement of most small- and large-scale events. People have been bereft of an important social glue and condition necessary for societal functioning (Evans et al., 2020).

Within this landscape, a new and rather novel approach to events is that of events-for-development (EfD), where events are envisioned and sometimes planned (although not always well) to help facilitate outcomes such as economic and social development, social inclusion, and conflict resolution and peace building. In essence, there is a strategic objective that goes beyond the actual hosting of an event. This is a shift in mind-set from thinking of an event as just providing entertainment and enjoyment, or for competition's sake in the case of sport events. EfD captures the ability of events to contribute to building community networks and social capital, to celebrate and enhance cultural traditions, and to develop community spirit and pride (Chalip & McGuirty, 2004; Kellett, Hede, & Chalip,

DOI: 10.4324/9781003002772-12

132 *Event management and leverage in practice*

2008; Misener & Mason, 2006; O'Brien & Chalip, 2008; Schulenkorf, 2016). In the sport landscape, for instance, the concept of EfD can be situated within the broader field of sport-for-development (SFD), which is defined as

> [T]he use of sport to exert a positive influence on public health, the socialization of children, youth and adults, the social inclusion of the disadvantaged, the economic development of regions and states, and on fostering intercultural exchange and conflict resolution.
>
> (Lyras & Welty Peachey, 2011, p. 311)

Historically, SFD interventions have been administered as programmes taking place over a specified time period (e.g. three months, six months) and designed to address an individual, community, or societal need/issue such as social inclusion and mobility, social capital development, conflict resolution and peace building between divided communities, prejudice reduction, gender relations, health-related concerns, and improved livelihoods, among others (Schulenkorf, Sherry, & Rowe, 2016). Now, however, an increasing number of SFD organisations are employing special events as part of their ongoing programme suite due to the potential they may have for addressing broader community development goals (Schulenkorf, 2012, 2016). Take, for instance, the case of Street Soccer USA (SSUSA), which is an SFD organisation based in the United States operating in 13 cities, with a mission to utilise soccer to help individuals suffering from homelessness and poverty make positive changes in their lives (Street Soccer USA, 2020). Each city sends its team to the SSUSA National Cup every year for a tournament that has broader goals than just crowning a champion – the event is designed to support, reinforce, and activate the goals of SSUSA in assisting individuals in making sustainable long-term changes in their lives (SSUSA, 2020; Welty Peachey, Borland, Lyras, & Cohen, 2013).

Many other events could be highlighted – and some will be discussed in this chapter – both within and outside the sport context, which engage in the EfD space to achieve economic and social development agendas. Importantly, in order for these events to be successful, they must be strategically designed and then leveraged to address the outcomes of focus (see Chapter 3 in this book, and Chalip, 2006; Schulenkorf, 2016). In other words, development outcomes from events will not simply materialise without coordinated and strategic planning that is linked to ongoing agendas of communities.

There is vast potential in the novel EfD space, and as such, the purpose of this chapter is to provide an in-depth discussion of the new social field of EfD, outlining avenues where events have and are being utilised for social, cultural, political, and economic development in disadvantaged settings. Managerial implications for EfD and thoughts on future outlook for practice and scholarship will also be advanced. As such, this chapter has a number of objectives: (1) to provide the reader with an understanding of the historical development and background of the new social field of EfD; (2) to help the reader grasp the theoretical/conceptual frameworks and groundings that have been used to undergird EfD thinking; (3) to

A new social field 133

help the reader gain an appreciation for the scholarship which has addressed EfD for economic, social, cultural, and political outcomes; (4) to illuminate challenges and considerations to the EfD field; (5) to advance managerial implications for EfD practice; and (6) to posit ideas for next steps in EfD practice and scholarship.

The chapter is organised as follows. First, we discuss the historical development of the EfD social field and important theoretical/conceptual understandings that have been tapped to undergird scholarship in this area. Next, the scholarship revolving around EfD as related to economic, social, cultural, and political outcomes is reviewed, followed by a discussion on the challenges associated with EfD. Managerial implications for EfD are then elucidated before we close with thoughts on next steps and outlook for the EfD arena.

Historical development and background

Events have been characterised as multidimensional, multipurpose phenomena that can potentially evince multiple impacts that are both tangible and intangible (Lu, Zhu, & Wei, 2019; Mackellar & Nisbet, 2017). As essential features of community life, events take place in third places – the home is the first place, and work is the second – where creative interaction with others occurs, such as in arenas, stadiums, and parks (Oldenburg, 1999). Without third places and the events that are held within them, isolation, loneliness, and boredom can emerge. Thus, events are central to community life and society.

From a development standpoint, host cities and communities are interested in incorporating events into their destination marketing mix and tourism portfolio not only due to their forecasted economic benefits from tourism activity but also for their potential social benefit (Chalip, 2006; Gibson & Connell, 2016; Lu et al., 2019; O'Brien & Chalip, 2008). The emergence of the EfD concept is firmly rooted in the historical precedence of events being envisioned as contributing to a nation or community's political, cultural, and social agenda, with sport events in particular being seen as platforms for bridging social divides and promoting community development (Welty Peachey, Borland, Lobpries, & Cohen, 2015a). There is potential for events to contribute to development agendas, provided they are strategically designed and managed and then leveraged for ongoing community-wide impact (Schulenkorf, 2012, 2016). Special events are often welcomed in communities, both large and small, not only for their potential economic and social benefit, but also because they can evoke feelings of celebration and camaraderie, instil community pride, and facilitate engagement and learning (Schulenkorf, 2016). Most work in the EfD space has focused on solving community problems and issues through a deficit-approach mind-set. Instead, it may also be beneficial to approach EfD from a strength-based paradigm where organisers try to enhance existing strengths of a community to mitigate social issues (Misener & Schulenkorf, 2016).

Thus, many ongoing community development efforts and initiatives are choosing to include special events as part of their programme mix when targeting disadvantaged individuals and communities. These events can serve to call attention to

134 *Event management and leverage in practice*

the issue at play (e.g. homelessness, gender inequality) and raise awareness of the issue in the public's eye, reinforcing the mission and agenda of the organisation and programme (Schulenkorf, 2012, 2016; Schulenkorf & Adair, 2013). Special events may increase excitement and motivation of participants in ongoing intervention programmes, renew their interest in participating, and engage the community around the issue through a festival effect (Schulenkorf & Adair, 2013; Weed, Coren, & Fiore, 2008). Community members may be drawn to the energy and positive emotions surrounding a special event and take action to watch or even participate in the event. Schulenkorf and Adair (2013) also suggested that through strategic management and planning, event organisers can highlight and promote the mission of the initiative to local, regional, and national politicians and to sport associations, potential sponsors, and the media. It is important to keep in mind, however, that special events must be integrated into the community-wide development agenda or they risk being isolated and ineffective (Schulenkorf, 2016).

This integration and strategic planning for situating events into the development mix reflects the concept of event leverage, which was reviewed in detail in Chapter 3 (please see this chapter for an in-depth discussion of the concept). In general, event leverage can be defined as "activities that need to be undertaken around the event itself, which seeks to maximise long-term benefits from events" (Chalip, 2004, p. 228). Event managers and policy makers essentially need to envision the desired outcomes for a community before the event occurs and then engage in strategies to achieve these outcomes, which may be economic, social, or environmental (Chalip, 2006; O'Brien & Chalip, 2007). Leverage thinking is critical for managers working in the EfD space, as developmental outcomes through the event will likely not be achieved without thoughtful and engaged alignment of the processes and goals of the event with targeted social and economic outcomes (Schulenkorf, 2016). Integral to the strategic leveraging of events are the concepts of liminality and communitas (Chalip, 2006). EfD can create a liminoid space, where event participants and attendees experience the unexpected, excitement, enthusiasm, and community cohesion that result through spontaneous celebration and building of relationships, or communitas (Welty Peachey et al., 2015a). When individuals step outside of their normal bounds and form unexpected relationships, communitas can emerge, as the event elicits feelings of equality, belonging, and group devotion to a goal that transcend individual lives and interests (Arnould & Price, 1993). Chalip (2006) articulated a number of strategies for an event to engender liminality and generate communitas (see Chapter 3), which are preconditions for social impact. As will be discussed in a later section of this chapter, the leverage concept has been applied to a number of studies examining both the economic and social outcomes of events and is thus a critical foundation and consideration within EfD.

Theoretical and conceptual frameworks

There are four key theoretical and conceptual groundings which are relevant to the EfD social field: the Sport-for-Development Framework (Schulenkorf, 2012),

A new social field   135

Sport-for-Development Theory (Lyras & Welty Peachey, 2011), Intergroup Contact Theory (Allport, 1954), and social capital (Putnam, 1995, 2000). Of course, other theoretical and conceptual understandings can be brought to bear in the EfD space – and we might suggest should be central to our thinking – but for sake of parsimony only these four, which have received significant attention in the literature, will be discussed.

Sport-for-Development Framework

Schulenkorf's (2012) Sport-for-Development (S4D) Framework presents a conceptual, process-oriented management tool that was designed to inform sport and event planning, management, and leverage. The S4D framework was conceived to help address management and leverage issues revolving around EfD and efforts in targeting a range of social and health-related outcomes, primarily through sport, although the applicability of the framework beyond sport events should be considered. The malleable framework advantages cultural heterogeneity and programme diversity, while shaping implementation, directing evaluation, and encouraging future planning of development initiatives. The framework is divided into three interrelated areas: (1) sport event management, (2) direct social impacts, and (3) long-term social outcomes. Within event management, Schulenkorf advocates that external change agents (such as development workers or event managers) are often needed initially in the process to launch an initiative, but that over time, responsibilities should be transferred to local stakeholders. To achieve direct social impacts, it is critical for community members to be actively engaged in the management process of the event. Finally, to facilitate long-term social outcomes, direct impacts must be leveraged into long-term social outcomes (Chalip, 2006), a process that requires structural, economic, and political support to capitalise on the liminality and communitas that are generated from the events. In addition, as discussed earlier, it is vital for the event to be linked into the ongoing development agenda of a community to maximise the potential for sustainable outcomes (Schulenkorf, 2012). Thus, the S4D framework is an important theoretical and practical grounding for engaging in the EfD space and has strongly influenced the development of the Strategic Event Management Framework presented in Chapter 2 of this book.

Sport-for-Development Theory

While initially developed to provide an overarching framework for ongoing SFD interventions, Sport-for-Development Theory (SFDT) emerged from a grounded theory approach with a local EfD initiative in Cyprus (Lyras, 2007). It has since been applied in the SFD space to the study of events and their impact on social and community development, such as conflict resolution and peace building and social inclusion of the disadvantaged (Lyras & Welty Peachey, 2011, 2015). SFDT draws from interdisciplinary theoretical and conceptual foundations including organisational theory, intergroup contact theory, humanistic psychology,

136 *Event management and leverage in practice*

educational psychology, and theory and methods of research (Lyras & Welty Peachey, 2011, 2015). Five components are central to the framework: (1) impacts assessment, (2) organisational, (3) sport and physical activity, (4) educational, and (5) cultural enrichment. In essence, SFDT advances that impacts assessments should measure multilevel change over time and that both top-down and bottom-up organisational structures are needed, ones that are culturally sensitive and give voice to all stakeholders (Lyras & Welty Peachey, 2011). Non-traditional sport programming and inclusive play are critical, with the level of competition matched to the nature of the population being served. Quality educational lessons should accompany the sport and play activities in order to facilitate transferability of learning outcomes to the real world. Finally, cultural activities such as music, dance, and the arts should be packaged with sport and educational programming. For an EfD approach, this means that organisers should consider incorporating a wide variety of ancillary activities into and around the primary event in order to maximise the potential for individual and community development and to facilitate transferability of lessons learnt at the event into the ongoing life and fabric of a community (Lyras & Welty Peachey, 2015).

Intergroup Contact Theory

Many EfD initiatives are designed around the premise of bringing individuals from different communities together to break down barriers and stereotypes between groups that may be historically in conflict, or between groups from different socio-economic backgrounds. Intergroup Contact Theory (Allport, 1954), or the contact hypothesis, draws from the social categorisation framework (Tajfel & Turner, 1979), in which people categorise themselves and others into social groups. In-group members are individuals similar to one's self and are generally viewed in a positive light and trusted. Out-group members, however, are individuals who are different from oneself and are not viewed as positively or trusted to the same extent. Consequently, intergroup bias can exist, whereby people express more positive attitudes towards in-group members than they do towards out-group members. Intergroup Contact Theory suggests that if four key conditions are met, personal interactions among in-group and out-group members should result in reduced intergroup bias. These include (a) equal status within the contact situation; (b) intergroup cooperation; (c) common goals; and (d) support of authorities, law, or custom. In the context of an event, quality and frequency of contact between disparate groups – for example, youth from Palestine and Israel – can potentially result in building trust and relationships, reducing prejudice, and facilitating cultural understanding and peace building (Lyras & Welty Peachey, 2011).

Social capital

Finally, many EfD programmes have as a focal outcome enhancing social capital among event participants and other stakeholders. While there are different

A new social field 137

conceptualisations of this construct, the modern debate around social capital largely derives from three main theorists: Bourdieu, Coleman, and Putnam. In the EfD space, Putnam's (1995, 2000) approach to social capital has thus far received the most attention from scholars. To Putnam, social capital is the "features of social organisation such as networks, norms, and social trust that can facilitate coordination and cooperation for mutual benefit" (p. 66). Trust, networks, and reciprocity play prominent roles, and once trust is built, networks can be developed which enable inclusion and social mobility, and then an exchange process can occur (reciprocity). Mechanisms to facilitate social cohesion and inclusion are bonding and bridging. Bonding social capital involves enhancing social networks between homogenous groups, such as family, neighbours, or close friends, while bridging social capital is formed when relationships are developed with individuals who are different from oneself, where social ties and bonds may be looser and more diverse in nature. These bridging relationships enable individuals to leverage a broader set of resources, which are critical for social cohesion, inclusion, and mobility (Putnam, 1995, 2000). Events have the capacity to facilitate these bonding and bridging relationships through diverse interactions and learnings which can occur and then be leveraged for longer-term social capital development (Welty Peachey et al., 2015a).

However, social capital is a contested and rather nebulous term, which scholars have criticised as being too amorphous and almost impossible to truly measure (Coalter, 2010). In fact, some scholars have taken this critique on board and advanced the concept of temporary social capital, which may come into prominence more with events. McNaughton (2014) advanced that temporary social capital is a form of social capital characterised by ties that are formed quickly, which often come about due to a challenging problem or issue, or an exogenous shock. These ties have relatively short lifespans and often dissolve once the problem or situation has stabilised. This concept of temporary social capital could be relevant to EfD, where events are often formed around a specific cause or issue and aim to bring stakeholders together to engage with and dialogue around the cause. Perhaps, this temporary social capital is truly the form of social capital evinced from events – as there are challenges in demonstrating long-term social capital development – and these ties last only until the issue central to the event is addressed or mitigated. Still, temporary social capital may well be important per se, and it could potentially be leveraged for longer-term social capital gains with strategic planning and strong linkages and partnerships between the event and community organisations and government entities.

Foci and outcomes of EfD

Building on the important contextual and theoretical background to the nature of EfD, we now turn our attention to discussing the potential economic, social, cultural, and political outcomes often linked with the EfD space.

As discussed in detail in Chapters 5 and 6, events – and in particularly large-scale, mega-events and festivals – have been touted as contributing to the

138 *Event management and leverage in practice*

economic development of regions and states. However, evidence to support these claims is contradictory and mega-sport events in particular, such as the Olympic Games and Federation Internationale de Football Association (FIFA) World Cup, have received their share of criticism (Chaberek-Karwacka & Ziółkowska, 2017; Levermore, 2011). Scholars have for example argued that public funds are better used for addressing critical needs in a community, such as enhancing social and educational programmes, rather than sinking funds into mega-events and their associated facilities (Conchas, 2014). Nevertheless, and despite these critiques and challenges, communities continue to invest in events and festivals of all sizes in hopes of developing the local economy. Certainly, events can and do contribute to economic development of communities and regions, but as discussed in Chapter 3, this potential will not be realised unless they are strategically planned and then leveraged for economic benefit (Chalip, 2004; Chalip & Costa, 2005; Chalip & Leyns, 2002). To maximise the economic benefits from events, there must be effective coordination with community stakeholders, government entities, and businesses, along with strong alliances and partnerships (Chalip, Green, Taks, & Misener, 2017).

In one of the few studies specifically on EfD and economic development, O'Brien (2007) made an important contribution by elucidating how local or regional, smaller-scale events can also apply leverage tactics to maximise economic development. In particular, O'Brien (2007) highlighted that smaller-scale events, such as the regional surfing festival in this study, need to capitalise on the centrality of the sport subculture for immediate and longer-term leverage potential. Overall, recent work has indicated that grassroots events can contribute to sustainable development, including economic development, in many ways better than large-scale, mega-events due to their smaller footprint, lower costs to implement, and shorter duration (Wang, Ju, Xu, & Wong, 2019).

Aside from economic development, a growing body of literature is emerging in the EfD space around the role of events in stimulating social, culture, and political development. This is an exciting advance, as the majority of work historically has focused on events and economic development, and while there are certainly still many challenges to organising events for social-cultural outcomes, as will be discussed later, there is also much promise. For instance, special events can be vital to the ongoing efforts of development initiatives in communities. Schulenkorf (2016) found that special event festivals, for example, delivered through the *Just Play* SFD programme in the South Pacific helped to create new interest and excitement for the SFD initiative focused on social and health-related problems in the region, re-engaged local stakeholders in the broader programme, and helped to build and sustain local management capacity. To activate the potential of these smaller-scale EfD initiatives for community development efforts towards social, political, or cultural outcomes, external change agents can play a pivotal role (Schulenkorf, 2010a). These agents of change need to facilitate community participation; be a trust builder, networker, leader, and resource developer; advocate for socially responsible practices; be an innovator; engage in financial support; and be a strategic partner for long-term sustainability. Over time, more and

A new social field 139

more responsibilities should be transitioned to local stakeholders to sustain the event and programme over the long term (Schulenkorf, 2010a).

Music and cultural arts festivals can also play a critical role in community and regional development (Gibson & Connell, 2016). Certainly, these festivals can stimulate local economic development through tourism, but they also have the potential to contribute to social inclusion, social cohesion, and other sociocultural development outcomes as they bring people together in transcendent spaces with music and the cultural arts as unifying emblems (Arcodia & Whitford, 2007; Bagiran & Kurgun, 2016; Pavlukovic, Armenski, & Akcanara-Pilar, 2017). However, the impact of music and arts festivals can also evince more negative outcomes in a community if care is not taken in their management and design, such as contributing to unwanted changes in community values and patterns, resident exodus, higher prices of services, conflict with event attendee xenophobia, and commodification and exploitation of culture and traditional ways of life, among others (Arcodia & Whitford, 2007; Deery & Jago, 2010; Pavlukovic et al., 2017).

Additional work has addressed EfD and social, political, and cultural outcomes from the event leverage paradigm, as reviewed earlier and in Chapter 3. For example, scholarship by Schulenkorf and Schlenker (2017) identified leverageable opportunities associated with EfD in low- and middle-income countries, illuminating mechanisms to facilitate sociocultural outcomes of a community festival in Samoa. Small-scale event organisations need to connect the event to well-respected individuals and institutions in the community to enhance support and visibility. In addition, it is beneficial for these events to give employment and volunteer opportunities to local stakeholders to involve them in the management of the event, thus helping to develop their managerial skill sets that will transcend the lifespan of the event and benefit the community over the long term (Schulenkorf & Schlenker, 2017). Similarly, Schulenkorf, Giannoulakis, and Blom (2019), in their study on a community-led mini-marathon event in Greece, have argued that a participatory management approach, leverage thinking, aligning the event with social issues, and involving community members are critical for maximising social, cultural, economic, and sport benefits (Schulenkorf et al., 2019). The main takeaway from all of this recent scholarship is that leverage thinking and community participation in event management are keys to effecting social, cultural, political, and other outcomes from EfD events. One social issue where EfD projects have been employed is with homelessness and social inclusion of the disadvantaged. For instance, work has shown that the SSUSA Cup played a role in facilitating social inclusion, social mobility, and social capital of event participants who were homeless, provided there was follow-up and continued engagement from the organisation with participants upon return home from the tournament (Welty Peachey et al., 2013). Importantly, the event achieved these outcomes through building a sense of community, creating hope, helping participants to think of others beyond just themselves, and in fostering goal achievement. The celebratory and festive nature of the event established an inclusive and welcoming climate, which was then leveraged by organisers to sustain positive impacts back in home communities.

140 *Event management and leverage in practice*

A follow-up study by Welty Peachey and colleagues (2015a) with the SSUSA Cup found that event organisers were successful in cultivating liminality and communitas and then leveraging these intangible resources for social capital development and integrating homeless individuals back into their communities. One additional contribution of this work was identifying the importance of inclusive play, where coaches played with the homeless players, as a key ingredient for social capital development through the event. However, it was also important to de-emphasise high levels of competition at the SSUSA tournament, as teams losing by lopsided scores did little to build self-esteem and positive outcomes among some participants marginalised by society (Welty Peachey et al., 2013, 2015a). Indeed, Magee and Jeanes (2013) tracked the experiences of homeless players from the United Kingdom in the Homeless World Cup, finding that because the team did not perform well at the Cup and suffered many defeats, this tended to reinforce participants' beliefs that they were failures at life, work, and social relationships. Thus, care must be taken in the critical management and structure of EfD projects targeting marginalised individuals to be sure that their focus on competition and winning does not supersede other developmental goals.

Aside from the aforementioned organisations, literally hundreds of organisations around the world are embracing sport and sport events in particular to work at issues of social inclusion and mobility among other disadvantaged and marginalised populations. For instance, Beyond the Ball is a sport-based non-profit in the city of Chicago in the United States deploying sport to help reclaim play space in areas of the city rife with gang violence and to work at building relationships and opportunities between youth from disparate backgrounds and neighbourhoods (Beyond the Ball, 2020). As foundational to its programming, the organisation includes many special events, from basketball on the streets to football tournaments, to bring together marginalised youth – particularly those involved in gang life – to play and build relationships through sport and events.

In addition to social inclusion, other organisations in the EfD space are employing events of various sizes to assist in conflict resolution and peace-building efforts through stimulating social, political, and cultural outcomes. One example is the Doves Olympic Movement programme that took place in Cyprus in the 2000s, an EfD intervention which employed sport, the cultural arts, and educational initiatives to help Greek and Turkish Cypriot youth bridge cultural divides and work at issues of cultural understanding and conflict resolution (Lyras, 2007). This programme was organised around special events, which had success in fostering better understanding between these youth and was the genesis of Sport for Development Theory (reviewed earlier; Lyras & Welty Peachey, 2011, 2015). Another similar event-based programme in Sri Lanka – the Asian–German Sport Exchange Programme, formed in 2002 – utilised sport to try to heal divides in the ethnically divided country between Sinhalese, Tamil, and Muslim peoples (Schulenkorf, 2010b). Importantly, strategically designed and managed sport events contributed to establishing interpersonal friendships and inclusive social identities that transcended ethnic community lines. To be effective, however, such special event projects must be woven into ongoing political and social agendas

A new social field 141

and receive sustainable sociopolitical support to address issues of reconciliation, inclusion, and peace building over the long term (Schulenkorf, 2010b).

An important sport-based event working at conflict resolution and peace building in the United States in the 1990s and 2000s – the World Scholar-Athlete Games (WSAG) – brought together more than 2,000 youth leaders from 200 countries at each event in an attempt to foster peace, understanding, and inclusion among these future leaders (Welty Peachey, Cunningham, Lyras, Cohen, & Bruening, 2015b). Through the utilisation of mixed-nation teams, cultural and educational activities, and conflict resolution workshops, the event helped to reduce prejudice and foster change agent self-efficacy in these youth (Welty Peachey et al., 2015b). This event highlighted the importance of grounding event design in sound theory (in this case, SFDT) and in strategically linking event activities to specified outcomes. Here, the mixed-nation team structure contributed the most to prejudice reduction, while cultural and educational workshops activated change agent self-efficacy to a greater degree (Welty Peachey et al., 2015b).

While most scholarship in the EfD space targeting social, cultural, and political outcomes has focused on participants in the programmes, there is some work that is beginning to look at impacts of these events on other stakeholders, such as volunteers. For instance, another study with the WSAG revealed that volunteers in the event from many nations increased their social capital through their volunteering experience by expanding their network and building relationships with other volunteers and event participants; learning about diverse countries and cultures; developing an enhanced motivation to work for social change back in their home communities; and through reciprocity and "giving back" to the event (Welty Peachey, Bruening, Lyras, Cohen, & Cunningham, 2015c). However, as with many event studies, the long-term effects of the event on volunteers' social capital development are not known, thus, calling for the critical need for more longitudinal research efforts to ascertain the long-term effects of events on sociocultural development.

Challenges to EfD as a new social field

The preceding section discussed the emerging EfD social field and explored its activation towards economic, social, cultural, and political development and outcomes. While there is much promise to EfD, like any paradigm or approach, it is not without its critiques and challenges. One historical challenge in the EfD space is the neocolonial, top-down approach organisers have taken, where an event is helicoptered into a local community and region and then organisers depart immediately afterwards, claiming development has occurred, but neglecting to integrate the event into the fabric of the community (see Coalter, 2007). While improving of late, this neolithic way of thinking about events and development, the "headquarters knows best syndrome" (Bouquet, Birkinshaw, & Barsoux, 2016), has been perpetuated by mega-events such as the Olympic Games, as well as by small-scale events that are organised in higher-income countries and then imported into regions in low- and middle-income countries in order to "develop"

142 *Event management and leverage in practice*

them. As Singer (2002) noted: "We still need to learn how to prevent global bodies becoming either dangerous tyrannies or self-aggrandising bureaucracies, and instead make them effective and responsible to the people whose lives they affect" (p. 199). Of special concern is when events are brought into underdeveloped areas, as they often necessitate increased financial and social commitments of communities perhaps ill-equipped to handle them (Reis, Vieira, & Sousa-Mast, 2016; Schulenkorf, 2016). Relatedly, as mentioned previously, there is a danger if special events are disconnected from the ongoing development efforts of a community. The isolation of events will do very little to enhance economic, sociocultural, or political outcomes, and unfortunately, this has often been the case, where event planners operate parallel to community agendas instead of integrating them and vice versa (Schulenkorf, 2010a, 2016).

In the EfD space within the SFD field – where social aspects like participation and engagement are key – a salient challenge is to identify and design the optimal level of competition within the event that will best facilitate positive individual and sociocultural outcomes. Specifically, too much or too intense of a focus on competition may serve to undermine the development process for marginalised and disenfranchised individuals who have received continuous messaging that they are "no good". Suffering defeats in competition and too much focus on winning may do little to build the self-esteem and self-concept individuals need to make positive changes in their lives (Welty Peachey et al., 2013, 2015a), and they may experience psychological pressures from needing to perform in front of large audiences (Schulenkorf, 2016). Another challenge associated with event design is linking event components with targeted outcomes. In other words, what specific features of the event evince a targeted outcome? Is the educational programming of an event associated more with a certain outcome over and above the sport component? What outcomes are best targeted through a team-based competition structure? What specific types of sports and play (e.g. traditional or non-traditional sports) are related to target outcomes? These are intriguing questions that future research should explore.

With regard to event evaluation, there are certainly many challenges associated with teasing out the unique contribution of an event to the economic development and vitality of a city and region. This is an incredibly difficult undertaking, particularly in a large metropolitan area with hundreds if not thousands of events, programmes, and initiatives which may contribute to the economy. In addition, as Coalter (2010) indicated, we often confuse micro-level outcomes (i.e., individual-level outcomes) with community development at the meso-level or even the macro-level (society). If participants in an event exhibit positive change in cultural tolerance, for instance, this does not necessarily indicate that the community has suddenly become more tolerant of diverse individuals. In a similar vein, are positive (or negative) outcomes associated with an event sustained over the long term? For instance, as mentioned earlier, perhaps the social capital developed through an event or festival is temporary in nature and wanes once participants, attendees, and others return to their home communities (McNaughton, 2014). If this is the case, how might these temporary social capital gains be

A new social field 143

sustained over time? More evidence is needed on the longer-term effects of events and festivals on many types of development indicators.

Managerial implications

Drawing from the earlier review and discussion, there are a number of key implications for event managers and organisers to consider for optimising EfD towards economic, social, cultural, and political gains. First, to optimally capitalise on the potential of events to support development efforts, these events must be strategically integrated into the ongoing economic, political, and social agenda and fabric of a community (Schulenkorf, 2010b, 2016). EfD organisers need to engage early and often with government entities, tourism bureaus, economic development agencies, chambers of commerce, visitors' bureaus, and other relevant agencies to integrate the event into the strategic priorities of the community. Not doing so will isolate the event and give it little traction in effecting positive change. Second, and relatedly, EfD organisers need to involve local stakeholders and entities in the planning of the event, forming partnerships with relevant entities in order to enable an effective and efficient event that could potentially be sustainable over the long term. Organisers may wish to consider servant and shared leadership models to best activate the potential of EfD, where power and leadership are shared and top leaders empower subordinates and local stakeholders to grow and develop into leadership roles (Jones et al., 2018; Welty Peachey & Burton, 2017). Initial work has shown that these follower-centric leadership approaches can be effective in contexts where social change and development are strategic outcomes (Welty Peachey, Burton, Wells, & Chung, 2018). Over time, once local management capacity has been developed, external change agents should transfer leadership responsibilities of the event to local stakeholders to ensure sustainability (Schulenkorf et al., 2019).

Third, EfD organisers should employ leverage thinking from the outset (see Chapters 2 and 3 for a more detailed and applied discussion) to strategically design and implement events for targeted economic and social outcomes. When events are first conceptualised, they should be done so with goals, strategic objectives, and outcomes in mind, and then planning and resourcing should be aligned to facilitate these objectives and outcomes. A primary danger is assuming an event will contribute to economic or social outcomes simply by offering it – this is furthest from the truth.

Finally, it is critical for EfD organisers to match the type and nature of the activities that are the focal point of the event with targeted populations and outcomes in order for the event to have potential to evince positive outcomes. For example, if the goal of an SFD organisation is to deploy an event to work at issues of peace building and conflict resolution between communities and cultural groups historically in conflict (e.g. Protestants and Catholics in Northern Ireland, Israelis and Palestinians in the Middle East), pitting teams comprising individuals from one community or cultural group against another in a sporting contest (e.g. football as the most popular) will do little to break down barriers

144 *Event management and leverage in practice*

and facilitate cultural acceptance. An unintentional outcome of this form of event design may be to actually increase cross-cultural intolerance through declaring "winners and losers" and supporting an "us versus them" mentality (Welty Peachey et al., 2013). Instead, organisers can structure the event around mixed nation teams, where Israeli and Palestinian youth, for instance, play on the same football team, working together to achieve common goals. Coaches should be trained in conflict mediation and cultural sensitivity issues so that the team-based environment can be used as "teachable moments" for the youth. Another event design consideration – particularly for a sport event – is the level, nature, and intensity of competition. Sport-based tournaments and events heavily focused on high-level competition, for example, will not be the best design modality if participants in the event are disadvantaged and have little self-esteem or self-concept (e.g. immigrants, individuals suffering from homelessness). While obviously important, competition should nevertheless be de-emphasised by valuing participation as the goal, employing tactics such as awarding all event participants medals regardless of whether they were "winners or losers" in the traditional sense, and creating special awards that recognise achievements in the event unrelated to skill performance (e.g. sportspersonship awards, supportive teammate awards, loudest cheer awards). These are just a sampling – there are many other event design considerations that should be taken on board by organisers as they strategically engage in the EfD space.

Conclusion and outlook

Moving forward, there is huge untapped potential for EfD as a new social field. Scholarship and practice are only beginning to recognise the importance of strategic design and leveraging concepts, and these need to be explored in much more depth. Certainly, at the time of this writing, the COVID-19 pandemic is ravaging the world and forcing the cancellation and postponement of grassroots, community, and mega-events. What will be the long-term impact of the pandemic on the viability of the EfD space? How will event organisers adapt and reconfigure the concept of events (e.g. virtual events) to engage in the development space in times of crises such as these? In addition, event organisers and scholars need to consider how to best integrate special events into the ongoing programme suite of organisations seeking to engage in community and individual development (e.g. ongoing, year-round programming of many SFD organisations; Schulenkorf, 2010b; Schulenkorf et al., 2019). What is the optimal number of special events to best complement existing programmes and not diminish these efforts? What strategies should be employed to link the event to ongoing programme objectives? Relatedly, research is needed as to how EfD organisers can best connect their events into the economic, social, cultural, and political agenda of a community to maximise potential for sustainable outcomes. What forms of partnerships are needed to activate this potential? With whom?

We would be remiss to claim that everyone in a community benefits equally from the hosting of events for development purposes, particularly when considering economic development. How can events best be designed and leveraged to

A new social field   145

facilitate outcomes across myriad social and economic strata? Do the elite just keep getting richer from the hosting of events, and how do we counteract this? Scholarship has indicated that the effects of events on communities and individuals may be more temporary in nature, such as when individuals develop temporary social capital at an event that then potentially dissipates as time passes (McNaughton, 2014). It has always been challenging to claim that events have long-term impacts and outcomes with communities and individuals, but certainly they may. More research is needed with participants in EfD initiatives to track long-term outcomes, to see how the event may have impacted them years past their participation. The outlook here is that these events are marking points for participants and communities and may stimulate future change and action, provided there is follow-up and integration of the event into various community spheres.

References

Allport, G. W. (1954). *The nature of prejudice*. Boston: Addison-Wesley.

Arcodia, C., & Whitford, M. (2007). Festival attendance and the development of social capital. *Journal of Convention and Event Tourism, 8*(2), 1–18.

Arnould, E. J., & Price, L. L. (1993). River magic: Extraordinary experience and the extended service encounter. *Journal of Consumer Research, 20*(1), 24–45.

Bagiran, D., & Kurgun, H. (2016). A research on social impacts of the Foça Rock Festival: The validity of the festival social impact attitude scale. *Current Issues in Tourism, 19*(9), 930–948.

Beyond the Ball. (2020). Retrieved from http://beyondtheball.org/?page_id=16

Bouquet, C., Birkinshaw, J., & Barsoux, J. (2016). Fighting the "Headquarter knows the best" syndrome. *MIT Sloan Management Review, 57*(2), 58–66.

Chaberek-Karwacka, G., & Ziółkowska, J. (2017). The impact of mega-events on the local economic development through the development of social capital. *Journal of Geography, Politics and Society, 4*, 25–31.

Chalip, L. (2004). Beyond impact: A general model for sport event leverage. In B. W. Ritchie & D. Adair (Eds.), *Sport tourism: Interrelationships, impacts and issues* (pp. 226–252). Toronto: Channel View Publications.

Chalip, L. (2006). Towards social leverage of sport events. *Journal of Sport & Tourism, 11*(2), 109–127.

Chalip, L., & Costa, C. A. (2005). Sport event tourism and the destination brand: Towards a general theory. *Sport in Society, 8*(2), 218–237.

Chalip, L., Green, B. C., Taks, M., & Misener, L. (2017). Creating sport participation from sport events: Making it happen. *International Journal of Sport Policy and Politics, 9*, 257–276.

Chalip, L., & Leyns, A. (2002). Local business leveraging of a sport event: Managing an event for economic benefit. *Journal of Sport Management, 16*(2), 132–158.

Chalip, L., & McGuirty, J. (2004). Bundling sport events with the host destination. *Journal of Sport & Tourism, 9*, 267–282.

Coalter, F. (2007). *A wider social role for sport: Who's keeping the score?* London: Routledge.

Coalter, F. (2010). The politics of sport-for-development: Limited focus programmes and broad gauge problems. *International Review for the Sociology of Sport, 45*(3), 295–314.

146 *Event management and leverage in practice*

Conchas, M. (2014). Research possibilities for the 2014 FIFA World Cup in Brazil. *Soccer & Society, 15*(1), 167–174.

Deery, M., & Jago, L. (2010). Social impacts of events and the role of anti-social behaviour. *International Journal of Event and Festival Management, 1*(1), 8–28.

Evans, A., Blackwell, J., Dolan, P., Fahlen, J., Hoekman, R., Lenneis, V., McNarry, G., Smith, M., & Wilcock, L. (2020). Sport in the face of the COVID-19 pandemic: Towards an agenda for research in the sociology of sport. *European Journal for Sport in Society, 17*, 85–95.

Gibson, C., & Connell, J. (2016). *Music festivals and regional development in Australia.* London: Routledge.

Jones, G., Wegner, C., Bunds, K., Edwards, M., & Bocarro, J. (2018). Examining the environmental characteristics of shared leadership in a sport-for-development organisation. *Journal of Sport Management, 32*, 82–95.

Kellett, P., Hede, A.-M., & Chalip, L. (2008). Social policy for sport events: Leveraging (relationships with) teams from other nations for community benefit. *European Sport Management Quarterly, 8*, 101–121.

Levermore, R. (2011). Sport-for-development and the 2010 Football World. *Geography Compass, 5*(12), 886–897.

Lu, S., Zhu, W., & Wei, Jei. (2019). Assessing the impacts of tourism events on city development in China: A perspective of event system. *Current Issues in Tourism.* Advance online publication. doi:10.1080/13683500.2019.1643828

Lyras, A. (2007). *Characteristics and psycho-social impacts of an inter-ethnic educational sport initiative on Greek and Turkish Cypriot youth* (Unpublished dissertation). University of Connecticut, Storrs.

Lyras, A., & Welty Peachey, J. (2011). Integrating sport-for-development theory and praxis. *Sport Management Review, 14*(4), 311–326.

Lyras. A., & Welty Peachey, J. (2015). The conception, development, and application of sport-for-development theory. In G. Cunningham, A. Doherty, & J. Fink (Eds.), *Routledge handbook of theory in sport management* (pp. 131–140). Abingdon, UK: Routledge.

Mackellar, J. (2015). Determinants of business engagement with regional sport events. *European Sport Management Quarterly, 15*(1), 7–26.

Mackellar, J., & Nisbet, S. (2017). Sport events and integrated destination development. *Current Issues in Tourism, 20*(13), 1320–1335.

Magee, J., & Jeanes, R. (2013). Football's coming home: A critical evaluation of the Homeless World Cup as an intervention to combat social exclusion. *International Review for the Sociology of Sport, 48*(1), 3–19.

McNaughton, R. B. (2014). The kindness of strangers: Temporary social capital and the internationalisation of SMEs. Paper presented at the *Otago Centre for Entrepreneurship Research Symposium*, Otago, New Zealand.

Misener, L., & Mason, D. S. (2006). Creating community networks: Can sporting events offer meaningful sources of social capital? *Managing Leisure, 11*, 39–56.

Misener, L., & Schulenkorf, N. (2016). Rethinking the social value of sport events through an asset-based community development (ABCD) perspective. *Journal of Sport Management, 30*, 329–340.

O'Brien, D. (2007). Points of leverage: Maximising host community benefit from a regional surfing festival. *European Sport Management Quarterly, 7*(2), 141–165.

O'Brien, D., & Chalip, L. (2007). Executive training exercise in sport event leverage. *International Journal of Culture, Tourism and Hospitality Research, 1*(4), 296–304.

O'Brien, D., & Chalip, L. (2008). Sport events and strategic leveraging: Pushing towards the triple bottom line. In A. Woodside & D. Martin (Eds.), *Tourism management: Analysis, behaviour and strategy* (pp. 318–338). Wallingford, UK and Cambridge, MA: CABI.

Oldenburg. R. (1999). *Great good place*. New York: Marlow.

Pavlukovic, V., Armenski, T., & Akcanara-Pilar, J. (2017). Social impacts of music festivals: Does culture impact locals' attitude towards events in Serbia and Hungary? *Tourism Management, 63*, 42–53.

Putnam, R. D. (1995). Bowling alone: America's declining social capital. *Journal of Democracy, 6*, 65–78.

Putnam, R. D. (2000). *Bowling alone: The collapse and revival of American community*. New York: Simon and Schuster.

Reis, A. C., Vieira, M. C., & Sousa-Mast, F. R. D. (2016). "Sport for development" in developing countries: The case of the Vilas Olímpicas do Rio de Janeiro. *Sport Management Review, 19*, 107–119.

Schulenkorf, N. (2010a). The roles and responsibilities of a change agent in sport event development projects. *Sport Management Review, 13*(2), 118–128.

Schulenkorf, N. (2010b). Sport events and ethnic reconciliation: Attempting to create social change between Sinhaleese, Tamil and Muslim sportspeople in war-torn Sri Lanka. *International Review for the Sociology of Sport, 45*(3), 273–294.

Schulenkorf, N. (2012). Sustainable community development through sport and events: A conceptual framework for sport-for-development projects. *Sport Management Review, 15*, 1–12.

Schulenkorf, N. (2016). The contribution of special events to sport-for-development programmes. *Journal of Sport Management, 30*, 629–642.

Schulenkorf, N., & Adair, D. (2013). Temporality, transience and regularity in sport-for-development: Synchronizing programmes with events. *Journal of Policy Research in Tourism, Leisure and Events, 5*(1), 99–104.

Schulenkorf, N., Giannoulakis, C., & Blom, L. (2019). Sustaining commercial viability and community benefits: Management and leverage of a sport-for-development event. *European Sport Management Quarterly, 19*(4), 502–519.

Schulenkorf, N., & Schlenker, K. (2017). Levering sport events to maximise community benefits in low- and middle-income countries. *Event Management, 21*, 217–231.

Schulenkorf, N., Sherry, E., & Rowe, K. (2016). Sport-for-development: An integrated literature review. *Journal of Sport Management, 30*, 22–39.

Singer, P. (2002). *One world: The ethics of globalization*. New Haven, CT: Yale University Press.

Street Soccer USA. (2020). Retrieved from www.streetsoccerusa.org/mission-model-impact/

Tajfel, H., & Turner, J. C. (1979). An integrative theory of intergroup conflict. In W. G. Austin & S. Worchel (Eds.), *The social psychology of intergroup relations* (pp. 33–47). Monterey, CA: Brooks/Cole.

Turner, V. (1979). Frame, flow and reflection: Ritual and drama as public liminality. *Japanese Journal of Religious Studies, 6*(4), 465–499.

Wang, H., Ju, P., Xu, H., & Wong, D. (2019). Are grassroots sports events good for migrant cities' sustainable development? A case study of the Shenzhen 100 km Hikathon. *Sustainability, 11*, 1–16.

Weed, M., Coren, E., & Fiore, J. (2008). *A systematic review of the evidence base for developing a physical activity, sport and health legacy from the London 2012 Olympic and Paralympic Games: Report to funders*. Canterbury Christ Church University, Centre for Sport, Physical Education & Activity Research, Canterbury, UK.

148 *Event management and leverage in practice*

Welty Peachey, J., Borland, J., Lobpries, J., & Cohen, A. (2015a). Managing impact: Leveraging sacred spaces and community celebration to maximise social capital at a sport-for-development event. *Sport Management Review*, *18*, 86–98.

Welty Peachey, J., Borland, J., Lyras, A., & Cohen, A. (2013). Street Soccer USA Cup: Preliminary findings of a sport-for-homeless intervention. *ICHPER-SD Journal of Research*, *8*(1), 3–11.

Welty Peachey, J., Bruening, J., Lyras, A., Cohen, A., & Cunningham, G. (2015c). Examining social capital development among volunteers of a multinational sport-for-development event. *Journal of Sport Management*, *29*, 27–41.

Welty Peachey, J., & Burton, L. (2017). Servant leadership in sport-for-development and peace: A way forward. *Quest*, *69*(1), 125–139.

Welty Peachey, J., Burton, L., Wells, J., & Chung, M. (2018). Exploring servant leadership and needs satisfaction in the sport for development and peace context. *Journal of Sport Management*, *32*, 96–108.

Welty Peachey, J., Cunningham, G., Lyras, A., Cohen, A., & Bruening, J. (2015b). The influence of a sport-for-peace event on prejudice and change agent self-efficacy. *Journal of Sport Management*, *29*(3), 229–244.

Part 3

Event management and leverage

Reflections and outlook

11 Critical issues and future research in event management and leverage

Introduction

Special events hold significant business and social value to countries and communities around the world. Throughout this book, we have highlighted the importance of managing and leveraging events to achieve desired business and social outcomes. We have related our discussions to recent events that have made significant impacts on different levels, ranging from small community festivals to large-scale or mega-events. With our examples, we have aimed to provide a critical yet balanced investigation into different event dimensions and strategic decision-making, recognising the need to carefully plan, implement, maximise, and evaluate events to achieve desired benefits. While social and business dimensions have dominated our discussions, in this final chapter we have the opportunity to both reflect and suggest future avenues for event research and practice. As such, we will look at areas in which business and social domains may be investigated or approached in new and innovative ways but also shift our focus to related event domains for an increasingly holistic and integrated approach towards managing and leveraging events.

Given that the purpose of this book was to explore and advance the latest concepts and developments in event management and leverage from an interdisciplinary perspective – and given the disruptive impacts of COVID-19 on the events industry during the time of writing – we also take the opportunity to reflect on critical issues and trends that will influence the way in which future events are designed, delivered, experienced, and evaluated. In doing so, we explore challenges and opportunities for events in the post-COVID-19 era that are expected to have significant implications for both event theory and practice.

Critical issues: business dimension

In today's dynamic, complex, and interconnected business environment, inter-organisational partnerships and networks are becoming increasingly important for events to improve their competitive position. As event managers consider how they will generate and sustain economic returns, increased attention should be given to the potential for alliances to create value through complementary

DOI: 10.4324/9781003002772-14

152 *Event management and leverage in practice*

resources, capabilities, and access to innovation. Relationship management and the co-creation of value have never been more critical for the planning, delivery, and sustainability of events. However, in the context of relationships and commercial sponsorship, it is important that event managers negotiate the likely tensions between commercialisation and event authenticity. That is, while business outcomes are critical for event success, so too are social impacts and maintaining event sincerity and positive consumer relationships.

Authentic relationships are also critical as a response to COVID-19 restrictions. While the pandemic has generated unprecedented challenges for the events sector, opportunities have also emerged. During COVID-19, we have seen live events shift to the digital world. While this has encouraged the creative delivery of content and maintenance of relationships, the financial return has often remained insubstantial. As we look ahead, there are opportunities for events to maximise their full potential by adopting a hybrid approach, where live events and digital delivery are meaningfully integrated and resources – including business and technological know-how – can be leveraged. However, while technology may help to address logistical challenges, save expenditure, and promote digital interactions, stronger infrastructure will be required. Live-streaming, integration with online video platforms, and lead capture and engagement tools will be important for event managers to leverage events to a wider audience in a convincing way. As such, this is a prime example for a space where relationships among business service providers, event technology, and channel partners will be critical. Overall, event managers are more than ever required to determine how various cross-sectoral partnerships can help in their post-COVID-19 recovery and future sustainability.

It should also be noted that the international appeal of physically held events – including business and sport events – remains high, despite the increasing number of virtual events being organised. For example, even though a number of large scale and mega-events including the 2020 European Football Championships, the 2020 Tokyo Summer Olympics and the 2020 World Expo in Dubai had to be postponed, they were considered to provide critical business opportunities, especially for international buyers and sellers, to interact and showcase and inspect the physical goods on sale (Davidson, 2018). Host cities also seek longer-term destination benefits associated with being a connected city, such as sustained international visitors and enhanced reputation as a favourable location to undertake business and social activities (Lee, Kim, Lee, & Kim, 2014; Sainaghi, Mauri Aurelio, Ivanov, & d'Angella, 2019). Here, the COVID-19 pandemic has brought the topic of individuals' health and safety to the forefront and in the future, advanced infrastructure development and business opportunities may no longer be enough for a country to win the right to host mega-events. It can be assumed that the aspect of health and safety will feature more prominently in future bid documents which may put countries like Australia and New Zealand in a favourable position (Howard, 2020). Both countries have managed to contain the spread of the COVID-19 virus and as such, they provide a blueprint of the requirement that event hosts must meet. From a research perspective, it will be intriguing to see

Critical issues and future research 153

if health and safety will indeed take a more prominent position in future bidding documents, similar to considerations around sustainability and legacy that have taken a much stronger role in the deliberations of awarding hosting rights to mega-events such as the Olympic Games or the World Cups.

Another event impact area that is strongly gaining in importance is the experiential learning that organisations and individuals gain from hosting events. For international endeavours such as the Olympic Games or the World Cups, which are reoccurring at different locations every couple of years, event-specific knowledge can become a significant competitive advantage if it is transferred across national boundaries through individuals' interactions, which in turn helps transform the tacit knowledge into an explicit form. Clearly, the COVID-19 pandemic disrupted this process significantly, with knowledge workers unable to travel. The lack of physical interaction required organisations in many business domains to change and seek alternatives to their knowledge management processes. The global health services sector offers a particularly flexible model that could be replicated by event professionals. In particular, at the pandemic's peak, legal and medical practitioners in many countries were forced to provide consultation services to their clients and patients via e-platforms (Wang & Wu, 2020). This required using relevant virtual meeting technology and designing digital research and workflow platforms that allowed the practitioners one-click access to pertinent information (Ammirato, Linzalone, & Felicetti, 2020; Legal Executive Institute, 2020). Looking forward, business event organisations can attempt to develop similar platforms and consider the potential use of virtual reality software to overcome physical barriers and facilitate sharing between knowledge workers. These practices will provide event business customers with an immersive experience similar to a physical event. For instance, virtual event start-ups such as Hopin (https://hopin.com) have entered the event marketplace by providing a "virtual venue" that offers users access to a wide range of digital events and features, including virtual rooms which attendees can move in and out of. In a virtual format, this approach resembles experiences of a traditional live expo, conference, or workshop where exhibitors and visitors can mingle, engage, and exchange ideas. With the first steps being made, it will be fascinating to see future developments in this space, including the use of virtual architecture to design the physical spaces that events will use in the future. As such, we are looking forward to developments that are truly innovative and disruptive and that build on current knowledge to go beyond the standard processes of simply putting conferences or meetings online.

Critical issues: social dimension

Throughout this book, we explored the social dimension of events with a particular focus on the contributions community events make to social connectedness, social capital, sense of place, and belonging. Recognising that community events offer significant opportunities for valuable social contributions to the communities that host them, there are also challenges that exist. Communities are not necessarily

154 *Event management and leverage in practice*

homogenous and there will be subgroups within a host community who feel differently about a festival and who are affected in different ways. This means that some people or groups may indeed experience social connectedness and a sense of place and belonging, while others feel excluded and alienated from their community. Future research should therefore pay attention to the existing power dynamics within a community and how this affects levels of involvement in, and therefore benefits from, community festivals (Bakas, Duxbury, Remoaldo, & Matos, 2019). This, in turn, has implications for event organisers to maximise community involvement – including from marginalised or minority groups – such that positive social outcomes can be realised for a broad cross-section of community members.

These considerations also have relevance for the newly introduced events-for-development (EfD) space. As we discussed, there is much untapped potential in the new and exciting social field of EfD, which organisers and researchers are just beginning to capture and strategically incorporate into programming and research agendas. The impact of COVID-19 on the EfD space has been unparalleled and necessitated that many organisations pivoted to virtual events in order to continue reaching their participants. Even with this major challenge – especially in disadvantaged community contexts where access to computers and internet is far from guaranteed – there are previously unconsidered opportunities. Looking to the future, EfD organisers could, for example, consider how to adapt and reconfigure their event offerings to reach groups through virtual hubs in community health centres – something that may lead to sustained virtual event offerings post-pandemic. In such scenarios, virtual events may after all be a viable strategy to engage some hard-to-reach populations.

Another important consideration for event organisers and researchers is to ascertain how best to integrate events into the ongoing, year-round programming of the organisation. Schulenkorf and Adair (2013) have previously argued that in a "for-development setting", events cannot be held in isolation from mainstream programming or their effectiveness in reinforcing programme objectives and outcomes will be severely compromised. Here, EfD organisers must consider the optimal nature of partnerships and collaborations that will be needed to link the event portfolio into the economic, social, cultural, and political agendas of a community in order to maximise outcomes. This is particularly important for large-scale and mega-events that are not linked to a specific place. For instance, more critical thinking is needed to find the best way in which the Olympic Games and the Football World Cup engage with "for-development" projects in the future, given that their previous involvement has not always led to the desired social and physical legacies that were promised to communities (see Levermore, 2011; Thomson, Schlenker, & Schulenkorf, 2013). Overall, we argue that critical research on event impacts and legacies needs to continue, and it will be particularly exciting to see how the EfD space evolves and grows over the next decade and beyond.

Critical issues: event impact evaluation

As the aforementioned examples highlight, event impact evaluations will continue to play a crucial role in ensuring a solid evidence base on which event

Critical issues and future research 155

management decisions can be made and justified to stakeholders. With respect to the measurement of social, economic and increasingly, environmental impacts as part of a triple bottom line approach, challenges remain, and we will briefly discuss two of the most pertinent issues in more detail.

First is an acknowledgement that while there is a need for comparability in assessing events and their contributions, this should not come at the expense of contextualisation. Although toolkits have been developed to provide a more standardised approach to event impact evaluation (see Pasanen, Taskinen, & Mikkonen, 2009; Schlenker, Foley, & Getz, 2010), "the reality is that a 'one size fits all' method still eludes the many researchers working in this field" (Nordvall & Brown, 2020, p. 166). Events are simply too varied in size and scale, ranging from small community festivals designed primarily for local audiences to mega-events that have the potential for significant impacts on a host destination and economy. The evaluative needs of these events also differ based on their specific objectives, the type and scale of the event, and the range of stakeholders involved. Thus, the challenge for any assessment tool remains that there must be sufficient flexibility to allow for customisation that meets the evaluation needs of a particular event (Schlenker et al., 2010; Wood, 2008). Moreover, the ideal toolkit would also provide standardised yet flexible tools for the evaluation of various event impacts, at basic, medium and advanced levels. The user could then tailor their evaluation approach selecting the impact dimensions of interest, and the required level, taking into account their evaluative needs, reporting requirements to other stakeholders, and their available resources (Nordvall & Brown, 2020). Looking towards the future, the development of advanced toolkits that allow for an integration of the seemingly conflicting aspects of standardisation and flexibility will present an intriguing challenge for event researchers and monitoring and evaluation specialists. In fact, the challenge is of critical importance, given that a flexible toolkit may well take decisions on methodology out of the hands of either those internal to the event who may not have expert skills in event impact evaluation, or external consultants, who may seek to manipulate methods to achieve a more positive result (Jaimangal-Jones, Fry, & Haven-Tang, 2018).

Second, with respect to the measurement and communication of event impacts, there is the challenge of finding a balance between being able to easily communicate the overall impacts of an event versus being able to understand these detailed impacts in a nuanced way. We see this issue brought to life in event impact studies that seek to achieve commensurability – reporting on the economic, social, and environmental impacts of an event in a common unit (typically a monetary value). Such evaluation approaches – including the model tested by Andersson, Armbrecht, and Lundberg (2016) in their study around the European athletics indoor championships – are valuable in that they are trying to make the typically more intangible impacts more easily comparable. Without commensurability, we indeed leave room for different stakeholders to interpret the findings differently and make their own judgements on the value of an event that produces, for example, tangible, positive economic impacts but at the expense of negative social impacts on a host community. However, if expressing intangible social impacts in monetary terms undermines their value – or if it obscures a detailed

156 *Event management and leverage in practice*

understanding of the areas of concern to a host community – then commensurability per se should be questioned. In certain cases, a more descriptive yet rich analysis of social impacts may indeed be more useful to event organisers than putting a rather sterile economic value on these types of impacts – especially when they are trying to respond to the needs and concerns of their host community. Future studies might therefore investigate further how to improve the reporting of typically intangible impacts (such as social and cultural impacts) in monetary terms.

Critical issues: event leverage

With regard to future considerations on event leverage, further thinking is needed to address the problem of event transiency (Chalip, 2014), examining how various networked relationships and event partnerships can be sustained to continue to capitalise on leverageable opportunities well after the event has concluded. Longitudinal studies that examine leveraging opportunities before, during, and after the event would further assist in strategic event planning, beyond the currently implemented one-point-in-time approach (Richards & de Brito, 2013). Future consideration should also be given to which stakeholders benefit the most from leveraging tactics, as marginalised and disenfranchised individuals may not receive leverageable benefits due to ideological forces that influence leveraging strategies of those in power (Ziakas, 2015). To truly capitalise on the potential of leveraging events for community outcomes, care must be taken to be sure these benefits are realised equally by all members of a community, not just for those who have more means and resources than others.

Relatedly, there also needs to be further work on who should initiate or "do" the leveraging, and how to best include community stakeholders in the leveraging process so that their voices are heard and considered. Here, a critical consideration is leadership in the event leveraging context, including how leadership should look and from where leadership should emerge. In the event context – and especially in the case of large-scale or mega-events – leaders may need to manage multi-team systems (Zaccaro, Dubrow, Torres, & Campbell, 2020) to coordinate teams of individuals from multiple organisations who are involved in event planning and leverage. What forms of leadership are best suited for guiding this multiplicity of teams? What role does leadership play in maximising the benefits of events for communities and individuals? How do we identify the most promising event leaders? Such questions will be critical to answer if we are serious about "moving the needle" in professional event management, leadership, and educational development.

Final remarks

For many decades, special events have played a central role in people's lives and they have provided significant business and social value to countries and communities around the world. Looking to the future, the post-COVID-19 era presents a challenging yet critically important time for event planners and managers. Given the significant changes in consumer behaviours and attitudes, managerial responses

Critical issues and future research 157

to the pandemic will require changes to previously taken-for-granted business models and delivery approaches, including a more flexible way of planning, implementing, maximising, and evaluating events. While some event organisers have already addressed these critical aspects, others are still adapting to "the new normal" where digital technology, online tools and services, as well as hybrid forms of delivery are here to stay. At the same time, it becomes obvious that COVID-19 has not diminished the value of in-person events and the latest research suggests that people are indeed keen and committed to returning to face-to-face events as soon as possible (Reed Exhibitions, 2020). In fact, the social engagement aspect of live events is likely to remain quintessential; in the sport sector, for example, fandom is all about actively supporting your favourite team in the stadium, while in the business sector, direct communication at expos or congresses fosters networking, collaboration, idea sharing, as well as buying and selling. After all, some of the greatest business ideas, scientific developments, and technical innovations have been sparked during an event workshop or, indeed, over a glass of wine afterwards.

For the post-COVID-19 era, there is critical demand for more event-specific research that will offer the events industry valuable insights into how to reshape events to the advantage of a multitude of stakeholders and fuel long-term profitability and growth. With this book, we have aimed to contribute to this discussion by showcasing the latest concepts and developments in event management and leverage. We believe that our book may well provide a launching pad for new and innovative engagements with event theory and practice. As such, we encourage other event researchers to build on our work and maximise the opportunities to contribute new knowledge on managing and leveraging events for a sustainable future – across business, social, and related dimensions.

References

Ammirato, S., Linzalone, R., & Felicetti, A. M. (2020). Knowledge management in pandemics: A critical literature review. *Knowledge Management Research & Practice*, ahead of print. https://doi.org/10.1080/14778238.2020.1801364

Andersson, T. D., Armbrecht, J., & Lundberg, E. (2016). Triple impact assessments of the 2013 European athletics indoor championship in Gothenburg. *Scandinavian Journal of Hospitality and Tourism: Event Impact*, *16*(2), 158–179. https://doi.org/10.1080/15022 250.2015.1108863

Bakas, F., Duxbury, N., Remoaldo, P., & Matos, O. (2019). The social utility of small-scale art festivals with creative tourism in Portugal. *International Journal of Event and Festival Management*, *10*(3), 248–266. https://doi.org/10.1108/IJEFM-02-2019-0009

Chalip, L. (2014). From legacy to leverage. In J. Grix (Ed.), *Leveraging legacies from sports mega-events: Concepts and cases* (pp. 2–12). London: Palgrave Pivot.

Davidson, R. (2018). *Business events*. Abingdon, UK: Routledge.

Howard, J. (2020, June 26). Australia and New Zealand to host 2023 FIFA Women's World Cup. *ABC News*. Retrieved from www.abc.net.au/news/2020-06-26/australia-and-new-zealand-to-host-2023-fifa-womens-world-cup/12394688

Jaimangal-Jones, D., Fry, J., & Haven-Tang, C. (2018). Exploring industry priorities regarding customer satisfaction and implications for event evaluation. *International*

158 *Event management and leverage in practice*

Journal of Event and Festival Management, *9*(1), 51–66. https://doi.org/10.1108/IJEFM-06-2016-0044

Legal Executive Institute. (2020, July 1). Knowledge management: COVID-19 has caused a boon: How do you make it last? *Legal Insights Europe: Thomson Reuters*. Retrieved from https://blogs.thomsonreuters.com/legal-uk/2020/07/01/knowledge-management-covid-19-has-caused-a-boon-how-do-you-make-it-last/

Lee, Y. K., Kim, S., Lee, C. K., & Kim, S. H. (2014). The impact of a mega-event on visitors' attitude toward hosting destination: Using trust transfer theory. *Journal of Travel & Tourism Marketing*, *31*(4), 507–521.

Levermore, R. (2011). Sport-for-development and the 2010 Football World Cup. *Geography Compass*, *5*(12), 886–897.

Nordvall, A., & Brown, S. (2020). Evaluating publicly supported periodic events: The design of credible, usable and effective evaluation. *Journal of Policy Research in Tourism, Leisure and Events*, *12*(2), 152–171. https://doi.org/10.1080/19407963.2018.1556672

Pasanen, K., Taskinen, H., & Mikkonen, J. (2009, January 1). Impacts of cultural events in Eastern Finland: Development of a Finnish Event Evaluation Tool. *Scandinavian Journal of Hospitality and Tourism*, *9*(2–3), 112–129. https://doi.org/10.1080/1502225 0903119546

Reed Exhibitions. (2020). *COVID-19 and how it's changing the event industry*. Richmond, UK. Retrieved from https://reedexhibitions.com/sites/default/files/pdfs/COVID-19%20and%20How%20it's%20Changing%20the%20Event%20Industry.pdf

Richards, G., & de Brito, M. (2013). Conclusions: The future of events as a social phenomenon. In G. Richards, M. de Brito, & L. Wilks (Eds.), *Exploring the social impacts of events* (pp. 219–235). Abingdon, UK: Routledge.

Sainaghi, R., Mauri Aurelio, G., Ivanov, S., & d'Angella, F. (2019). Mega-events and seasonality: The case of the Milan World Expo 2015. *International Journal of Contemporary Hospitality Management*, *31*(1), 61–86. https://doi.org/10.1108/IJCHM-10-2017-0644

Schlenker, K., Foley, C., & Getz, D. (2010). *ENCORE festival and event evaluation kit: Review and redevelopment*. Gold Coast: CRC for Sustainable Tourism.

Schulenkorf, N., & Adair, D. (2013). Temporality, transience and regularity in sport-for-development: Synchronizing programs with events. *Journal of Policy Research in Tourism, Leisure and Events*, *5*(1), 99–104. doi:10.1080/19407963.2012.678600

Thomson, A., Schlenker, K., & Schulenkorf, N. (2013). Conceptualizing sport event legacy. *Event Management*, *17*(2), 111–122.

Wang, W.-T., & Wu, S.-Y. (2020). Knowledge management based on information technology in response to COVID-19 crisis. *Knowledge Management Research & Practice*, ahead of print. https://doi.org/10.1080/14778238.2020.1860665

Wood, E. H. (2008). An impact evaluation framework: Local government community festivals. *Event Management*, *12*, 171–185.

Zaccaro, S., Dubrow, S., Torres, E., & Campbell, L. (2020). Multiteam systems: An integrated review and comparison of different forms. *Annual Review of Organisational Psychology and Organisational Behavior*, *7*, 479–503.

Ziakas, V. (2015). For the benefit of all? Developing a critical perspective in mega-event leverage. *Leisure Studies*, *34*, 689–702. doi:10.1080/02614367.2014.986507

Index

Note: Page numbers in *italics* indicate a figure and page numbers in **bold** indicate a table on the corresponding page. Page numbers followed by "n" indicate a note.

Adair, D. 134
Anastasiadou, C. 124, 126
Andersson, T. D. 20, 42, 48, 51, 155
Antchak, V. 67
Armbrecht, J. 20, 42, 155
Asian–German Sport Exchange Programme 140
Asmussen, C. G. 79
ATKearney 79

Bach, T. 94
Backlund, E. A. 122
backward linkages 77
Barnard, S. 67
Beesley, L. G. 27
belonging/place, sense of 121–123
Beyond the Ball (2020) 140
BIE *see* Bureau International des Expositions (BIE)
Bixler, R. D. 122
Black, N. 119, 122, 123
Blom, L. 139
Bond, M. 112n1
Boronczyk, F. 62
Bourdieu, P. 120
brands 63; authenticity 67; equity 61, 62; exposure 60; image 60, 61, 62, 66; marketing 63
Breuer, C. 62
Brown, S. 42, 44
Bureau International des Expositions (BIE) 80, 82
Burns, P. 48
business dimension, critical issues of 151–153

Business Events Council of Australia 5
Butler, K. 67
Byun, J. 94

cause-related marketing 59–60
CBA *see* cost–benefit analysis (CBA)
CCTV5 93
CGE models *see* computable general equilibrium (CGE) models
Chalip, L. 18, 27–34, 134
Chen, S. 33–34
Chen, X. 81
Cheung Chau Bun Festival 122
Chien, P. M. 77
China Sports Daily 93
Cisco 63
Clunes Booktown Festival 121
Coalter, F. 142
Cobbs, J. 62
co-branding 89, 96
co-creation of value 12, 96, 99, 152
Coghlan, A. 12
Coleman, J. 120
commercial engagement 59–70
commercialisation 59, 66–68, 152
Commonwealth Games 2014, Glasgow 32
communitas, liminality and 18, 30–32, 134, 135, 140
community: engagement strategies 123–125; involvement 124
community events 117–118; challenges to 125–126; definition of 117; issues of 125–126; sense of belonging 121–123; sense of place 121–123; social capital

160 Index

120–121; social connectedness 119–120; social dimensions of 116–127
community festivals 117, 123, 124; challenges to 125–126; definition of 117; issues of 125–126
Community Involvement Framework 124–126
computable general equilibrium (CGE) models 46, 77
consumers 12, 30, 61–65, 68; attitudes 156; communication with 60, 63; evaluation of commercial sponsorship 67; search for authenticity 67; spending 45
consumption: abroad 109; alcohol 84; and production of festival 123, 125, 127
Contingent Valuation (CV) method 12, 48
corporate social responsibility (CSR) 60–62
cost–benefit analysis (CBA) 51, 77
Crompton, J. L. 65
cross-border knowledge transfer: formal institutional challenges 108–110; informal institutional challenges 106–108
cross-border trade 109
CSR *see* corporate social responsibility (CSR)
Culpan, R. 90
cultures: differences in 95, 104, 106–107, 108; dimensions 107, 108; organisational 105, 110, 111
CV method *see* Contingent Valuation (CV) method

Das, T. K. 95, 96
Deery, M. 47, 76
Delamere, T. A. 49
Derom, I. 33
Derrett, R. 117
destination marketing mix 29, 34, 36, 133
Dimou, I. 13
Direct Economic Contribution 47
Direct Expenditure Approach 47
Dossena, G. 81
Doves Olympic Movement programme 140
Dubai Exhibition Centre 83
Duffy, M. 121, 122, 125
Dwyer, L. 12, 20, 76

Economic Impact Analysis (EIA) 46
economics/economic: activities 25, 45, 76, 78; benefits 19, 27, 29, 31, 67, 77, 83, 90, 133, 138, 139; development 25, 27,

36, 77, 131, 132, 138–139, 141, 142, 144; gains 90, 143; impacts 16, 29, 40, 42, 43, 45–47, 50, 51, 94, 155; justice/well-being 4, 17; knowledge-based 82; leverage 18, 26, 28–30, 33; outcomes 26, 34, 77, 133, 134, 137, 141–143; values 12, 48, 68, 156
Edwards, D. 31
EfD *see* events-for-development (EfD)
EIA *see* Economic Impact Analysis (EIA)
Ellis, D. 94
ENCORE Festival and Event Evaluation Kit 50
e-sports 69–70
European Sport Management Quarterly 6
event impact evaluation 40–52; considerations in 43–45; context for 41–42; critical issues of 154–156; definition of 42–43; economic impacts 45–47; holistic 50–51; social impacts 47–50
event leverage 25–37; critical issues of 156; definition of 26, 134; distinguished from legacy 26–27; economic leverage 28–30; managerial implications of 35–36; for other outcomes 34; for physical activity/health 32–34; social leverage 30–32; for sport participation 32–34; theory development and principles 27–28; thinking, challenges to 34–35
events: alliances 93–94; authenticity 66–68; and destination marketing mix 29, 36, 133; and international business opportunities 76–85; management 96–97; parasport 32; social responsibility 68; sponsorship 60–62; sport 3, 4, 5, 18, 26–34, 37, 50, 80, 94, 98, 131, 140, 144; *see also* community events
events-for-development (EfD) 131–145, 154; challenges to 141–143; definition of 132; foci and outcomes of 137–141; historical development and background of 133–134; managerial implications of 132–133, 143–144; theoretical and conceptual frameworks 134–137
events industry 90; business/social perspective of 3, 5, 13; challenge in 67; commercialisation and 59, 67; COVID-19 impacts on 5, 98, 151
experiential learning 153
explicit knowledge 105
Expo 2020 Dubai 82–84, **84**

Index 161

Farrelly, F. 64, 96
Federation of International Basketball Associations World Cup 2019, China 35
FEET *see* Finnish Event Evaluation Tool (FEET)
festivals, community *see* community festivals
Festival Social Impact Attitude Scale (FSIAS) 49
FFA *see* Football Federation Australia (FFA)
FIFA Women's World Cup 2023 94, 98
Finkel, R. 121
Finnish Event Evaluation Tool (FEET) 50
Football Federation Australia (FFA) 94
forward linkages 77
Fredline, L. 76
FSIAS *see* Festival Social Impact Attitude Scale (FSIAS)

GATS *see* General Agreement on Trade in Services (GATS)
GCI *see* Global Cities Index (GCI)
General Agreement on Trade in Services (GATS) 108–109
Gerke, A. 98
Getz, D. 45, 47
Giannoulakis, C. 139
Gillooly, L. 63
Glastonbury festival (2015) 63
global cities, as host locations 78–79
Global Cities Index (GCI) 79, **80**
Global Reporting Initiative (GRI) 78
Goerzen, A. 79
Gold Coast Honda Indy, Australia 29
Golding, P. 67
Great Exhibition 80
GRI *see* Global Reporting Initiative (GRI)
Gross, P. 62
Groza, M. D. 62
Guo, Y. 111
Gwinner, K. 61

Hall, C. M. 117
Hammitt, W. E. 122
Hatch, J. 48
Henderson, C. M. 62
Hiller, H. H. 77
Hinch, T. D. 49
Hofstede, G. 107, 112n1
Homeless World Cup 18, 140
Horne, J. 17
Horticultural Expos 80

ICT *see* information and communication technologies (ICT)
individualism 107, 108, 112
Infantino, G. 95
information and communication technologies (ICT) 79
Input–Output (I/O) modelling 46
inscope expenditure calculation 45, 47, 50
intangibility/intangible: knowledge 106; outcomes 104; social impacts 47–48, 155; and tangible impacts of events 12, 133
Intergroup Contact Theory 136
international business opportunities, events and 76–85; Expo 2020 Dubai 82–84, **84**; global cities, as host locations 78–79; managerial implications of 84–85; mega-events, legacy of 77–78; World Expos 80–82
International Olympic Committee (IOC) 94
IOC *see* International Olympic Committee (IOC)
I/O modelling *see* Input–Output (I/O) modelling

Jago, L. K. 47, 76
Jasovska, P. 111
Jeanes, R. 140
Jebel Ali Free Zone 82
Johnson, R. 12
Journal of Sport Policy and Politics (2017) 6
justice, economic/social 4, 17
Just Play (SFD programme) 138

Katsikeas, C. S. 91–92
Kellett, P. 19
knowledge: acquisition 95, 104; explicit 105; intangible 106; management 97, 104–106, 111–112; stickiness 106–107; tacit 105, 106, 108, 110–112; transfer 35, 91, 104, 106–111
Ko, Y. J. 68
Kumar, R. 95, 96

Laing, J. 123–125
Lane, A. 33
Last Dance, The (documentary) 69
Lau, C. Y. L. 122
League of Legends Mid-Season Invitational 2018 69–70
learning: experiential 153; by observing/doing 110; organisational 7, 104–106, 108
legacy *versus* leverage 26–27

162 *Index*

Leopkey, B. 94
Leyns, A. 27–29
liminality, and communitas 18, 30–32, 134, 135, 140
Lindberg, K. 12
Liu, W. 12
Li, Y. 122
Los Angeles Olympic Games 1984 59
Lundberg, E. 48, 51, 155
Lv, K. 81

Magee, J. 140
Magno, F. 81
Maguire, J. 67
Mailman Group 93
Mair, J. 121, 123–125
Manzenreiter, W. 17
marketing: authenticity and 67; brand 63; campaigns 63, 66, 68–70; cause-related 59–60; relationship 64–65
Market Potential Index 82
McCartney, G. 67–68
McNaughton, R. B. 137
Meenaghan, T. 63
mega-events, legacy of 77–78
Melbourne 2006 Commonwealth Games 19
Mellor, R. 12
Mikkonen, J. 50
Minkov, M. 112n1
Misener, L. 32–34
Mistilis, N. 12
Morgan, A. 65, 96
Mosoni, G. 81
Mules, T. 12, 48
Mykletun, R. J. 122

Nagano Winter Olympic Games 1998, Japan 78
National Basketball Association (NBA) 93
NBA *see* National Basketball Association (NBA)
NBC 96–97
networked societies 78–79
New Zealand Football Federation 94
Nielsen, B. B. 79
Nikou, C. 94
Nissen, R. 66
Nonaka, I. 105, 108
Nordvall, A. 42

O'Brien, D. 29–32, 138
Olson, E. L. 61
Ontario Parasport Legacy Group 32
operational risk 66

organisational learning 7, 104–106, 108
Osti, L. 67–68
O'Sullivan, P. 63

Page, S. J. 45, 47
parallel linkages 77
parasport events 32
Pasanen, K. 50, 51
physical activity/health, event leverage for 32–34
Pirelli 61
place/belonging, sense of 121–123
political economy model 77
power distance 107, 112
Pramböck, B. 91–92
Prendergast, G. 65
Preuss, H. 26
process-based qualitative frameworks 13
Putnam, R. 120, 137

Qantas Airlines 69
Quester, P. 96
Quinn, B. 119–120

Rammal, H. G. 106, 111
Reebok 96–97
reputational risk 66
return on investment (ROI) 66
return on objectives (ROO) 66
Rich, G. 62
risk: associated 44; operational/reputational 66
Ritchie, B. W. 77
Robson, M. J. 91–92
Rogers, P. 124, 126
ROI *see* return on investment (ROI)
Rolex 61
ROO *see* return on objectives (ROO)
Rose, E. L. 106, 111
Rousseff, D. 93

Scheinbaum, A. C. 68
Schlegelmilch, B. B. 91–92
Schlenker, K. 50, 51, 139
Schulenkorf, N. 13, 31, 134, 135, 138, 139
SECI (Socialisation, Externalisation, Combination, and Internalisation) 105–106, 110–112
SEM Framework *see* Strategic Event Management (SEM) Framework
sense of belonging and place 121–123
Service-Dominant logic (S-D logic) 96–97, 99
Shanghai World Expo 81

Sharples, L. 117
SICE Framework *see* Social Inter-Community Event (SICE) Framework
Singer, P. 142
Sino Weibo's Spider Web of strategic alliances 92–93
SIP scale *see* Social Impact Perception (SIP) scale
Small, K. 49
Smith, A. 34, 77
social benefits/costs 11, 18, 19, 49, 90, 94, 116, 117, 118, 133
social capital 4, 13, 17, 32, 47, 120–121, 126, 136–137, 139
social cohesion 41, 119, 125, 137, 139
social connectedness 119–120, 123
social development 36, 77, 131
social dimensions of community events 116–127, 153–154
social and environmental impacts 45, 50, 51, 155
social event impacts 3, 13, 40, 50
Social Impact Assessments 12
Social Impact Perception (SIP) scale 49
social impacts 12, 47–50
social inclusion 43, 119, 131, 132, 135, 137, 139, 140
Social Inter-Community Event (SICE) Framework 13
socialisation 47, 50, 105
social justice 4, 17
social leverage 18, 30–32
social media 63–64
social mobility 132, 137, 139, 140
social outcomes 26, 27, 28, 34, 36, 135
social spaces 4
sociocultural benefits 13, 83
sociocultural impacts of events 42, 50, 78
sociocultural outcomes 139, 142
Solberg, H. A. 78
Soteriades, M. D. 13
Sparks, B. 12
Spartan Race 96–97
Specialised Expos 80
sponsorship: activation 62–64; definition of 59; event 60–62; fit between sponsor and sponsee 61; management 64–66
sport: events 3, 4, 5, 18, 26–34, 37, 50, 80, 94, 98, 131, 140, 144; participation 27, 28, 32–34; sponsorship 61, 91; subcultures 29–30, 31, 138
sport-for-development (SFD) 18, 31, 32, 132, 142; framework 135; theory 135–136, 140, 141

Sport Value Framework (SVF) 98
SSUSA *see* Street Soccer USA (SSUSA)
Stevenson, N. 121, 126
Stewart, S. I. 121–122
strategic alliances 89–96; challenges within 95–96; definition of 90; governance 91–92; opportunities within 95–96; partner legitimacy 92; portfolio 92; Sino Weibo's Spider Web of 92–93; types of 90
Strategic Event Management (SEM) Framework 11–20, *15*, 135; evaluation 19–20; implementation 16–17; maximisation 17–19; planning 14–16; process-based qualitative frameworks 13; review of 11–13
strategic responses and organisational learning 110–111, *111*
Street Soccer USA (SSUSA) 32, 132, 139, 140
Summer Olympics 2012, London 78
Sun, Y. 81
SVF *see* Sport Value Framework (SVF)

tacit knowledge 105, 106, 108, 110–112
Takeuchi, H. 105, 108
Taks, M. 35
tangible/intangible impacts, of events 12, 133
Taskinen, H. 50
TBL *see* triple bottom line (TBL)
Teng, B. S. 95
Tianyi, Z. 92–93
Tokyo 2020 Summer Olympic Games 25–26, 69
Toscani, G. 65
Tour de France 50
tourism 13, 16, 41, 82; activities 81, 133; attractiveness 77; bicycle 33; dependency 30; and events scholarship 67; and festivals 139; impacts 12, 29, 49; income 43
Tour of Flanders, Belgium 33
Trans-Tasman World Cup alliance 94–95
Triennale di Milano 80
triple bottom line (TBL) 12, 51
Turner, V. 30

uncertainty avoidance 107–108, 112

value, co-creation of 12, 96, 99, 152
Vans 64
VanWynsberghe, R. 33
Visa 69

164 *Index*

Wagner, U. 66
Waitt, G. 122, 125
Wang, M. 81
Wankel, L. M. 49
Weibo Sports 92–93
Welty Peachey, J. 32, 140
Werner, K. 97–98
Wiedmann, K. P 62
Wild, P. O. 78–79
Wilks, L. 119–120
Williams, D. R. 121–122
Winter Olympic Games 1994,
    Lillehammer 78
Women's Mini-Marathon, Ireland 33
Wood, E. H. 42–43
Woratschek, H. 98

World Bank 82
World Expos 80–82
World Scholar-Athlete Games (WSAG) 141
World Trade Organization (WTO) 109
WSAG *see* World Scholar-Athlete Games
    (WSAG)
WTO *see* World Trade Organization
    (WTO)

Xue, K. 81

Yu, M. 81
Yuval-Davis, N. 122

Zheng, X. 81
Ziakas, V. 13, 35, 67, 68

Printed in the United States
by Baker & Taylor Publisher Services